The Clock Keeps Ticking

by

Sharon Gayter

**Grosvenor House
Publishing Limited**

This book is published by
Grosvenor House Publishing Ltd
28-30 High Street, Guildford, Surrey, GU1 3HY.
www.grosvenorhousepublishing.co.uk

A CIP record for this book
is available from the British Library

ISBN 978-1-907652-43-1

Dedication

To my husband Bill. You gave me a life, let me live my dreams, led me forward and supported me in every goal I set. There are many more challenges ahead. Thanks for sharing my life.

Foreword

When we are born the clock begins to tick. Life is measured by time, the hours, days, weeks and years that we live. At the end, the clock stops. Between is your life. How will you live it? Will you let the clock tick and watch life go by? Or will you go out and create some adventures? Dreams? Goals? For me the clock ticked slowly during childhood. My adventure began when I left home. I found my love and freedom in the hills and in running. But more was needed to live this life to the full. I set small goals and one by one achieved them. My first goal to run the London Marathon started simply by me taking nearly three weeks to run a single mile without stopping. I achieved many of the goals I set in my life. From humble beginnings, from that marathon performance which was nothing special, I went on to compete for my country. I have been ranked the best in the country for many years within a branch of athletics which must surely be the toughest discipline – running ultra distance races. Ultra distance is anything beyond the marathon. Never content to sit still; that still wasn't enough for me and I continued on to take over 17 hours off the world record for running from Land's End to John O'Groats, a dream I yearned to achieve for twelve years.

From a quiet, withdrawn child, running awakened me and drove me forward. I became a person and grew. From a bus driver to a university lecturer: a fun runner to the best in the world: from barely speaking to brimming with confidence. This is a story not just about watching the clock tick, but living every minute to the full. Setting goals and dreams and going out and achieving them. We can all do this. The goals start small, in small steps until the dream is realised. I challenge you to be inspired by this story, to go out and set your own goals, challenge the clock and live your life to the full.

Acknowledgements

I have had many helpers on the way; the dreams were always mine, but a little help was needed to make them come true. To my various sponsors over the years – Mannatech, Arki Busson (EIM), Elle MacPherson Intimates, Asics, Expeditions Foods, Teesside University, Darlington Building Society, Vitabiotics and Spira, thank you.

To the dedicated crew for my world record run, Alan Young, Ivor Roberts, Andy and Ramona Thevenet-Smith, David Nicholson and Murdo McEwan, for keeping me in a 4 hour time warp for 12 days, 16 hours, 22 minutes and 3 seconds. Thank you. To Ella Towers and Vicky: for continually updating the website for you all to read. Thanks to those who kept me fit and healthy, Pip Chinn, Julie Sparrow, Dr Martyn Speight, Darren Cooper, Matthew Wright and Claire Harrison. To those individuals whose "little favours" mounted up – Ian Johnson for keeping my vehicles on the road, Signz of Skelton for the ever changing van livery and my wonderful neighbours who have looked after my dogs over the years – Martin, Denise, Matthew and Sarah, and Ann and Tony. Thank you.

Lastly, thank you to Isobel Longley-Cook, for removing so many "gots" from this text, shortening the sentences and highlighting my mistakes, editing this into a readable format.

Contents

Chapter 1

Where Am I?

My feet are rebelling, screaming at me to stop. They can't take much more. They are killing me. Swollen to two sizes bigger than normal, blistered, burning, throbbing agony, causing me excruciating pain with every step. It is like treading on glass with each foot strike, with every step I am staggering, moving sideways more than I am forwards. I am ignoring these signals; suffering the pain, soldiering on in ignorance – why? Well, I am on a mission, one mighty mission to become a world record holder. My head may be telling me to stop but my heart is insisting I should carry on. I am doing this of my own free will. Hell and agony all rolled into one. Self inflicted torture. An ordeal, call it what you like, but it is what I want to do, my own desire to become a world record holder, and believe me, it's not about to get any easier.

It's midnight and I am approaching Carlisle. Not good timing and sleep deprivation is hitting in. I am unable to maintain my co-ordination. It's like being drunk, but not a touch of alcohol has passed my lips. Maintaining forward momentum is difficult, but time is distance and distance is important and the clock keeps ticking. I want the time to pass to get nearer the finish, but it's also the enemy, the miles need to be run before the clock ends the day. And so why am I here? Why am I pushing myself so hard? Testing my body to its limits and pushing beyond all boundaries while in such a state? Well I am just over half way into my biggest dream event ever. Years and years of training, two years of planning and eventually here I am on my epic journey – Land's End to John O'Groats, but not just any Land's End to John O'Groats, this is a world record attempt and I have been running, walking, staggering and suffering for nearly seven days now, accumulating blisters and muscle injuries, my feet throbbing with the constant pounding and hammering as the tarmac beats them and sleeping on a minimum of just 4 hours per night.

I am lit up like a Christmas tree. Flashing cycle lights tied on my back and around my waist. Torch strapped on my head. I am dressed in a bright yellow gilet with fluorescent strips. I am the focus of the local binge drinkers staggering all over the road just like me. I am unable to walk in the direction my head is telling my legs to go; the local drinkers the same. Crash! Another direct hit with a party reveller. I stubbornly continue forward pushing these intoxicated party goers out of my way. Alan is following on the cycle but he is not faring any better, hijacked by a group of merry jokers, "What are you doing? A sponsored walk? John O'Groats is a long way", they laugh, not realising that that really is my goal. A few shocked minutes later they realise I am for real and kindly find a few coins to donate to Asthma UK.

The torture continues. This is the last stint of the day but this mission is getting harder and harder. Can I really make it just one more hour until the Little Chef on the A74 which is to be my overnight stop? Did I say overnight stop? It is gone midnight. It will be past 2am by the time I make it to my support van and bed. The alarm clock is set for 5:30am every day. I really want to stop now. Why can I not keep moving forward? I have got to concentrate. It is just 3 miles now. I remember the route, but it is dark now. It will be difficult to find the cut through from the industrial estate to the A74 dual carriageway, not that this bit will save time or distance, but it will save noise and the risk of being run down. I look at the map; the next mile is taking forever. Surely I must nearly be there? The tears are rolling down my face now. I can't stop. I have just got to make it. I have already lost a few hours on my schedule. This is relentless. Time doesn't stop. It is a continuous fight against the clock. It's an emotional roller coaster: as much as I want to stop, I don't want to stop. It's a battle, head against heart. Head is saying stop. Heart saying continue. Heart wins over yet again. I will not be beaten.

It is pitch black in this industrial estate, no street lights. I am well away from the night life of Carlisle now, but still unable to put my feet where my brain is directing them to go. The finish for the day is so close, but it feels so far: not sure if it's the pain of my feet or the emotion that makes these tears keep rolling, frustration even. My body is just not doing what it is supposed to do. I am staggering badly. Luckily it is quiet here and I'm not in danger of being hit by traffic as I don't think I could keep on a footpath even if there was one. I think even Alan is staying well clear of me. I would probably bash into him if he came alongside. I am not sure if he can even see the state I am in. Not a word is said, but I probably prefer it that way. I hate sympathy, this is my choice. No-one is making me do this. I am making me do this, as I said, self-inflicted torture.

Finally, I find the cut through to the A74, just a mile or so along the hard shoulder of the A74. This hard shoulder is a good width and the road pretty quiet, good timing to make up for the bad timing of Carlisle. Ouch! I kick something black. My feet are sore enough already but my head torch just isn't lighting up all the debris that is now getting in my way and it hurts. Bits of tyres and all the rubbish people lazily chuck out of the vehicle windows. It's disgraceful. The misery and distress just continues. I keep looking at my watch; the time keeps ticking but the miles are not. Surely it can't be more than a mile now? Surely no more than 15 minutes? Just where is that sign that tells me the services are just a mile away? I know there is a sign indicating the services. Maybe I have missed it with my head down kicking and stumbling over yet more rubbish? Finally the sign appears. I am almost there. There is just half a mile now. At last I can heave a big sigh of relief and the tears stop. I will make it. Another day finished. Sleep at last and a break for the feet.

Once I can read the services sign the lights can be seen and I just focus on that with such great satisfaction. My goal is still in my sight. I am another day closer. What a welcome sight, but I can't see the support van. Where is the support van? Over there, phew, that's a relief! One last effort to climb the steps Bill has put out for me and finally I sit down on the edge of my bed. Shoes off and my feet are instantly into iced water while I drink a nice hot cup of tea. What sheer luxury; pain over and sleep beckons. I feel content now, over half way, 473.6 miles to be precise (that means 363.4 miles still to go) but it has been one hard day. I am now a few hours (around 4 hours) behind the planned schedule of twelve days, but my plan is allowed to be delayed by 34 hours. My schedule is a punishing twelve days compared to the existing record of 13 days, 10 hours and 1 minute. I have completed my worst mileage yet, only 59.1 miles today and the first time I have lost a few hours off my schedule.

By the time I drink my tea, wash and undress ready for bed it is gone 2am. That means less than 4 hours sleep tonight. I lay my head on the pillow, relaxing with such a great feeling of self satisfaction that I am a day closer to my goal, but don't dare think the horrendous thoughts that I have to go through this all again tomorrow. This is only a temporary reprieve and the agony of putting my shoes on first thing in the morning will be real again in just a few hours time. I go out like a light now, not like the first few days where I lay awake unable to sleep after the day's exertion. I feel I have only just dropped off when the alarm sounds. Surely it's not 5:30 already? But yes, Bill is immediately out of bed and making tea and Ready Brek. The ordeal is to start all over again. The clock just never stops. Last night it ticked so slowly going through Carlisle, while sleeping it went like a flash.

So how did all this start? What drives me to do this? Where does my motivation come from? What keeps me going where many would fall by the wayside? How did I become such a freak of nature that I want to run such extreme distances? Well I have been running for many, many years now, all kinds of ultra distance, all kinds of terrain, all kinds of weather and all over the world. Is it nature or nurture? Was it my family life that made me need to continuously inflict pain on myself or was it just genetics? Well my family certainly don't do exercise of any sort. But maybe that's where I should start. Family life may well have created this need for pain, for self harm, but maybe it was just the need to feel like a worthy person. As a very introverted person may be it was the need to feel I had achieved something. I still don't really know the answer to that, but I certainly feel like I live life now rather than just exist. I have learnt that life doesn't come to you, life is what you make it, you have to go out and live your life.

Chapter 2

Family Life

This was the hardest chapter for me to reveal. It is not something that has ever been made public and in some ways I would rather it still remain a secret, but it is probably what shaped me into creating a tough coping strategy to get through life. I am not going into a year by year chapter and verse account, just a few significant examples of life so that you can read into it how life really was for me.

I don't remember much about my early life. My brother Paul was six years older and my sister Julie was four years older. My father Alan left before I can even remember him (my mother was the first of five marriages he has been through) and he never kept in contact; so even now I do not know him. The subject was never talked about much, only sufficient for me to know that money was tight and my mother struggled to bring three of us up on little money and lived in a caravan with an orange box as my cot to indicate how young I was when he left.

My first memory was when we moved into a three bedroom council house in the Romsey area of Cambridge, about a mile from the city centre. I can remember the massive kitchen and sink and running around the house. Although there was never much money around, it was a normal childhood at that point and never had any bad memories. Julie remembers occasions before Alan left when we used to go on family outings camping or to the sea side and it was a happy time and Alan was a good father when he was around.

My mother was always concerned about money and used to work at a pub in the evenings, leaving us three at home together. She used to put us to bed early, so she could go to work and leave us in the house alone - not something that would be allowed nowadays with three children so young. As soon as she left we were never tired and all came out and got up to all sorts of mischief in the house, but it took us some time to work out how she always knew we had been out of our rooms until Paul found her little trick. Mother would put little paper strips up against the closed bedroom

Sharon, aged 6.

doors, so as soon as we opened the door the strip would fall down and mother would know we had left the rooms. Paul was the one that always got into trouble, so after becoming wise to her tricks, we would come out at night, do our usual play things and when we went back to bed, put Paul's paper strip back up the door and Julie would claim innocently that she went to the toilet during the night and got away with it.

It was while working at the pub that she met John, who was to change our lives dramatically. I vividly remember the first time he was introduced to us in the house when he moved in, "This is John who will be living with us". Initially life was okay, there seemed to be a bit more money around and we visited a few of John's relations. He had twin sisters living in St Ives and a brother who lived in Trowbridge. He was never the kind of person I would call a father; he was just someone that lived in the house and put up with us. He wasn't the kind of person to play games or even try to get to know us – we just existed in the house alongside him. He was a big smoker and a big drinker and we often used to see him drunk. He had an infectious laugh when drunk and then used to fall asleep in the chair and snore loudly. I was always running up to the corner shop to get twenty Piccadilly at a price of twenty-two and a half pence, something that is ingrained in my head even today, I don't think Piccadilly cigarettes are even sold nowadays, but he used to smoke sixty to eighty a day.

It didn't seem that long before they got married; another big drunken affair. Then step sister Melanie came along, when I was nearly ten years old. Now John was a father to Melanie and everything showed from a very early stage. He idolised Melanie while the rest of us got ignored. By now the relationships were breaking down badly, Paul had got into bits and pieces of trouble, and ran away to be with his own father, whom he knew very well, being that much older than me.

Wedding of my mother to step-father John, Julie and Paul.

Paul has never really spoken much about his childhood. Although we get on very well and always have done, we rarely see each other, just an occasional dinner at Christmas time or when I briefly visit Cambridge. All I know is that Paul was put in a home and still kept running back to his father and was eventually shipped off to Oxford so that he was much further away and there he stayed until he was kicked out at eighteen years old. He came back to Cambridge and got an apprenticeship with a joiner's and lived in a bedsit behind the Police Station.

John finally became ill from his smoking habits and had to go to hospital to have a biopsy on his lungs. He was told he would be dead by the time he was forty if he didn't stop smoking. He was around thirty-seven then. He stopped smoking instantly and I never had to run to the shop to get twenty Piccadilly ever again. But this must have been the trigger for more drinking and life became more and more difficult.

There were constant, very aggressive arguments. John worked as an asphalter and mainly laid asphalt on roofs. We constantly had it rammed into us what strenuous, hard work this was, so that all he wanted to do when he came home was relax and go drinking. He would come home from work and whereas we were given stew and dumplings nearly every night, he would get pork chop and chips and just chuck it up at the wall saying, "I've had that once this week already". He should have tried having stew and dumplings five nights a week – that would have sorted him out! The drinking became heavier. At weekends he would leave for the pub around 11am, sometimes coming home around 3pm, snore his head off for a few hours and wake up just to go back to the pub until the early hours. Sometimes he never even bothered coming home in the afternoons and carried on continuously drinking. Sundays were the same, but the difference was we always got a roast dinner on a Sunday while he was up the pub, the only meal we could enjoy in peace without him and without arguments. Paul usually came around for a Sunday dinner when he came back to Cambridge.

The arguments and violence increased. We witnessed our mother being thumped in the face with such force it threw her backwards and her head smashed through a glass kitchen door. Luckily it was one of those reinforced glass panels that just made a large football-sized dent in the glass. There was never any remorse, there was constant talk that, "I am leaving" and I secretly wished he would, but my mother's nightmare was that he would take Melanie, not that he was ever capable of looking after his own daughter and could never understand this. His threats were that he would smash the house up, leave us with nothing, take Melanie and go to somewhere he would never be found.

I remember on one occasion his bags were even packed. The atmosphere in the house was horrific. When Julie and I got home from school we always looked for his car to see if he was home. When it rained it meant he couldn't work and would be home early, so we dreaded seeing his car. If he was home we would either hang around outside dreading coming in or sneak in the house and go straight to our bedrooms. If he was not home we would stay downstairs and have dinner (stew and dumplings of course). When we did come home and he was there it was like treading on eggshells, never quite sure what the reaction would be, whether he was in a good mood and bearable or just in a rage and best avoided. Just one wrong word said would change him instantly into a raging angry monster, shame he didn't turn green as he could have been the incredible hulk!

The effect on us three children was dramatic. As I mentioned earlier, Paul wanted to live with his own father Alan, but this was not possible, as he was in another relationship by then I guess. I remember him being beaten very badly by John on one occasion. Julie used to retaliate every now and then and also got a taste of John's violence too. As for me, being that much younger and wiser, I just looked on at the situation and worked out how to best avoid being treated like a punch bag. I retreated into myself, became extremely withdrawn, never used to speak to anyone, lost all my friends at school as I could never bring them back to my house and became a real loner. Many a night I cried myself to sleep listening to the ensuing rows and just hoped my mother would not get hurt again. I could not understand how she could continue living a life like this. I hated it and wanted out, but what could I do?

Julie grew up, left school at sixteen and got a job and a boy friend, but life at home was getting worse. Although back then Julie wanted to take a training post to be a typist she had to go to work to earn money, half of which was taken up for housekeeping to live in this horrendous house. As for her boyfriend, well John rejected and insulted just about anyone brought to the house. It finally hit a peak where Julie could take no more and she took a lethal dose of aspirin and walked out the house. Although it was a cry for help, no-one was listening. She stopped at a phone box to ring a friend to tell her what she had done and just walked away. Dizzy, disorientated and close to passing out she was found in time by her friend Sue and rushed to hospital to have her stomach pumped. Would this change our lives? Would our parents finally realise what they were doing to us children? Would they see exactly how unhappy we were? Could they see that they had driven a child to take an overdose? Would social services let her go home to such a family that had driven her to this after she pleaded with them in hospital not to send her home? No such luck, she was sent home to a very hostile reception, no sympathy just venomous glares from John.

Julie eventually reached the magical age of eighteen, and it was very shortly after that she left. She had a big party in a local hall to celebrate her birthday and as usual John ruined that as well. Constant fault picking all night ended in an almighty row on the doorstep to the house for everyone to hear. As the cake was about to be brought in John threw it to the ground. Julie was taken in by a friend's neighbour as a lodger, never to come home again, lucky her! Paul gone, Julie gone, just me left to go now and then John should be happy with his own little family once he got rid of me.

I was now fourteen and hitting rock bottom myself. I was the most withdrawn child you could imagine: no confidence, no friends, no desire to go to school and I hated life. I was very much a loner, only did the essentials that I was forced to do every day, go to school, do my paper round and live in my little bedroom. I often thought about Julie's suicide attempt and thought how brave she was. It was an easy way out of existing in this life and I dearly wanted to have the strength to do this myself. I thought about many options: throwing myself in front of a train, taking an overdose, but it was just that I wasn't strong enough to do any of these things. My greatest desire was to actually run away from home, a very realistic option that I dreamt of most nights and one which kept my mind busy thinking of the positive benefits – no more listening to the fighting every single night, no more feeling like an outcast in society amongst all these people that knew me, a new life. The only drawback: I had no money, no-where to sleep. Would I freeze to death? If not, would I starve to death? Either way none of these sounded like good options, as they involved a long and agonising death. It was not death that I feared but how to get there peacefully and pain-free in an instant.

There were a couple of high points in all this – when I escaped away from home on school trips. Our school used to have an annual trip to the Lake District. I had to save up my paper round money to pay for the trips, not excessively expensive, at around twenty pounds, which meant saving a pound a week for twenty weeks. It was on these amazing trips that I found a real love of the hills and of being outside. The trips consisted of staying at a hostel in Ambleside and walking in the hills all day with a packed lunch. I did not have to conform to society and interact with others. It was sheer pleasure, walking in the most amazing landscape I had ever seen, being at one with nature, no conversation, being alone and yet somehow not being a loner. In the evenings there were lessons on map reading and mountain rescue. I could forget about all the stress and worries back home: they did not exist for the week I was away. I fell in love with the hills and always vowed I would live in the hills one day. Unfortunately I had to return home again though and nothing had changed.

As a family we only ever had one holiday, and guess what? It was arranged by the pub John went to and was a trip to Butlin's at Skegness, another boozy affair where the kids could be dumped all day and parents drink to their hearts' content. Early on in the holiday John became very sick one night and a doctor had to be called, probably alcohol poisoning, but according to the doctor it was gastro-enteritis. He was back boozing again by the end of the holiday so it obviously wasn't that serious. Not a holiday I would ever want to go on again, as it really wasn't an escape from home, only another excuse to drink all day, every day, instead of just weekends, and the holiday didn't stop John from being his normal abusive self.

Julie now seemed happy in her new life away from home, Paul also seemed to be happy with his little bedsit – this was the answer. I had to make it to eighteen years old and then I could leave this living hell behind. I could rent a little bedsit like Paul's and have my own life. Life would then be for me to make it and not dictated by those around me. This was my only salvage, to watch the clock tick by until I was eighteen and old enough to leave home. This was what I had to do, to develop a strategy to cope with each day as it came, tick it off at night and say it was another day nearer to the day I could leave. I had a plan and I now simply had to cope with life, bear it until the day I could leave, just four more years.

At infant and junior schools I remember having many friends and being a normal child. Now attending Coleridge School I was a different person. As a child I was probably the most academic of the three of us, easily did all the work at school with no hassle. At senior school it was initially the same but home life was now taking its toll on my work. I barely did the minimum to get through class. I never had any concentration; it was a case of getting through the day. I did have one close friend in junior school called Glynis. Initially we used play with each other after school and go around to each others' houses, but this petered out as a result of my home life and Glynis went on to be best friends with Jenny. Sometimes after particularly bad weekends I was scared to come home. John really did have a vicious streak, when he grabbed hold of you by the scruff of your neck and held his fist up to your face looking at you with the most evil eyes you can imagine and anger written all over his face. He would say, "Do that again and I will smash your face to bits".

Luckily I was never the focus of any physical violence. I had moments like the above that scared the living daylights out of me but just made me withdraw more into myself, never daring to tell a soul what was going on at home and never really having any friends or relatives that I could confide in. It was really a kind of mental torture, constantly living a life of fear, never quite knowing what would happen next, waiting for John to instantly snap and go off into another fit of temper.

At the age of fifteen I managed to get a job at the local supermarket as a checkout operator. That was a bit more money than my paper round and worked on Wednesday, Thursday and Friday evenings (5pm until 8pm) followed by 9am until 5pm on the Saturday. This was great as it was more time out of the house and less time to hear the arguments. Although I was not officially allowed to do a job like this with so many hours while still at school, mother made sure I got the job as a friend was already working there at the same age.

There were a few times that I must have got to a low point and needed attention and turned to self harm. Nothing very serious occurred, but once I poured a kettle of boiling water deliberately over my hand several times and badly scalded it. The pain was immense as I gritted my teeth and squirmed as the boiling water flowed over my hand. This was a real pain as opposed to the mental pain I suffered every night. I didn't cry in agony, only felt content that I had hurt myself and someone would now have to take notice. When my mother came home and I showed her my hand she said I should go to the doctors' to get it sorted and promptly sent me to cycle the 2 miles to the doctors'. So much for sympathy and attention, it was pure anger from my mother that this achieved. The doctor refused to treat me saying I needed hospital treatment and that a parent or guardian should take me there. They were quite surprised that I had turned up at the doctors' on my own. After cycling home again there was still no sympathy. My mother was still angry and annoyed that she would now have to waste time taking me to the hospital. There was no such luxury as to be driven in the car or get a taxi for the 3 mile trip to the hospital; it was back on the bike. By now blisters were developing on my fingers and my hand was beginning to swell quite badly. I had my hand smothered in cream and bandaged and held up in a sling to relieve the swelling. There was still no sympathy though, as my mother made me cycle home with one hand, but as I was wobbly and could not keep up with her on the bike she left me to make my own way home as she had to get dinner ready for John which was a much bigger priority. I suppose it wasn't life threatening, but no love and care was ever shown, not here and not in the rest of my life. She was never an affectionate mother, never really cuddled or hugged me as a child. In one argument with Julie later in life she even declared she couldn't stand children and that Julie was the most miserable child she had ever met.

I suppose I got off lightly compared to what happened to Julie one day. She got knocked off her bike early one morning while doing her paper round. She was hit from behind and went straight through the windscreen of the car landing on the driver's lap. She ended up covered in cuts and bruises from the windscreen, had concussion and a broken collar bone. After being released from hospital I guess they must have assumed she had a caring mother that would look after her. I was surprised when I came home at lunch time to find her home and in bed. She looked awful, covered in blood, arm in a sling being very sick – and there was no-one else home. Mother had thought it more important to go to work as a cleaner at private houses. I am sure under the circumstances her employers would have understood, but obviously working and money was more important to her than her shocked, battered and concussed daughter. A neighbour was finally kind enough to come and sit with Julie and she was extremely worried about her due to her bash on the head and sickness. This was not tough love; this was totally uncaring and absolute neglect. The neighbour obviously knew what went on in our house, as it was a classic council terraced house with thin walls. She had a daughter Gail, the same age as Julie, and they often used to play together. They all heard what we put up with but as with all things in our life, nothing was ever done. Julie was often dragged back into the house to tidy her bedroom or simply pick up a slipper that had been left lying around. Gail would hardly dare put a foot in our house due to John.

I could go on about other examples but I think this gives enough insight into the lack of care we had as children and our hard and insensitive mother. She may have had a hard life with John, but that was her choice and there was no need to take it out on the children. We did not deserve this. But there was a marked contrast with John's daughter. I remember Melanie falling off her bike one day and getting a cut on her chin and a bloodied nose. She was immediately taken to the hospital in the car, and

I mean immediately. I came home to find the front door wide open, the television blaring out and no-one home. There was no major damage, no bones broken, only some cuts and grazes, but much more concern than was ever shown to us. So my mother could be a caring person but not with us, just to John's precious daughter.

Looking back, we were treated so differently it was unbelievable. We were never given pocket money, always made to work for it, doing jobs such as paper rounds, but by the time Melanie got to this age it was deemed too dangerous for her to risk doing a paper round. Not that I am grumbling that we didn't get pocket money as there was nothing wrong with the discipline of doing paper rounds every day and learning the value of money, simply that we were never treated equally. Melanie was lucky enough to be treated like a daughter rather than an outcast that wasn't wanted.

I often dramatised what my real father would be like and hoped that one day he would come and take me away from there and love and care for me in the way that normal families live, but it never happened. It wasn't until later in life that I was aware my brother still had contact with my father, but I felt that to me he would be a stranger after so much time and I have not made contact. Too much time has passed and I don't really feel there would be any bond there. He would be purely my biological father and a stranger in real terms.

Life went on though and soon it was time to leave school. I was always good at maths and technical drawing and careers suggested being an architect, which was rather appealing. Having worked (or was still working) at the checkout in a supermarket I did not envisage doing this the rest of my life and so fancied something a bit better. To do this I knew I had to go to university but again that was another way out of home. At school it was the days of GCEs and CSEs before GCSEs came along. To be an architect I needed A levels in technical drawing, maths and English but I was told my predicted grades would not give me the five GCEs needed to do my A levels at college so I would have to go to college to re-sit my GCEs.

As it happened I did get my five GCEs, but was still forced to go to college to re-sit qualifications I already had. On top of that the technical drawing course that I should have done was stopped at the college and I had to do engineering drawing instead, nothing to do with houses! I was the only female on the course. I hated it but did feel as though a couple of the teachers gave me special attention as I was the only female, but I didn't attend many lessons, I had no motivation to waste a year doing exams that I already had. In addition to this I was being told that there was no point in being an architect as drawings were now all being taken over by computer designs. Computers were only just about coming into their own now; it was 1979 and no schools had them yet.

I saw out the course and passed my driving test, but there was no incentive to carry on. I was told there was no point training to be an architect and I was fed up studying in a man's world. Although now seventeen it was plan B and I needed to get a job. Mother was not going to pay my way; I got a job as a clerical assistant in the local government office, then called Ministry of Agriculture, Fisheries and Food. I was put in an office with two women and a man, much older than me and studiously wanted to work. But I was baffled. I would do my work and sit there with nothing to do and had to be taught to pretend to look busy when all the senior officers came in. It felt like a false job and I hated it.

Eventually I got moved to the registry department. The office staff probably thought I was a freak of nature as I was such an extremely quiet person who only really spoke when I was spoken to. Registry was a much more lively and vibrant office with younger people. I got on well here, very busy with post and files to sort and make up and I began to make friends. But after being here a year it was obvious that by now I should have moved onwards and upwards and become a clerical officer as all those around me had done so. The reason I was still sitting here was obvious: I didn't have the gift of the gab. I was quiet and carried out my work precisely, probably the hardest worker in the office but this counted for nothing. What counted was how you got on with people and communication. I was still a very shy and withdrawn person with few social skills. I was frustrated. I was still a person and worked harder than anyone but that would never be good enough. I was not going to sit here and be walked all over by others, doing all the work while they got the promotions, so it was back to the drawing board to find another job. I had my principles and this was now my life. I was in control. I had been walked all over at home and I was not going to accept this in the life that I was creating for myself.

But the days had ticked by, the years had passed and the magical age of eighteen was finally achieved. Life began at last as I left home and got a bedsit at the same house as my brother Paul. It was heaven, sheer bliss to come home every night, not to have to look out to see if the car was there and John was home, not to have to listen to shouting every night and the obnoxious John after his drinking binges. Life was just me and my own little palace and my whole life ahead of me.

Sister Julie was now married to David and started her family. This was all she wanted in life, to have a family and show them love, care and affection, the complete opposite to what we had as kids. You often hear how kids grow up and treat their kids the way they were treated and claim they know no different. This is not the case. You know what mis-treatment is, you know if you don't like something as a child and so you should never do this to your children. Julie is a prime example of this, abused as a child but such a loving, caring parent to her children (eventually all five of them!). She has probably gone the other way and done too much for them, but they have so far all developed into loving, caring and well balanced people.

Surprisingly though, many years later, there have been a couple of relatives that have come forward and apologised for not realising what was going on at home. They always knew life was unhappy at home but not the extent to which we suffered and they could never understand why I would never speak to them when visits were made. This aunt and uncle made comments that they were surprised that I turned out to be a "normal adult" as I was such a withdrawn child and they probably thought I was abnormal in some way. They sincerely apologised for not taking me out of the hostile environment I lived in but it really was not their problem and at the time I was so scared I did not know they were a friendly family that would understand. As a child I really did feel all alone in this situation. It was not a situation that was easy to talk about and I could not just blurt this out to any relation. Would they really believe me? I could not tell the teachers at school for fear that if I did tell anyone and my parents were questioned it would be another excuse for a violent outburst and so it was best kept secret. Even now in writing this book and revealing my life as a child, my parents are still alive and can read this, but there can be no come-back as these are factual parts of my life as a child as I remember them and I now have no fear of my parents.

Julie also had not realised how I suffered as a child. As I never confronted John and stood up for my mother the way she did, she assumed that I was unaffected by all that went on at home. She knew that I was quiet and always ran away from all the problems at home. I stayed in my room and was never on the violent side of John so I suffered in a different way to her, but still suffered. Had Julie realised that I was living a nightmare also she would have taken me away from this life at a far earlier stage, but again, this was not her fault and how could she ever have known? This was not a house that she would often visit because of the memories it held and certainly not with John still in the house.

I have told my childhood story to try to make sense of why I became such an extreme runner who can tolerate a high level of pain that is really self inflicted and can push myself beyond barriers that most feel are humanly impossible. I think I simply developed a very strong will mentally to reach the age of eighteen, to survive and live day after day wanting this to be over, and of course, there was a goal post, a finishing line at the age of eighteen, the day I would become an adult and not have to live my life dictated to by my parents.

I want no sympathy about my childhood. Childhood is supposed to be the happiest time of your life; for me it was something I had to bear. It is a chapter of my life that I want to put behind me and forget – but it does keep rearing its ugly head. Family issues did create a few more problems later in life but I find it very easy to detach myself from my parents now (and have not had contact with them for many years). It's more about supporting my sister Julie who obviously suffered (and still suffers) from our childhood treatment. The best way of really describing it for me was "mental torture". I was not personally hit by John, just normal smacking from a mother, but was severely abused as a child.

The family issues did arise more when Julie had her children and more family problems ensued. There were frequent confrontations between families and my parents utterly refused to accept our childhood as we saw it and denied that we had any problems and asserted that we had a normal happy childhood. My mother claims she had a hard childhood, and she probably did, but as Julie can prove, you do not have to treat your children as you were treated yourself. It was some time ago that my mother was diagnosed with early stages of liver cirrhosis and apparently was devastated. I can't sympathise with a self inflicted illness and the fact that she still drank alcohol despite this diagnosis; so how devastated was she really? The thing to do was to stop drinking. Amazingly my mother and John still live together all this time later, even after Melanie grew up and left home. They must enjoy a life of conflict and pain.

Having seen this life my parents lived, I vowed never to live life like this. I would never be dictated to by a monster such as this. I would live an independent life and claimed I would never get married. I would have a life of bliss that I would create, my own little world, my own little heaven and live the way I wanted. I guess this would have been a very lonely existence. I had built up a big barrier that would be hard for anyone to crack, hard for anyone to get close to me and really get to know me. Deep down I thought I would be an independent, happy person, but I was to find happiness with one very special man; our lives would develop dramatically together.

Chapter 3

The Start of My Life and Running

My first job was as a civil servant. While here I met David Blyth; he was the stores person who dished out all the stationery. He was a small, thin, balding, Scots-man, no taller than me, who used to run to work and home again most days. He spent most of his life in the Army and was now seeing out his remaining few years in this post, as he was not far off retirement. As I was such a shy person he always made an effort to talk to me to get a response and I developed a good relationship with David. We would occasionally go to lunch together. I did have a fascination for running and had seen the London Marathon on television a few times and I did have a deep-down desire to run this as a challenge one day, but getting out and doing it was another thing.

David said I had the right build for running and could make a good runner. I was quite small and very thin at that stage. I was a feeble six stone on leaving school and really stick insect thin, but now I had left home and was not so stressed and was eating more regularly I was beginning to look a more "healthy thin" and was up to seven stone. But time ticked by and as usual I did nothing about it. I did, however, go and watch David run the Cambridge Half Marathon, which happened to start on Parkers Piece, in central Cambridge and opposite the Police Station where my bedsit was. I tagged on behind the last runners and ran diagonally across the field, not even half a mile and I was completely out of puff. I was amazed. I could not believe that people could really run this fast or far and promptly sat down feeling quite sick from my exertion and waited for the runners to finish. I was stunned at the speed of the runners and watched in awe, I had such great respect for them. It didn't seem that long before I saw David run through. He stormed through in just under 1 hour 30 minutes. It was unbelievable for his age of nearing retirement. I could not even imagine running this distance, let alone with such amazing speed. It was incredibly moving and inspiring. It was a big field of runners: around two thousand in total and there was a real carnival atmosphere on a lovely sunny summer's day. There was a marquee and several stalls and I sat around with David and vowed I would run this race the following year.

I was never a sporty person at school. The main sport my school offered was netball and occasionally hockey. On the odd occasion that we did sport inside it was again netball with the occasional trampoline lesson, which I did enjoy, but as there were so many in the class you were only allowed about 5 minutes each on the trampoline. I absolutely hated netball. I had no hand-eye co-ordination, often dropped the ball and was useless at throwing the ball in the right direction and at the right velocity for others to catch. Also, being quite small, I was no good at defending and could never get the ball in the net no matter how much I practised, so this was always a subject I hated. At the start of each game one of the strongest players would always be picked to choose their team. I was always the last to be chosen and it was always by default that someone got me on their team. As I was such a bad player nobody would ever throw the ball to me, so I stood around on the court getting shouted at by the Physical Education teacher because I was not moving, a very demoralising situation all round. Our school rarely did the classic cross country runs that so many people complain about and say was the bit they hated about school, but had I done this at school I might have found out that I actually liked running. The only exercise I had ever done was to cycle to school, about a mile from where I lived, and the paper round of course.

When I left school I still cycled everywhere until I got my first job and could then afford to buy a cheap, second hand car. So the bike got dumped in the shed, never to be used again. But the car was a disaster, constantly breaking down. I never dared drive far, for fear of it not getting there, so I only used it for work and taking my mother shopping occasionally. After I left home I used to go to see my mother for a roast dinner every Sunday when John was up the pub and I would often visit Julie and her children. In the space of a few years Julie had her first three children, Donna, Michael and then Jamie. Michael was quite ill as a baby and had to have an operation on his heart. He often suffered with immune problems and chronic asthma that put him in hospital several times in his younger days.

It was that first Christmas after I watched David run the Cambridge Half Marathon that something happened that was to make me get out of the house and finally start running. David bought me a pair of good running shoes to start running. I felt so guilty that he had spent so much money on me to buy me this stylish pair of Brooks's running shoes that felt like slippers on my feet. The cushioning was like running on air compared with the cheap pair of non-running trainers I was wearing. That was the trigger to finally put my foot out of the door and start running. But as I was not a confident person, very self conscious in fact, I didn't want to be

19

seen, as I knew I could barely run and was so unfit; so I snuck out in the dead of night when it was dark and people would not be able to recognise me and laugh at my attempt at running. I drove around the block which I estimated to be about a mile by the odometer on the car. A good challenge: run a mile. Here I was in my twenties, in the prime of my life and I could barely run 400 metres without getting totally out of puff and my legs aching like mad, but I persevered and set my goal to run around the block non-stop. It took about three weeks before I finally achieved this, running a whole mile without stopping to walk and it felt fantastic. It was such a great feeling of self satisfaction and contentment. Only a runner could really understand this feeling of deep internal achievement.

That conquered, I had to set a new goal – two laps of the block and then eventually a new loop that was 3 miles in length. This felt like such a challenge; could I really attempt a whole 3 miles? But I was bitten by the bug; I was running usually every other day now and gradually increasing the distance; so I sent off my entry for the Cambridge Half Marathon on 15th July 1984. I did have one hiccup in training, not running-related, but I broke my second toe and could not run for a few weeks. I often met up with David after work and went for a run with him, if you could call it that. I was so slow compared to him that he probably didn't enjoy the run at all and it certainly would not have contributed to his fitness. He usually made me go out in daylight hours to gain more confidence, as there was nothing about my running that I should be ashamed about.

When the big day finally approached I was a bag of nerves. Due to my toe injury the furthest I had run was 7 miles and this was 13.1 miles. It was a two lap course and as I lived right at the start of the race I had often practised running one lap on the race course. It was exciting and scary all at the same time. I really wanted to run the full 13.1 miles and not have to stop and walk. As I was going to do a race with so many other "real" runners I knew I would be at the back of the field and had a real fear that I would be last home. David was really re-assuring, insisting that I would not be last and also predicting my racing time. I had not really even thought about a time prediction, but based on the fact that it was taking me around an hour to run one lap of this course, I thought I would probably slow down dramatically and finish in 2 hours 30 minutes. David thought I would not be that much slower than 2 hours. The gun went and I started right at the back of the field. I ran across Parkers Piece with such a great feeling of contentment. I had been here the previous year and had barely been able to run across this field and yet here I was attempting to run 13.1 miles, absolutely astonishing!

20

I went out on the first lap concentrating on keeping the pace really easy. There were loads of runners around me and at this stage I had absolutely no fear of coming last. Into the second lap and, although perhaps feeling a little apprehensive, I was really looking forward to seeing exactly how far I could run. I was now running into new territory. I had never run this far before. Could I keep it going? On and on, I was doing this. Yes, I, who could not even run a mile a year ago, was ticking off the miles as they came, 8 miles, 9 miles, 10 miles until I finally circled round for the home run back. I was feeling tired but I was still running and I had not stopped to walk once. I was running with such a feeling of deep satisfaction. I was going to do this, it was to be my first ever achievement in life and it was all for me, no great reward at the finish, just a medal like all the other two thousand or so finishers. I turned into Parkers Piece for the final finishing straight. There was David cheering me on, he had finished ages ago and had already changed his kit. The finishing funnel was deep with crowds of supporters all shouting and cheering. It was such an uplifting experience, it was hard to put into words, such a great feeling that for once in my life I had done something positive and got my medal hung around my neck. I had run a full 13.1 miles non-stop. It was great but I felt really fatigued once I stopped and I sat down for a bit to reflect and wallow in self satisfaction.

My time was 2 hours 4 minutes and 17 seconds, 1764th out of 1885 finishers. There were over a hundred runners behind me and it was far better than I had anticipated, but my time really meant nothing to me. Finishing running 13.1 miles without stopping had been my goal and I had achieved this. David, by comparison was very disappointed with his run, 1 hour 33 minutes which was slower than his sub 1 hour 30 minutes performance the previous year, not something I could quite comprehend yet, as I thought it was a marvellous performance.

My legs ached for a week afterwards, but I was now ready to do the London Marathon. It was a bit of a lottery as to whether or not I would get in, as so many people apply to do this every year and only about thirty thousand accepted back then; so this was my first obstacle.

I stayed in the civil service for about three years and while there went on an Outward Bound course in Fort William. This was a real eye opener for me. It was a three week course of activity and I got up to all sorts. Each week's activities included a "big expedition". The first week was canoeing, which was a disaster as it rained so heavily and was quite windy; so we had to abandon the water after a couple of canoes capsized with the water getting very rough. Our kit got pretty wet and where we camped turned into a boggy stream with water flowing through the tents. As we had to be out for three days and be self sufficient with the food we carried, we walked up to a bothy, pooled what food was left and not wet and stayed our time there until we could get back. The second week was my favourite and I found my real love. We went backpacking and the weather was glorious, although I really struggled with the backpack and heavy equipment we had to carry (big canvas three man tents back then). I loved the freedom of being out in the hills, setting up camp where we wanted and being in such a tranquil situation. I always knew I would come back to the hills and had forgotten how much I really loved being there; it was the only place I had really felt like I belonged and could feel happy. No pressure on me from any sources – apart from here where I was the slowest and most unfit of the bunch and struggled to keep up with the others.

The third expedition was a sailing trip, a big teamwork event that I was not too taken with, but I did enjoy being on the water. We did lots of other things. Rock climbing and abseiling were something else I knew I didn't like: dangling from a rope with enormous drops and clinging on to the rock face for dear life while being eaten alive by midges. This was not my idea of fun, nor was climbing a tree, getting slapped by branches and being a contortionist to twist between the branches, following the ropes of the lead man. It was a great three weeks though, and, although I didn't enjoy some of the activities, I really learnt a lot in terms of what I wanted from life and the things that I really did enjoy. I probably got a lot fitter as a result, as shortly after I returned I completed my second half marathon in September, near Bury St Edmunds and finished with 1 hour 56 minutes and 2 seconds, not a bad improvement.

It was shortly after I returned from this trip that I changed my job. As I mentioned earlier, I was stuck as a clerical assistant and could not gain promotion due to my shyness. I felt as though I was being walked all over and laughed at, as most young people who worked there got promotion within six months to a year. My next job was nothing special, merely another job that brought in the money. I worked as a stores person and driver for a chemical company near Saffron Walden. The company provided a free bus service to bring in the workers from Cambridge. I enjoyed the job far more, but again was working with mostly middle-aged people in a small office of around four people. I enjoyed my time here though, as I was not tied to the desk all the time. The job entailed getting up and sorting out stock, serving employees who came in for stock and driving for the company, picking up either people or deliveries. It was a more varied job and was a pleasant stop gap for a few years.

It was a week or so before Christmas when I got my first blow; I had been rejected from the London Marathon. It was very disheartening. I hadn't realised how important goal setting had been and, without the goal of the London Marathon to run, I didn't feel much enthusiasm to get out and train, but shortly after this I went on my first backpacking expedition. I had been reading up on the subject, looking at all the equipment needed and all the National Long Distance Paths that there were in Great Britain. This was a great way to start by walking a standard way-marked path that had a definitive start and finish line so I could again sense that satisfying feeling of saying I had done something. David had a lot of backpacking experience from the past and was very helpful in enabling me to get all the equipment together. The backpack itself and tent were the most expensive, but David generously donated a quality down sleeping bag that he had surplus to requirements.

We did our first hike together in the Lake District as a practice run for the equipment and I had forgotten what stunning beauty there was in this National Park. I loved every minute of it and the backpack was much more comfortable, being a bit lighter and actually fitting me.

Next we were to embark on the first of many of the National Long Distance Walks. This was to be Offa's Dyke, 168 miles from the bottom to the top of Wales, Chepstow to Prestatyn. It was good to have David with me, as I gained more confidence in myself and it was also good to at least have some company. Navigation was quite easy, as this was a way-marked path with the traditional "acorn" signs to follow that labelled this as an official "Long Distance Path". It was a much more varied walk than just slogging it up and down mountains and we frequently went through little towns. It was again very satisfying to complete this walk and feel as though I had achieved something. It also gave me somewhere to go in my time off, as I had never really gone on holidays and not being a real socialiser preferred the quiet spots away from everyone. Although campsites were very cheap, I still preferred to wild camp away from everyone to really experience that feeling of complete freedom, to be at one with the world and completely self-sufficient.

Over the festive season at Christmas that year I finally had the excuse to give the family ordeal a miss. I hated Christmas, yet another reason to get drunk and I could never quite tell when John would turn into his nasty self. It was always after the drink that he would turn unpleasant and always nit-picked over such tiny issues that got blown out of all proportion; some were over the type of wine or whether or not cranberry sauce was provided. As Julie had a family of her own now and the children wanted to stay at home and play with their presents, we now had our family dinner there. Julie did a really superb job: all the trimmings, very pretty decorated table with cranberry sauce just for John, a back-up horseradish sauce, just in case it was that item that was essential to avoid an argument, and of course, a bottle of quality dry wine just for John to prevent any complaints about this.

Instead I was to travel up to Scotland to walk the West Highland Way, 95 miles with David. He lived alone and never really went anywhere for Christmas; so was just as happy as me to go backpacking at this time of year. As it turned out, it was not the best decision about the time to walk this because of the weather. We started on Christmas day at Milngavie train station, near Glasgow and walked a few miles the first day before darkness. The next day we climbed over Conic hill to drop down to Loch Lomond at Balmaha, but we were to experience a few problems sleeping in the tents; the temperature dropped below freezing and the camping gas was not working too well. As we had stopped before darkness, the temperature was still high enough to cook our dinners, albeit very slowly, but by morning the water in the bottles had frozen solid, so we could not have any breakfast or morning tea. That day we walked to Rowardennan Hotel and camped here so we could have dinner in the hotel. It was actually quite cosy having dinner there and passed some of the time instead of shivering in our tents. We now had to make sure we made it to some sort of civilisation every evening, as it was impossible to eat in the tents, so this dictated how far we walked each day.

The walk to Inversnaid the next day was amazing. There had been such a hard frost that waterfalls had formed into massive icicles hanging down, and with the sun shining onto them, they were glinting like shiny, precious necklaces dangling from rocks engraved on the landscape. Underfoot conditions were quite tricky, and being thrown a little off balance carrying a heavy pack on the slippery ground led to a few falls, but thankfully nothing too serious. The next freezing night was spent at Inveraran and the snow began to fall the following day on the way to Tyndrum, roughly half way on the route. Then we reached one of the most remote sections on the walk; after the Bridge of Orchy an old Military Road led us over the bleak Rannoch Moor. It was snowing heavily as we crossed, the snow piling up beneath us making the going very slow, but we dared not stop as the temperature was dropping. There was no reprieve, no quick short cut down to civilisation or shelter and warmth. We had to dig deep to continue walking the 19 miles that day to reach Kingshouse, and dinner for the night.

24

This isolated hotel was very busy for the night. We had contemplated staying in the hotel as conditions were so harsh, but we had forgotten it was the festive season and many people came away for the holidays to stay here. It was fully booked. After staying in the warmth for dinner we were very reluctant to venture out to our tents that were quite hard to find under the snow.

The next day was new year's eve and it was difficult to follow the path over Devil's Staircase, as the snow was falling again and making the route almost impassable, but a few hardened walkers had already been out and left footprints to follow so we made it over and finished the day at Kinlochleven. Like everywhere else we had stopped, there were no campsites open in the dead of winter and we struggled to find a suitable place to camp in the snow. The only feasible spot was along a grass verge that had been slightly protected from the snow by trees, right alongside the road, but it was a very quiet village.

However, it was not a quiet night, as it was new year's eve and we had to go to the pub to get our dinner. We had a few drinks for the first time. I was never really a drinker, having seen very drunken parents it was not something I ever wanted to do, to become dependent on alcohol and get in such a state.

After a few drinks, David got on well with the locals, being a Scotsman with a very strong accent still, and we were invited back to someone's house. I don't really think they believed us when we said we were camping and were walking to Fort William the next day. But we saw the new year in and walked to Fort William on new year's day to complete our journey. As it was a bank holiday there was no public transport and the only food available was at a Chinese restaurant and we had to camp in a local park until we could start our trip home the next day.

Upon returning home I opened my mail to some good news. I had been accepted to run the Mars London Marathon on 20th April 1986. For the last year I had completed the odd race here and there and not improved on my time at all. In fact I raced on seven occasions that year; five of them were half marathons, all around the 2 hours mark. Now I had the goal to aim at and a reason to step up the miles, it was a great incentive and really made me push myself every time I went out. Each time that I went out and ran further than I had ever run before it felt satisfying and I did another four races in the lead up to London, the longest being the Rutland Water 17 miles (my longest run before the London Marathon) and my fastest half marathon at Swavesey with a great new personal best time of 1 hour 46 minutes. I even got a trophy for being the 1st lady in the seventeen to twenty-three years old age group. David also did this race in a time of 1 hour 41 minutes, so as I was getting faster he was getting slower, but considering he was now retired this was still fantastic running.

The day of the London Marathon dawned and it was exciting. I had never seen so many runners and the queue to the start line was horrendous. I couldn't get anywhere even near enough to see the start line; so joined the masses. I was not that bothered about a fast start, as like my first half marathon my goal was just to finish running. The furthest I had run was 17 miles and I was now going to step up to 26.2 miles. It almost felt dreamlike; as if this really wasn't happening to me. How had I become a marathon runner? But the start was signalled and I stood and waited. Eventually there was movement and a slow walk; 20 minutes later I reached the start line, but I wasn't bothered about the time, I just wanted to get going now and start this dream. It was slow going to start with, due to the crowds, but bit by bit we spaced out and managed to get moving. Part of me liked being with so many like-minded runners, but part of me hated feeling so jammed in with others, having to watch every step, occasionally being shoved and accidentally kicked. The miles started to tick by and it began to happen, I was running the London Marathon, over Tower Bridge and the half marathon mark shortly afterwards, on to the Isle of Dogs. It was an amazing experience and I had now hit the 17 mile mark and the start of a new challenge. I was still feeling surprisingly comfortable, much better than when I had run the 17 miles previously. I had never seen such crowds, shouting out runner's numbers or people's names printed on their shirts. What with the bands that were playing, and the entertainment, it was like a 26 mile long party and I totally soaked up the atmosphere. This was a really fantastic event and I had never experienced anything like it; I really was a part of this event.

Mile by mile went on and on almost effortlessly and then I hit the cobbles, and yes, I was now made very aware of the fatigue I was feeling. I was thrown off balance and began to feel my knees aching. The fronts of my legs were sore too, and my calves screaming at me, but I looked around at the magnificent uniforms of the Beefeaters and remembered I was living my dream of running the London Marathon. The euphoria continued, along the Embankment, down Birdcage Walk and eventually to London Bridge and the finish as I looked up and could see Big Ben.

I held my hands high as I ran under the banner and achieved my dream. I, Sharon Kember, had run the Mars London Marathon of 1986 in a time of 4 hours 27 minutes and 7 seconds with an overall position of 14, 658th. I was on cloud nine, overcome with emotion and cried my eyes out. It's hard to explain, but I hadn't realised how much I had really wanted this. I looked around feeling pretty stupid at my reaction, but I wasn't alone, there were others weeping too, grown men reduced to tears. It was a really humbling, profound feeling; acutely overwhelming, intensely satisfying and my dream had really come true. I really had run, and I mean run 26.2 miles and had not stopped to walk once. But walking now, I certainly knew I had overstretched the mark. I was aching and beginning to stiffen up, but I couldn't care less, it was worth every ache and pain to be an achiever. I had a medal hung around my neck; was given my goodie bag with a massive t-shirt and made my way home. I could hardly walk up and down the stairs to my bedsit that week as stiffness beyond belief set in.

It wasn't until a couple of weeks later when my legs were returning to normal and the euphoria wearing off that I realised I had no incentive to train any more. I had set a goal to run the London Marathon and now that my goal had been achieved there was no reason to go running and training any more. It was a weird sensation and quite a disheartening thought; nothing could rekindle that inner desire to feel a worthy person who deserved a place in society. I needed a new goal, but I had not really realised what goal setting was at that stage, and how much I needed a new incentive, a new goal.

Where I lived near the Police Station was also close to the only indoor swimming pool in Cambridge and I used to go swimming regularly in the mornings before work when the pool was divided into lanes. I often used to bump into David here. He pointed out someone called Sarah Springman, who was the British and European Women's Triathlon Champion – that was a 2.4 mile swim, 112 mile cycle and then finishing with a marathon, 26.2 miles of running. I found this astounding; the marathon was tiring enough without all the swimming and cycling. She was a sub 3 hour marathon runner too!

It wasn't long after that I read in the local Cambridge Evening News that Sarah was backing the Cambridge Triathlon, a smaller introductory event of a 20 mile cycle to Newmarket and back, 1 mile swim in the local outdoor swimming pool, followed by five laps of Coldham's Common field, a fraction under 5 miles. For something new to do I thought I would have a bash; so I got a cheap new bike and started practising cycling to Newmarket and back, as well as doing the swimming and a bit of running.

27

My next race was the Cambridge Half Marathon in July, nothing significant with a finishing time of 1 hour 52 minutes. The Cambridge Triathlon was on 10th August 1986. It was exciting doing a new challenge, but I had not really trained long or hard enough to do it justice and in reality knew I could cycle, swim and run the distances involved; so it was not really into new territory like before when I really didn't know if I could do it, although I had never done all three sports together. It didn't feel so much like a race as the first event was cycling and we were set off at intervals to avoid congestion and we were not surrounded by other athletes and I never really knew where I was in the race. Next it was into the swimming pool and I found that I had never thought much about the changeover. Others were far quicker here. The pool was full of flies and dirt, so I didn't enjoy it and finally I was off for the run. As it was a lapped event on grass I could see I was overtaking a few other athletes and was running strongly, but on finishing there was none of the overwhelming emotion that I had when I finished the London Marathon. It was merely like finishing any other event, just a different one. I came 12th of the 26 female competitors and was 6th fastest on the running section finishing the event in 2 hours 12 minutes.

I then had an array of racing numbers. Each one felt special as every race had been an achievement. I couldn't bring myself to throw the numbers away, and even got certificates with some of the races; so I started my collection of scrapbooks. Every race number I have collected has been glued in a scrapbook, along with certificates and including race date, venue, time and position.

It was a week after this that I set off on my first backpacking expedition on my own, along the Pennine Way. Although I guess David would have liked to have tagged along, it was something that I wanted to do on my own. I had the confidence to do this now and wanted to go back to that great feeling of being at one with the world in the wilderness. This was a 270 mile point to point walk up the spine of England, starting at Edale in the Derbyshire Peaks and finishing over the border in Scotland at a tiny village called Kirk Yetholm.

In walking this I found my real sense of freedom again, completely locked in my own world, away from all the news and unaware of what was happening in the world. This was the way I liked it, no peer pressure or expectations to live up to in order to conform to society, just me and my house on my back wondering the footpaths of the country. I wished I could carry on living the rest of my life this way.

I set off from Edale at 7:30am for the start of my long, lonely trek. I really loved being outside, doing a bit of exercise and doing exactly as I wanted. The route was not great, as recent wet weather had made the going very tough in the "peat groughs" that had to be negotiated. I was fearful of going off route, but in some ways it didn't really matter as I had all I needed on my back; so I didn't need to make it to a campsite as I was completely self-sufficient. The weather was also deteriorating. The windy morning, where I witnessed the small trickle called Kinder Downfall being blown upwards; had now turned into heavy rain and I was sinking up to my knees in some of the peat bogs. I only made it as far as Crowdon Hostel, 15 miles into the walk, as the weather was closing in with the mist and I was not enjoying this now.

The next day dawned dry and cloudy and the aptly named summit of Black Hill (1,908 feet) was a black quagmire of peat. I had bumped into several other walkers all attempting the Pennine Way and I felt as if we all had a kindred spirit, the same inner strength of mind to complete this challenge. I continued on my way, religiously following my maps across the M62 motorway to camp with a few others in a disused quarry after 19 miles of walking.

The weather was grimly overcast again the next day, but I continued on my trek. I made a short detour into Hebden Bridge to re-stock my supplies, but hated being back in the hustle and bustle of town life, with cars and people busily rushing around getting jobs done and I was glad this was only a short visit before heading back to the hills and tranquillity again. I went by Stoodley Pike and into Bronte Country. The section near Withens, a decaying skeleton of a house, the Wuthering Heights of Emily Bronte's classic novel, was very popular with day walkers. I camped near Ponden Reservoir, having done another 20 mile trek.

A wonderful sunny day dawned, dry at last and I thoroughly enjoyed the walking, a little less strenuous than the previous day, coming to camp beside the River Aire. The next section I found was becoming more beautiful and I was becoming more at home with the landscape and my journey, as I was into the Yorkshire Dales, by way of Malham Tarn, the amphitheatre of Malham Cove and the climbing of Fountains Fell (2,192 feet) and Pen-Y-Gent (2,273 feet), one of the "Three Peaks" that are part of a challenge walk. The path then led down to Horton-in-Ribblesdale where the Three Peaks Challenge starts, the other peaks being Ingleborough and Whernside. The cafe there welcomed Pennine Way walkers and had a range of supplies especially selected for the Pennine Way. Fully loaded,

I set off for my night alone about a mile from Sell Gill Holes, having walked 21 miles that day. This was what I wanted, glorious landscapes, camping in the middle of no-where, not a soul in sight, solitude and isolation, like a separation from the world in my own remote little paradise. I felt at one with myself.

My ecstasy continued, setting off at 6:30am way above the clouds on the high level pack horse road that led to Hawes and the completion of the first 100 miles. I stopped there shortly for lunch and the heavy rain began to fall. A steady climb of 5 miles followed to go over Bluebell Hill, Little Fell, and Black Hill Moss to reach the trig point on Great Shunner Fell (2,340 feet), the highest point so far on the Pennine Way. The walk was miserable as the mist came down, visibility was poor and the path deteriorated into a slippery mire. Better was to come though, as on descending below the mist I came to the River Swale, a magnificent collection of swirling waters and waterfalls cascading in full force with the weather. I opted for the soft option of the Youth Hostel at Keld in view of the foul weather, as I needed to dry my kit out.

The next morning continued with the same wet, misty weather onto Tan Hill Inn, the highest licensed house in the country at 1,732 feet. I took the alternative, longer route to Bowes Castle after the horror stories I had heard about the deep peat hags on Sleightholme Moor where walkers sink up to their waists in black swamps. The weather finally began to improve, but further detours were to follow, as the fords at Deepdale Beck had swollen massively to make this impassable and I had to find a bridge. I continued onwards by Baldersdale and the half way point to camp near Grassholme Reservoir (26 miles that day!).

A bright day at last for the trip to Middleton-In-Teesdale and I followed the pleasant riverside path by Low Force until the thunderous crashes of the water of High Force could be heard. Half hidden from view initially, it was hard to miss, the sheer volume of water plunging over a 70 feet drop to a rocky bed in a wooded gorge. It was the biggest waterfall in England. Quite a spectacle but also a tourist attraction and the place was flooded with viewers. Further on my hike I enjoyed the approach to the next waterfall at Cauldron Snout. By contrast this waterfall cascaded 200 feet, its tumbling water jumping left and right, interrupted by rocks. I scrambled up the steep rocks to reach the top where the waterfall was fed by Cow Green Reservoir. On and on I walked, with a 4 mile crossing of featureless moor at 2,000 feet to descend to Maize Beck and another swollen beck crossing, but the best was yet to come, a cairned path led to the top of High Cup Nick. I came across it all of a sudden, a natural wonder, a massive symmetrical bowl rimmed by a formation of basalt crags that maintains a level contour all the way around, absolutely stunning and something that can only be witnessed on foot. This was why I loved the outdoors, the breathtaking, astounding natural wonders that just appeared. I had to sit and admire this panorama. The path skirted the rim on a high level course before descending to the village of Dufton, where I camped with many other Pennine Way walkers.

After that 24 miles of glorious visual attractions, I had 16 miles of the hardest climbs the following day and the weather was vying with me: cold, cloudy and very strong winds on a day that involved four summits over 2,600 feet. First was Knock Fell (2,604 feet), then Great Dunn Fell (2,780 feet), with its radar masts and a weather station with the tarmac road leading to the village of Knock; the highest surfaced road in the country. The descent followed to the marshy depression of Tees Head and another abrupt climb to Little Dunn Fell (2,761 feet). Then there was a dip and a sharp rise to the fringe of boulders that rings the plateau of Cross Fell (2,930 feet). The summit had a trig point, a display of cairns and a very welcome wind shelter. There was one last descent to negotiate before resting at Garrigill for the night.

It was Monday 25th August, a bank holiday, when I walked another magnificent 21 miles as the wind continued to strengthen. As the day continued, I felt a little tired and the going was slow after the massive climbs of the previous day; so I called it a day to wild camp near Todholes Barn, about a mile from Greenhead. Although grassy in appearance the ground was quite stony underneath and it was difficult to get the tent pegs in. I was alongside a brick barn of some kind and so had some shelter from the wind. It was a deafening, sleepless night as the wind and rain buffeted the tent all night long. I crawled out a couple of times to hammer in the pegs a bit better but at 4am disaster struck and the whole tent collapsed. The wind was flapping the tent all over and my kit was beginning to scatter. It was impossible to put it up again in the darkness; so I just bundled everything up and tried to squeeze through the door of the barn. It turned out to be full of junk and impossible to move! I just squashed everything through the door, put every piece of kit on and waited until daylight. Most of my kit was soaked through by this stage and, fighting against the shivering, I needed to get moving to get warm. There was no space to pack my bag properly; my clothes were all mixed up with a very wet tent and sleeping bag in my attempt to salvage my belongings before they blew away into the night.

By 5:30am the light was beginning to seep through and I was eager to get warm and somewhere safe; so after stuffing everything in my rucksack I went out to battle the weather at 6am. It took nearly 2 hours to stagger down to the shelter of Greenhead Youth Hostel, which had conveniently been barely more than a mile away. The weather was unbelievable. I had never been out in such strong gale force winds, which later transpired to be Hurricane Charlie. It was impossible to stand upright and I was continuously thrown in all directions, rain coming at me sideways and barely able to see where I was walking. It was very unnerving, the one situation where I did not want to be out on a limb all on my own and I sought the company of others.

Greenhead Youth Hostel was my salvation, welcoming me into the warmth of the drying room and offering a hot bowl of porridge, absolute heaven! The forecast was for the weather to continue all day and clear by the evening. There was no point continuing that day. I was cold, wet and tired, my stuff was all wet and I had not slept a wink all night. I booked into the Youth Hostel for dinner and a bed for the night and spent the day drying out all my kit and refuelling for the days ahead.

Wednesday brought showers and blustery conditions but I was full of life again and eager to get going on the next stretch along Hadrian's Wall for 10 miles. There was a section called the Nine Nicks of Thirlwall, a string of nine steep up and downs, with the highest point on Hadrian's Wall at Winshields Crag at 1,230 feet. The route then left the wall to continue its northward journey and I finished my day at Bellingham.

There was no real improvement in the weather the next day: heavy showers and blustery winds, but a long 6 mile section through Redesdale Forest, the biggest man-made forest in Europe at least offered some protection away from the wild moorlands and I progressed 17 miles further, wild camping on a rough spot in the forest on Ogre Hill at 6:30pm. I had hoped to get further as this left 28 miles now to reach the finish line at Kirk Yetholm and I needed to finish as time was running out for the journey home.

I was on my way by 6:30am for the longest day's walk yet. The weather was still overcast with showers and very misty. I followed the fence line, frequently sinking in the bogs, twice up to my waist, I did begin to think that it was possible to sink so deep I might disappear from sight, never to be found under the bogs on this footpath; not a nice way to go and with no one having any idea where I was. Over the summits of Lamb Hill

(1,677 feet), Beefstand Hill (1,842 feet), and Mozie Law (1,842 feet) to reach Windy Gyle (2,034 feet). I continued from here on the Scottish side of the border fence to reach Border Gate and a grass track known as Clennell Street. Through Border Gate and back onto English soil again to surmount Butts Road (1,718 feet), King's Seat (1,743 feet), Score Head (1,910 feet) and a long climb to Cairn Hill (2,419 feet).

There were more peat hags now and underfoot conditions were very difficult on the climb to the Cheviot (2,676 feet). Back into Scotland again, I felt quite exhilarated walking the last few miles to the finish at 6:30pm in the tiny village of Kirk Yetholm, 270 miles completed, all on my own. My journey had come to an end and it was back to the world of civilisation. I signed the Pennine Way Book in the Border Hotel.

It was Saturday 30th August when I began my day long, multiple bus journey back to Cambridge. A big part of me felt very tired, very happy to be finished walking and not being battered by the weather, but an even bigger part of me felt very sad. I had enjoyed my journey and really didn't want it to end. I felt as if I wanted to carry on walking for the rest of my life and never have contact with the outside world ever again; just a few little peeks as I went through the little towns and villages. This had been my first journey on my own, I had wanted it that way and wanted to feel the independence and solitude, navigate for myself and develop my love of freedom in the hills.

The Pennine Way was such a classic path that many know and have heard of. Few people venture out to do this on their own, even fewer were females on their own. I don't think I met another individual female Pennine Way walker, and although I guess many have done this on their own, it was not the norm. Again I felt that deep down satisfying feeling of accomplishment. I didn't feel the need to have to have people around me and was more than happy with just myself for company. My little one roomed bedsit now felt massive compared to my tent, sleeping bag and stove that I had called home for the last two weeks.

I soon slotted straight back into society again, backwards and forwards to work, weekends to myself. I didn't do much running after that, just the odd run to keep a little fitness together, but longed to be out walking again. I felt the need for change again. Doing a nine to five job; the same thing every day, and a long journey to work was giving me itchy feet again and I wanted something new. Flicking through the papers I came across a job for a bus driver. I quite enjoyed the driving side of my job, escaping out of

The double-decker bus in which I passed my test.

the office and almost feeling outside in the car, travelling to different places. That sounded like a nice change; so I turned up at one of the open days for driver testing. The local bus company had just bought a new fleet of minibuses and needed a lot of new drivers. I was offered the job and was soon wearing my new uniform. I had a week of training in both driving, route learning and the ticket and money side of the job and passed my test a few days later.

It was kind of a fun job to start with, different shifts, different start time every day, working weekends, days off during the week, evening shifts, and yet still somehow away from everyone, obviously meeting the public as they stepped on the bus, but also still being on my own driving.

The next year was 1987 and with my new job I actually earned more money and brought myself my first brand new car, a Ford Fiesta. This gave me more freedom to go places and do more of what I wanted. I started running again and could now travel to do a few more races, still mainly around the half marathon distance and I ran a total of thirteen races that year. The highlights of course were my holidays.

My first holiday in 1987 was a trip out in the car to the Isle of Wight in March. I camped and used the car to travel to a different point on the Island every day in order to walk the entire coast of around 60 miles and also visit the many attractions on the Island. It was a good trip but I didn't get to experience that real "out on your own" feeling. So I started planning my next backpacking expedition, something bigger and better and came up with the South West Way – 560 miles, now how was I going to fit all that distance into a holiday!

That was roughly 26 miles a day for four weeks. The weather in the South West should be much more pleasant than what I had experienced on the Pennine Way and there were no big climbs over 2,000 feet. So this was to be my holiday; I was off from the 1st to the 29th July 1987. This was also to be the first occasion that I got in the local press. I was going to do this as a sponsored walk, as it was such a long walk and fellow drivers supported me in this. Julie's young son Michael had heart surgery at a young age and a fellow worker that I still had contact with from my previous job had been taken ill with a heart attack and I was still quite close to him; so I decided to walk this for the British Heart Foundation.

The route was nowhere near as remote as the Pennine Way, but I still managed to find enough solitude to feel that I had made a journey. I met many friendly people along the way, as there was a sign attached to my backpack with a small container for donations. It was such a different journey from the first one experienced, there was little chance of getting lost as I was by the sea most days – I got quite a sun tan too!

I also found that on returning, colleagues now wanted to know how I had done and actually came up to speak to me, something that had never happened to me as a lonely teenager. No one had wanted to know me. I had no conversation. I had never been a person with anything valuable to say, but this trip had created a conversation and created a need for people to want to talk to me and it felt good. After I had collected all the sponsor money I handed it over in one of those big cheques for publicity and got myself in the paper again, having raised just over five hundred pounds.

1988 was pretty much the same, a few half marathons, a few long distance walks; the longest was the Southern Upland Way at 212 miles. Although I planned to walk this on my own, I had bumped into David in the swimming pool and he had wanted to come with me, although he was

Handing over £500 cheque for the British Heart Foundation, raised by walking the 560 miles of the South West Way alone. ©Cambridge Evening News.

suffering from a back problem at the time. We travelled up together and started but on day two he camped by lunch time to take things a bit slower. Unfortunately I was on a time schedule, as I only had two weeks off work to walk this, whereas David was now retired and time was not such an issue. The walk did turn into a more eventful trip than expected. After a few days I camped with a group of three men who were walking the first half of the Southern Upland Way in a week. We had a good rapport and walked together for a few days and afterwards I even became good friends with one of the group called Ray Wallis, from Hull. It was on day five of the walk that we came across an injured walker. I ran back down with Ray to the nearest farmhouse to raise the alarm while Mark and Tony looked after the injured walker, Margaret. We got the best deal, as the farmer's wife gave us a pot of tea and cake. It became obvious this was going to take some time and daylight was not on our side. So it was decided that I would return and let Mark and Tony continue walking to the planned campsite while I stayed with Margaret.

It wasn't long before Ray arrived with a doctor and an ambulance crew to relieve Margaret's pain and we started to carry her down on a stretcher. Further down we met the mountain rescue team who were far stronger with much better equipment. They took over and we returned on our way. Our plan had been to try to make it to the planned bothy where the overnight stop was, but the weather turned and as darkness fell we could see the storm with forked lightning and thunder heading our way. Navigation was difficult and we were walking by torch light with map and compass. We were eventually forced to camp, as we were not entirely sure we were still on course. It was a wild, wet and windy night and we camped at a very vulnerable, bleak spot on the open hillside, with no protection from the elements where I doubted my tent would hold up in the strong gusts. I don't think either of us slept well and I ventured out several times to check my guy ropes.

The next morning the mist was still down but we got on our way and eventually caught up with the others. I continued with the group until we reached Beattock, and the place they were departing and continued alone for the second week. I later got a letter of thanks for my public spirited actions from the Chief Constable of Dumfries and Galloway Constabulary.

Later that year I also completed my second marathon, a local one at Harlow, and surprised myself by bringing my marathon time down to 3 hours 43 minutes. My fastest half marathon that year had been at Huntingdon in a time of 1 hour 46 minutes.

Chapter 4

The Big Move North

It was always after returning from a long walk that I used to get "itchy feet" and try to put my life in perspective. I was a far happier person now than I had ever been, content in most ways but still lacking in others. I hated Cambridge and longed to be nearer the hills. It was always so far away to go for a weekend off and I had no real family ties here; in fact I had a desire to be further away from the family and the associated problems that were always appearing, and I wanted something more than a one roomed bedsit. The price of property in Cambridge was flying through the roof and a big "property boom" had left the average waged person unable to buy the smallest, cheapest property.

I also had a short term relationship with someone that had not worked out and feeling depressed by this gave me the incentive to "get out and go somewhere". But to where? I had no idea, I wanted somewhere that had cheap houses and was near the hills. I simply got the map out and travelled the entire country looking at places I thought I might like to live. I came up with two places that fitted my criteria, had houses I could afford and were near the hills. The choice was Carlisle or Middlesbrough. I opted for Middlesbrough as the North East was always drier than the North West, and the Lake District has a lot of lakes for a reason. I found a new Wimpey estate going up close to the Eston Hills area of Middlesbrough and put my name down on a house, just under twenty thousand pounds for a new house compared to seventy thousand pounds for the cheapest flat that could be found in Cambridge.

My house was on one of the later phases of development; so I had about six months to prepare for the move. That year was to be 1989 and it started with something that I didn't realise at the time was to shape the rest of my life. I did an event called the "Fat-Ass Fifty Miler Finishing in Farnham, no entry fee, no aid, no awards and no wimps!" It was just an event I had seen that could enable me to experience that "new territory" feeling of running further than I had ever done before. There was little support on this event and I had to carry quite a lot of kit and food for the day. It was also off-road along the North Downs. My view was that it was a bit like backpacking but more distance was covered in a day and I had less to carry.

The event started around 7am on 7th January 1989 as daylight peeked through, just twenty-five starters and thirteen finishers. I enjoyed most of the day but struggled with navigation a bit. Navigation was easy when walking; when I had the time to stop and look around to confirm where I was, but when running I didn't have the time or the desire to keep stopping. The winner was a well known name in ultra running, Norrie Williamson, in a fraction under 9 hours. The 1st lady was Hilary Walker, a world record holder at ultra distance events, in a fraction over 10 hours. As for me, well I was 10th person and broke the 12 hour mark. I was chuffed to finish and didn't find it anywhere near as hard as some of my previous marathons. I could not understand why, as I had run almost twice as far as previously. I put it down to the fact that I had run much more slowly, stopped frequently for navigation, or to get drink or food out of my backpack and this was also off road. I had never run an off road event, only done road races.

I managed to get my entry accepted to run in the ADT London Marathon that year and remember travelling with a friend called Tony Swindlehurst. At his best Tony was a sub 2 hours 30 minutes marathon runner and was also a good friend of David. He came to watch the event and gave me moral support. I also got in the paper again raising money for charity for Asthma UK, this time with the angle of "Cambridge to London coach driver swaps wheels for running shoes" as I was now on the National Express division of the company. Driving the "big buses" was also quite fun. I loved standing in London's Victoria Station looking baby faced as I was still in my early twenties, collecting the tickets from the passengers who thought I was the hostess on the coach. Then when I sat in the driver's seat I could hear the hushed silence, followed by, "She doesn't look old enough? She doesn't look big enough?"

The big move to the North East of England came in June 1989. I was going to pay less for a new three bedroom Wimpey house in view of the Eston Hills than I was paying to rent a one room bedsit sharing a bathroom and toilet with the five other male residents in the house. Brother Paul had long since gone. While working for the council he had been lucky enough to get a council flat, but I had no chance, the only way I could get a flat was if I had a child! But he had moved on again since then and was now with his partner Kathy and expecting their first child. Paul and Kathy got married and in the space of three years were to have three boys, Christopher, Mathew and Ryan. Paul helped with my big move. I hired a Luton van and

Paul came up in the car. Paul laid a new carpet for me and helped unload all my stuff into the house, which didn't look like much now that I had a three bedroom house to spread out in. I had been gathering bits and pieces and storing them at my mother's house. She had also donated some bits and pieces to the house move. It was to be a few more weeks before I personally moved in.

Tony had become a good friend by this stage, mainly as a running partner and we also had a shared love of the open country and walking. When I left Cambridge I had to leave my job and take a chance I could get a job pretty quick in Cleveland. I had two weeks annual leave left, so I hoped to get a job in this period to avoid going without wages. Luck was on my side, as there were loads of bus companies in Middlesbrough; so I headed straight to the biggest company that had buses running near my house. This company was called United at the time, but were to frequently change ownership and names. I walked in, got an interview and Ian Charlton kindly offered me a job, to start work on Monday 19th June 1989. My employment was sorted, I had just over a week to spare and I decided to go for a backpacking trip. This was to be the Coast to Coast, starting in Cumbria at St Bees Head and finishing locally in the North York Moors at Robin Hood's Bay.

Top of Kidsy Pike, 2,560 feet walking the Coast to Coast.

Tony had travelled up with me to see the new house, as he also had a vested interest. It was difficult to get a mortgage on the house because I was living and working in Cambridge and my house was over 200 miles away. The mortgage company knew I would have to change jobs to move in and wanted a guarantor in case I didn't get a job for a while. I had approached my mother but John was strictly against the idea, although they could have done this for me as they had purchased their council house and their particular property was then worth about ten times what they had paid for it. However, they flatly refused saying I would not be able to get a job and why on earth did I want to move to such a dirty, industrial place. Well yes, there was a bit of industry around in the chemical works between Redcar and Eston, but all I could see was the hills. So Tony had generously stepped in; he had more confidence in me than my own family did. Tony lived alone in a shared house in Cambridge and worked at one of the universities. He also had some annual leave, so we decided to walk the Coast to Coast together. It was a fantastic trip, very varied with the mountains of the Lake District, a flat section in the middle and the hills of the North York Moors to finish with.

As Tony went home I started my new job, it was quite a daunting prospect and I began to wonder what I had let myself in for. I knew absolutely nobody, had not even met the neighbours and struggled to even find the bus station. Although I knew I could drive buses, this was a different kettle of fish. I did not know the area at all, not a single friendly face, and I had nobody to tell the traumas of the day to, just me and my big house that I had longed for. There were so many different routes! I had known Cambridge so well, lived there all my life, but here I didn't know place names, road names and even the accent was a big barrier. I remember one of the drivers telling a joke one day about a "dook". As everyone fell around laughing he looked at me and said, "Didn't you find that funny?" My reply was, "What is a dook?" There was even more laughter as he kindly animated, "Quack, quack" and I realised the joke was about a duck!

But I learnt how to use the electronic ticket machines, got used to the antiquated buses, some that did not even have power steering and got to grips with some route learning. Before being let loose on the public I was given three days with a driver, where I did all the work but was supervised by another driver. Ray Harrison was my companion for those few days and probably had to act more like a translator and navigator than anything else. It was really hard work, concentrating on remembering all the routes, trying to remember place names and getting used to the accent. In some ways the passengers up here made life easier as regular users just got on and said "Sixty-five pence, please", so I knew how to tap it in and didn't have to work out where they were going and the fare. The driving was the easy bit.

I think many of the drivers were baffled by me. I knew nobody, so why had I moved here? Also there were hardly any female drivers and I was quite small compared to some of the drivers, so I did not fit in with "the norm" yet again, but I was used to that. The first week I was let loose on my own I was a bag of nerves; I really didn't know confidently where I was going. My biggest fear was getting lost and going off route. Timetables were strict and I could not afford to do this. I was pretty slow anyway, trying to figure out where people were going until I recognised places and different names passengers called the bus stops. On my first week when I was on a service to Redcar, I came to a roundabout where I could not figure out where to go. I pondered a bit and went straight on. I didn't recognise anything and appeared to be on a bit of a country road which I began to think was wrong, but there was no way I could turn around a bus so I just carried on. None of the passengers said a word. Eventually I came to another roundabout several miles later and found I was in Marske! I had never been here and knew I was off-route. I turned around to the passengers in search of the right direction. No one had said a word, just assumed there was a diversion of some kind, but I got directed back to where I had come from and, a few frustrated passengers later, I was directed all the way to Redcar. That was the answer. Every time I found myself somewhere I didn't know where to go I asked the passengers and soon got the answer. I had a strong southern accent still so they probably guessed I was new to the area.

I had hardly raced that year with the big move, merely three races to date: the Fat Ass Fifty Miler, a half marathon at Swavesey and the London Marathon. For me the best way to get to know the area was to get out running again and regain my fitness. There was a big half marathon in the area called the Cleveland Major, so I decided to get fit and run that in the September. I often used to run to work and run home again, as there was a shower in the bus station and it appeared that I was the only one to ever use it. So I got a few stares from other drivers that I confused yet again! Here I was as a driver with a free bus pass to travel to work and I decided to run there and run home – it was a distance of around 5 miles. The Cleveland Major soon came and went and the Langbaurgh Half Marathon was the only other race I did that year. I also backpacked along the 108 miles of the Cleveland Way with Tony in September.

1990 was another pretty insignificant year. I did a few more races over a variety of distances and terrain, tried a fell race, did some really hilly races and found a few long off road trail runs which I realised I really did enjoy. The main races were the Crosses, Hanging Stone Leap and the Cleveland Classic. The Crosses was a 53 mile trail event which had checkpoints every few miles with water and visited many of the historic Crosses in the North York Moors. I got lost several times through not looking at the map and watching where I was going. I soon learnt the hard way as I repeatedly overtook the same competitors again and again. Eventually I teamed up with Mike Harper, a veteran of many Crosses events, who knew the way without even using the map and arrived at the finish without getting lost again, I was the 45th person out of 229 finishers and 2nd lady. If I hadn't got lost I would have won this, so I was determined to come back and try again. The Hanging Stone Leap started about a mile from where I lived and ran up Eston Nab, the local hill top I could see from my house, then across to other local landmarks such as Roseberry Topping, Captain Cook's Monument, Highcliffe Nab and down to the hidden spot at Hanging Stone, surrounded by thick woodland. I made another navigational error that cost me a place and was 3rd lady this time. The Cleveland Classic was a 56 mile race, similar in structure to the Crosses and I came home 4th lady and 30th person of the 233 finishers, it was evident that the longer the run, the further up the field I was finishing and I began to enjoy this slight realisation of success.

I did a couple of backpacking walks with Tony, a reasonably local one called Wolds Way, a short 80 mile trip done in a long weekend and then a more adventurous one driving to France to walk the Tour du Mont Blanc. This was the most magnificent mountain range I had ever seen and the walking was extremely strenuous, but I was rewarded with the most stunning panorama. The altitude was also significant, as a couple of times on the high cols Tony felt sick and dizzy and had to lose height to camp. We also had quite a bit of snow on some days, even though it was June, that forced us to stay an extra day in some places. This Grand Randonnée route circumnavigated Mont Blanc itself, walking from France, to Italy and Switzerland before returning to France in a 120 mile trek. It was just the most peaceful, picturesque landscape I had ever been in; everything was on such a big scale compared to our little mountains in Great Britain.

After the walk we had a few days left over and as I had driven across we spent a few extra days travelling around Switzerland and the Grindlewald area, camping under the "North Face of the Eiger" and we also did a few touristy things like a boat trip on the Lake Thunersee at Interlaken and a visit to the caves of Beatushohlen. We had thought about taking the train trip up the Jungfrau, Europe's highest railway, but the weather was poor

Camped in snow above Chamonix, France, walking the Tour du Mont Blanc.

again and would spoil the views. To finish the trip we went to St Maurice and the Olympic bob sleigh run, which was a bit of a disappointment, and ended up in Austria for the night. On the way home we had lunch in Germany, and an evening meal in Luxembourg, then on through Belgium and back to France to get the ferry home; a truly European trip with many money exchanges, how much easier the Euro would have made things!

On returning from Europe it was straight back to the norm again, back to work and back to running. There was another bus driver who was a runner, called Jim Blower. He got me to join the local running club, Mandale Harriers and we started up a team to get some drivers running in the Great North Run that was to be held in September. We recruited a good few drivers to get together as much as possible and began training in the local Stewart's Park. One of the drivers, who was reasonably fit was Bill Gayter, he had joined the bus company shortly after me and wanted to start running. We eventually ran the race as a team and kept together and carried a team banner around, in just over 2 hours. It was a long drawn out race but was fun to run a bit differently and support others.

Once the Great North Run was out of the way the drivers drifted apart and we no longer did our weekly runs together, but as Bill quite enjoyed the

44

running and wanted to carry on, we used to meet up and run together sometimes. I told him about my backpacking trips and he said that he had done backpacking in the Army and would like to do some walking, so we arranged to walk the Westmoreland Way 200 miles in the Lake District. It was a disaster! This so called big, strong Army lad packed everything in his bag, great big heavy towel, jeans to wear in the evening etc. Had he really done backpacking before? I left him to it, not wanting to interfere and trimmed down my backpack to make it as light as possible as usual. Unsurprisingly Bill didn't last the trip and we made a detour back after half the route was done. Bill's feet were sore, his shoulders bruised and all his kit wet. He learnt a lot of lessons on "real backpacking" that trip, as he told me how the trips were done in the Army and most kit was transferred by lorry!

Bill and I became quite close but Tony was still visiting for the odd weekend and we competed in a few races together. These were both purely friendly training partner relationships. It was hard dividing time between training partners and now I just wanted to get away on my own for a change, it was hard to understand that we could not all run races together. One long weekend when Tony had planned to come up I wanted to get away on my own and decided to do just that and go walking on the Isle of Arran. I really don't think Tony believed me. He was aware that I had become friendly with other people now, unlike when I first moved to the area and knew no one. I now had several running people I knew and several of the bus drivers who had become runners. I had lost that feeling of freedom and isolation again and wanted to be away from everything.

The Isle of Arran is a gorgeous Island, very few people in the walking areas and I got back to my own little world for one long weekend off work. I had been working on the four day week rota, this meant that every few weeks I could get three days off the end of one week and three days off the start of the next week and get six days off without having to use annual leave, but the hours were long, usually 12 hour days. It was shortly after this that Tony stopped visiting and Bill and I became closer. It was after a busman's holiday to Blackpool that we actually became a couple after Bill screamed his head off on one of the scary rides that I dragged him on, not wanting to chicken out his only consolation was that he got to sit behind me on the ride and put his arms around me – or, more precisely, squeezed the life out of me as the ride progressed!

He had thought that Tony and I were a couple and he had not realised until I was talking about a particular walk that we had taken two tents and were purely training friends who did races and trips together. Tony was a really nice man, very good company and would make someone a wonderful husband as he was a really sensitive, thoughtful and generous person, but probably too sensitive for me. I really enjoyed my trips with him, but also liked the space on my own without him during normal working life and I was not a settling down kind of person. I had never envisaged settling down and having a real relationship. I liked my life as it was, the freedom it gave me to do as I pleased and live life the way I wanted to. I never wanted to be dictated to by any person the way my mother had been and the only way to do this was not get involved.

Chapter 5

Bigger Events

Bill kind of grew on me, initially he was like a training partner, then we did a few other things together and on our first real date he took me to the pictures at Redcar – to see 'Gremlin's 2'. I don't think I was ever a kind of sensitive, emotional person due to my family upbringing and was always an independent person and would do most things myself that I was capable of. I first met Bill when he joined the buses. I had not even given him a second glance. He was just another driver to me and he also smoked, one of my pet hates. Bill had now stopped smoking, but was still living at his family home with his parents, who smoked. He claimed that being with me helped prevent him from going back to the cigarettes.

The next year, 1991, we did a few more short backpacking trips together and Bill learnt the art of "lightweight" packing. We did a weekend trip to Wales for the Carneddau Walk, just 49 miles in January, the Nidderdale Way, closer to home and 53 miles and had a trip to Scotland, all in preparation for the big one – a trek along the Pyrenees of 540 miles (869 kilometres). The plan was to walk the entire length in two trips, the first section from Hendaye to Luchon (267 miles) and the second section from Luchon to Perpignan (273 miles). Each trip would have to be our main holidays from work and would take three weeks.

I had been to the Alps; so now I wanted another taste of mountains that were higher than Great Britain and the Pyrenees didn't let us down. They were very different from the Alps, far greener on the French side and more barren and dry on the Spanish side. The walk took a bit of getting used to, as the climbs were far harder than expected. We settled in at just 13 to 15 miles a day for the first few days following the red and white markers of the GR10 route. As the backpacks started to feel a bit lighter we started to go further averaging around 18 miles a day. It was another amazing trip that I thoroughly enjoyed, yet another very different experience and somewhere that I had not been before. Although Bill said he enjoyed it I think his family began to take pity on him. Although not overweight, Bill was a rather solid, muscular man and on his return had lost significant weight and even his mother commented, "You are looking very thin in the face", so whereas most people put on weight on their holidays the annual trips began to be Bill's annual slim downs. We did another couple of long weekend trips before the year was out and did the odd race here and there, nothing of any great significance.

The only race that was a bit sad to run was the Ray Harrison Memorial Run of 10 miles. Ray had been the bus driver who had to put up with me for three days during my training when I had no idea where I was going; so I had got to know him quite well. He had a short illness and died within a few weeks while only in his forties. This race was run by several of the bus drivers and was held for several years.

1992 began pretty much the same but with one major event taking place; on Valentine's Day Bill took me out for a meal with the plan to propose, but after wanting one last drink for Dutch courage he found the bar had shut; so chickened out. The next day at work he said he had something to ask me; I was rather surprised that he didn't just come out and ask me. I had to wait until we finished work. After stopping off to collect "fish and chips" for dinner on the way home he finally proposed – not the most romantic of proposals, but I had become rather attached to Bill and immediately accepted. He had wanted someone to "keep him fit" and I matched the bill – I think he got a bit more than he bargained for!

Bill had come to understand me very well; he had met my family and met John. He was easily able to cope with John's mood swings far better than the rest of us. He had seen John fly off the handle over nothing and found him quite amusing. Julie always used to make sure Bill sat next to John at Christmas dinners as he had far greater tolerance than the rest of us. I had opened up on our past and he was the man who had finally cracked my hard outer shell. I had come to love Bill. He came with nothing and wanted nothing from me, just companionship and to care for me. There was nothing more I wanted from a man. He let me do as I wanted and supported me in every way possible, he never tried to restrict my way of life or change me in any way. I thought I would never get married, and never find someone who would care for me and allow me a life to do as I pleased. Bill liked an identical life to me, full to the brim with activity, always races and goals on the horizon. He enjoyed the outdoor life, our hyperactive holidays and worked hard on all jobs in the house and more than anything else, never raised his voice to me, or used abusive language, instead he encouraged me in everything I did.

For my part I realised how much I missed him when he wasn't around. I had not realised how much I had come to depend on Bill, how much

I confided in him and really did need him in my life. This independent, single person really did need a man in her life, not just any man, but this man. Bill had taken time to get to know me, to understand me. He had banished a fear in me that no one else had been able to do, that fear of letting go and being dependent and sharing my life.

After telling both families who were all delighted I then got some plans from my mother – who told me, "Well you can get married in this church, the after party can be here, these relations can be your bridesmaids etc". This was supposed to be my wedding. I lived up here in the North East and although I had not even thought about where to get married or our wedding plans, getting married in Cambridge was not part of my plans. I sat down with Bill and we shared our thoughts on where to get married. Bill was always so easy to get on with and nearly always had identical thoughts and ideas and would have got married where ever I wanted, but practically speaking Bill's father had taken early retirement through illness and was not in the best of health, so it would not have been practical for him to travel. With my family there were always conflicts as to who (or who not) to invite with having divorced parents and a step father on the scene. I always hated even going to family weddings and avoided them like the plague – only attending my immediate family's weddings.

I didn't want a big "do" and didn't even want a big church wedding with the white dress. In reality I wanted the smallest wedding possible with the least guests possible as I did not like being "centre of attention" and hated getting dressed up. Bill was of the same opinion and preferred a small event. When I suggested, "What about Gretna Green?" and having nobody at the wedding it got us excited. We loved the thought of a completely hassle free wedding, free from all prying eyes as to what you are wearing and no sneers such as, "Didn't think much to the food" and we could have the wedding how we really wanted it – which was what it was supposed to be about. We did have a couple of dilemmas such as "Wouldn't it be nice to have our parents as witnesses?" but then you couldn't invite the parents without inviting the brothers and sisters and so it continued, so we had to make the decision to do it the traditional way and drag two people off the street to be our witnesses.

That sorted the next thing was to sort the date – sooner rather than later was my response to avoid the plans that my mother seemed to be making – our next long weekend of six days was three weeks later – how about that? No problem. So it was a frantic three weeks, getting in touch with the registry office at Gretna, sending off the paperwork, buying rings, making a cake, booking the honeymoon and buying the outfits. That was all that was needed, how simple!

So on Friday 6th March 1992, we ran away to Gretna Green to get married. Bill was dressed in casual light blue cotton trousers and a jumper and me with red jeans and a bright jumper of red, yellow, green and blue to signify a bright future. We enticed our two witnesses off the street – one elderly lady who was really pleased as she wanted to see the inside of the newly built registry office and a younger lady who was more concerned about getting changed to look smart enough for the wedding. It was so exciting; there were so many weddings all going on at the same time in various rooms. Ours was in the room that seated about fifty people. There was a smaller room that was for just ten people but this was already booked. The room was pleasant, a large circular stained glass window at the back, a few rows of seats and a pretty desk with a few flowers on.

As our commitment to each other began I got the giggles. The registrar obviously had a routine that she went through and a speech that she must

Just married at Gretna Green, a colourful suit for a bright future!

50

have recited a thousand times; she spoke as if talking to a big room full of people and this set me off, as there were just four people in a line in front of her and she was continuing with her speech as if to this large room full of people. It nearly set Bill off and I had to compose myself by the time I had to do "my bit". It was a relief to get it over with as I could not contain myself. We were finally pronounced husband and wife and signed the statements and were free to go.

Our honeymoon was not far away, in the honeymoon suite at the Mountain Ash Hotel in Windermere, Cumbria. We had a bottle of champagne, four poster water bed and en-suite luxurious bathroom. We had a fantastic few days and even took the ferry across Windermere and ran back to the hotel.

Soon it was time to head to Cambridge. We had told the family we were paying them an overnight visit to discuss the wedding. We dropped the bombshell and mother was not best pleased, not too sure why! Whether it was because she had not been invited or whether it was because it was not in Cambridge, either way it didn't matter to me. My sister Julie, although slightly annoyed could see the funny side and said, "It's just how I imagined you would do it" knowing that I never liked big occasions.

One family down it was back to Cleveland the next day to face the music at Bill's family house. As I remember it I think he had actually telephoned his mother when we told my family to make sure they would all be home when we arrived the next day. I walked in to a completely different response; there was a big bouquet of flowers waiting to welcome me into the family. They all thought it was very romantic and were really pleased that we had "tied the knot".

It was then back home to the house we now shared. Bill had moved in a long time ago. There had been a night when the subject of moving in had been brought up. He never went home from that point onwards or spent another night at his mother's house. There had been one rather upsetting incident just a week or so before we got married. We had been burgled and the entire house had been turned upside down. On getting home from work one day we walked in to find the video recorder in the middle of the floor. Baffled by this we immediately checked all the doors, only to find the patio doors had been "melted" with a blow torch. Upstairs all the contents of every drawer were strewn over the floor and several personal items stolen. I had a charm bracelet that was an eighteenth birthday present and several aunts and uncles had all brought a charm to put on the bracelet.

This had gone along with a watch that David had brought for me in Cambridge and I was sad to lose. As for Bill, he had a sovereign ring that he received for his eighteenth birthday; the thief had also found this. The only surprise was that in the spare bedroom our wedding outfits had been laid out on the bed with the wedding rings on top, but these obviously hadn't been noticed; so it was a relief that we still had these to exchange our vows.

That incident had upset me enormously and I hated coming home now. I felt extremely violated because someone had invaded my privacy and my home. There had been several incidents of burglary at the house, the radio in my car had been stolen several times; so I had given up having a radio and the spare wheel had also been stolen – as it still had a brand new tyre on it cut off from the bottom of our new van. This was the final straw, the house was not in the most desirable place in Cleveland and I now knew where I wanted to live – in Guisborough, the opposite side of the Eston Hills, a small market town nestled below the Guisborough Woods and right on the edge of the North York Moors.

Financially we were not so badly off now. We had two lots of wages to pay for the house that I could easily afford on one wage, so we began saving for a new house. I had always known that I would not live in Eston for a long period of time, as it was a starter home in the middle of an estate and surrounded by houses, left, right, back and front. I wanted somewhere a little more private and a bit closer to the major hills in the area. It was also an easy decision for Bill, as I don't think he ever really felt as though it was "our house". The mortgage was in my name and Bill had moved in with me with the house already set up as "my house". By moving house he could now feel that the next house would really be "our house".

The next month we both ran the ADT London Marathon, me in 3 hours 46 minutes and Bill in exactly 4 hours and 1 second. I hated it; I had not run such a crowded race for a long time and after being accidently tripped over at the Cutty Sark, 6 miles into the race, I really struggled with bumps and grazes only to finally be tripped over a second time in the last mile. I was in tears again at the finish but for different reasons. I hurt so much and never wanted to run this race again. I hated the crowds that I had loved so much on my first event. To add to my humiliation the television coverage had picked me out falling over and being dragged to my feet again and commented, "And this is the spirit of the London Marathon with fellow runners helping each other". For the next few years while ADT were still the sponsors the clip was shown at the start of every London Marathon. I was glad when new sponsors took over and new footage was shown.

Backpacking with Bill in France.

We did a few more races that year and finished off the rest of the Pyrenean Trail, the 273 miles from Luchon to Perpignan, where Bill had his annual slim down again. I ran quite a few off-road marathons that year and was the 1st lady in most of them. I did twenty-five races that year totalling 530 miles, two of them ultras, the Lyke Wake Race of 42 miles and the Cleveland Classic of 56 miles.

If I thought 1992 stated with a sudden pleasant shock of getting married, 1993 started with an even bigger unpleasant shock – I got attacked and beaten up on the buses and lost my job! There were always attacks on drivers every week, some more serious than others. We were often the focus of abuse, from school kids, drunken people or teenagers out for fun. That afternoon I left Redcar with a full standing load of passengers at around 5pm. By the time I got to Eston near where I lived the bus was half full and three young passengers got off. As I pulled up to the bus stop and touched the "door open" button my head went flying towards the side window, not quite recovering or knowing what had happened as a barrage of blows hit the side of my face and head while I tried to protect myself. One lad was laying into me while another was trying to pinch the money. I remember seeing the third lad walking in front of the bus laughing as all three ran off when a lady on the bus came to my rescue.

I felt helpless and abused and didn't know what to do. I realised then that the bus was rolling backwards. It was on a slight incline and I had not even put the handbrake on. As I was shaking and in a state of distress the lady encouraged me to drive just a quarter of a mile further to the Police Station. Yes, that was the best bet. Tearful, shaking like a leaf I cautiously drove up the road, in a great state of shock and not really knowing what I was doing or aware of much around me. I really wanted to get off this bus and retreat away from the world that was violating me again. I walked into the Police Station only for them to think I was a passenger on the bus despite being fully dressed in official uniform. On realising that I was the driver the police did react and immediately sent a van off in the direction the thugs had run – towards my house just half a mile down the road from the bus stop.

It didn't seem long before the manager arrived with an inspector to see how I was. There was nothing they could really do. Although feeling battered and bruised, there was no real damage that needed treatment, nothing was cut or broken it was more the shock that I had been physically attacked at such a busy time of day with around twenty people still on the bus. Bill took me home and I took a day off the next day as things began to sink in. I did get a big bouquet of flowers from work which was a nice caring touch. Bill really didn't want me to return to work, but being the independent person I was I didn't want this to beat me and anyway it was my job; so I went back to work later that week. The driver who picked up my bus and finished off the journey told me that I had parked half way across a pelican crossing and that I had not put the hand brake on yet again – it's amazing there wasn't another accident right outside the Police Station! I hadn't realised what a state I must have been in.

My return to work didn't last long though. It was probably around a week later that a few young lads got on the bus; they didn't do anything to me, they were simply clowning around and messing on, but I was now very nervous. I had been a bag of nerves since the attack; these young lads probably lived just up the road from me and I feared that I might bump into them. I sat on the bus in the middle of the compound crying my eyes out again. I couldn't face driving out there in front of the public again and felt powerless to do anything. It was a relief really that someone had seen me and reported me and the manager had the job of collecting me yet again.

Although the physical part of the attack had been easy to recover from, the realisation that this had really happened to me had a great impact on my mental state. I hated leaving the house. We had been saving since we got burgled the previous year in order to move house and now the time had come to move on. I had the fear of these thugs living just doors from me. I wanted out and wanted out quickly. The house was very soon on the market. It was hard coming to terms with what had happened. I didn't want to go back on the buses, as I felt so vulnerable now. Although there were many attacks on the buses, I didn't expect it to happen to me. There were the usual excuses: it's because you are a female, it's because you are so small. For me there was no answer, but I certainly wasn't going to go to work to be treated like this.

As I wasn't working for a bit I was challenging the bus company to have screens installed to protect drivers. Attacks such as the one on me would be harder to carry out and I had to do something with my time. Initially I got back to running. Running had been my escape from the world many years ago. It had given me the lifeline I had needed, had given me a purpose and goal in life and now I used it as my salvation from the assault. Running was calming and satisfying, I could be out in the hills all alone, no thugs would have the energy to reach out into the hills and it always gave me time to drift away with my thoughts and relieved other tensions in life.

Without having to work and be tired running to work and home, and also having more time to race at weekends without work commitments I had the most incredible year imaginable. The statistics for 1993 were forty-three races totalling 895 miles of racing, twenty-three races of 20 miles or more (thirteen where I was 1st lady) and four ultra distance races where I was easily the 1st lady in all four. I even won a race with Bill called the Smugglers Trod and we got a trophy (picture) for the "1st husband and wife" team as well as breaking that course record. Maybe now I would shake those thugs' hands for making me change jobs; without the assault when would I have made the decision to leave the buses and when would I have found the time to train and race to my heart's content and realise my potential?

As for the holidays that year, I had to take Bill on a trip to the Alps. Having now walked the entire length of the Pyrenees I had to show him the height and beauty of the Tour du Mont Blanc that I had witnessed with Tony several years ago. It was just as wonderful second time around and Bill was also struck with the panorama. Having spent a couple of weeks walking around Mont Blanc and various other paths we finally committed to actually climbing Mont Blanc, a far more challenging climb than either of us had ever experienced. It was called Mont Blanc for a reason and there

*In the news again for winning the husband and wife trophy
on the Smugglers Trod, 26 miles over the North York Moors.
© Evening Gazette.*

was always snow on the summit. After hiring out the kit such as crampons and ice axes and booking the bothy half way up the climb we set out on our mammoth expedition. The start was by cable car to gain height and then scrambling up the rocks to the bothy. There appeared a long line of walkers doing exactly the same as us, as we were doing the "tourist route" to the top since this was the least dangerous way to go and we were not exactly experienced climbers. The bothy was so fully booked we were allowed three quarters of a bed each in a line of mattresses.

I didn't sleep much in the cramped, noisy conditions, but everyone was there to do the same thing – climb Mont Blanc. It was an early start around 3am. The reason for this was to get to the top before the heat of the sun came out and could melt snow that might cause an avalanche. We heard many a horror story during our afternoon stay in the bothy, including those about a section of the climb where there were daily rocks falls that killed people and crevasses that suddenly appeared and swallowed people up. Many walkers paid to have guides and were roped together. We kind of teamed up with a couple of British men. One was a guide in the area and the other the owner of Nevisport in Fort William; so we felt in good company.

We were almost the last to leave the bothy the next morning. It was still dark, we struggled to put on the crampons and we were really quite nervous about what lay ahead. The air was bitterly cold and very thin and we were warned to look for the signs of altitude sickness and wisely told to retreat immediately if we had any effects. We were both feeling fine after our night at significant height and stepped out into the snow for the first time. Up to the bothy there had only been small patches of snow that had not warranted wearing the crampons, but from this point onwards it was a white sheet of deep snow. Step by step we followed the amazing snaking line of torches. It was obvious to us that the guides would know the way well; so by following the pack it would be easy to find the route rather than risk navigating in the dark by ourselves. We occasionally saw the two British men but trudged on slowly, breathlessly, taking a "breather" every now and then. The snow was very soft and we sank quite deeply into it in places.

We were both fit by this stage, having already walked quite a few high paths in the last two weeks, and we were well acclimatised. As we only had very light day packs the going was easier. Onwards and upwards, gradually overtaking big groups of walkers roped together – we got many comments about not being roped, but realistically there was no point, should Bill happen to fall there was no way I could support his weight and would probably fall with him, so we thought we would take our chances.

Daylight slowly came upon us and the going got slower and slower as the air got thinner and thinner. The next section was quite "hairy" going along a steep narrow ridge with a massive drop either side and a small trench where we had to walk with one foot in and one foot out as we passed walkers in the opposite direction. Although at times it felt like an age and progress was slow, we passed a big stick in the snow. I thought it was just a guide post, but I noticed a few people standing around before the route began to descend. I was wondering if that was just a dip before the climb to the summit, but it was not until I turned around to make a comment to Bill that I realised the walkers following us had all stopped by the "big stick" and were taking photographs of it. Could that have been the top? We retraced our steps to find out that it was in fact the summit of Mont Blanc, a bit of an anti-climax really! At 15,781 feet (4,810 metres), Mont Blanc is reported to be the highest mountain in the Alps, another great goal achieved together.

Top of Mont Blanc (15,781 feet).

The weather was quite foul now; it was very windy, bitterly cold and we were surrounded by clouds so it was impossible to see the views below. Where we had camped in Chamonix a couple of days earlier we had had good views of the summit and had waited a few days until we knew the weather would be good to attempt climbing to the summit, but we were now very disillusioned. This was a once in a life-time opportunity and, although we had made it to the summit, we could not take amazing photographs of the view, we could hardly stand still long enough to have our photograph taken with the "big stick", being buffeted by the wind and with snow now falling.

We couldn't stand around long, conditions were worsening by the minute and our breathing was laboured. The mist and clouds were very unlikely to lift in the next half an hour and were not exactly warm; so we had to start the descent. That turned out to be just as arduous, frightening and scary along the narrow ridge with the wind picking up strength all the time and us having to keep one foot out of the trench as others barged by. At one stage Bill was knocked; the fall would have been fatal. All we wanted was to be off that ridge as quickly and as safely as possible.

As the slopes became gentler, broadening out to a wider plateau, we could relax more. Walkers were scattered all over now taking different routes, so it was difficult to know the exact route we came up. We then came across a deep cut in the snow which was obviously a crevasse. Bill was becoming increasingly un-nerved and I sensed that that was not the way we came. I got the map out and scoured the horizon. The sun was coming out now and the warmth felt good as the winds died down. We were at a lower altitude now and visibility was good. I could see we had drifted too far to the right and in the distance could see walkers in the direction we should be going. We kept our eyes peeled to the ground as we crossed the plateau, giving several more crevasses a wide berth. These looked deep and black and I was hopeful that the snowfall had not been heavy enough to cover the surface so we could walk with confidence.

Back on route it was plain sailing now back down to the bothy. It was a lot more relaxed atmosphere now, but still very disappointing that the summit had been spoilt by the weather. We replenished ourselves with the food at the bothy and were soon joined by the couple of British men. They had become separated and only the guide had made it to the summit. The owner of Nevisport had retreated to the upper bothy and waited before the weather had turned and he had to return with the mission not accomplished. We now felt more satisfied that at least we had achieved our goal and reached the top, as it was evident that many walkers had not made it that day for various reasons.

It was a pleasant clamber back down the rocks to the cable car to take us back to Les Houches and on to Chamonix. It had been a long day. As we lay in the sunshine at the campsite we were frustrated that the summit was now bathed in sunshine and we could clearly see the weather on top had lifted. It wasn't until the next day that we saw the headline news in the papers: the day we made the summit of Mont Blanc twelve climbers had been killed in an avalanche on the Italian side of the mountain and reality hit home as to how dangerous this big mountain was.

For Bill it had been a massive achievement, the highest mountain either of us had ever climbed. It had also been quite an experience, what with the squashed bothy experience, the early start by torch light, the lack of oxygen, the freezing weather, the use of crampons, the fear on the ridge and later the crevasses on the plateau. In reality I think Bill was really chuffed at this achievement but I doubt that he would ever want to climb it again – it was another of those classics, been there, done that and never again thanks. But Bill was becoming accustomed to our way of living, where life was one big adventure, waiting to be discovered; experiences to be sensed and achieved. This was something he never would have thought he could ever have dreamed of, let alone done, but with me he was capable of achieving greater things than he ever thought possible. This wife that he wanted to keep him fit had now dragged him the entire length of the Pyrenees, trained him to run marathons and now tested him to his limits in climbing Mont Blanc.

Of the ultras that I did that year, the first one was the most amazing for me. It was the Long Distance Walkers Association annual 100 miles event. That year it was being held in Cleveland and started at Great Ayton, a few miles down the road from where I lived. This was a very popular event and the entry limit of 500 entrants was easily exceeded. I was one of the 499 starters that day in May. My plan, as usual, was just to finish as this was almost double the distance that I had ever run in the past. It was a big jump from 50 miles events up to 100 miles events including navigation and carrying essential kit. As it was a local course I had run all of it in sections during daylight hours and was aware of a couple of places where it could be difficult to navigate in darkness. I had no idea where I would be in the field and how I could cope with the distance.

There was a mass start at 10am and I was immediately away with the leading group, a few of whom gradually pulled away. I settled in as the 1st lady, probably in the top ten in the field. The weather had been glorious sunshine all day and daylight began to fade as I left Goathland at around the half way mark. There were a couple of men a few metres ahead and I was now in 5th place overall. Darkness was a challenge and on one of the sections which I knew would be tricky the rain began to fall and I lost the path. I knew I had gone too far to the left when I started dropping too steeply and ended up knee deep in bogs. The two men who had been a few metres ahead of me suddenly put on a spurt and as the path was quite thin I lost them while trying to keep my balance and stay on route. I tripped and stumbled and fell many times off balance in the soft underfoot conditions until I could see the road up ahead and could get back to firmer ground. Bill was waiting for me at the road side, wondering what had happened as the two men ahead had gone through long ago and they commented that I had just disappeared!

Never mind, this was a long race and the goal was to finish. I had expected a few hiccups like this, but it was nothing major. The rain continued and I arrived on the coast road at Robin Hoods Bay as a police car passed by. I expected some kind of comment as to what this idiot was doing in the early hours of the morning, soaked to the skin, running down a country road. I guessed they must have been informed, as the car continued on its way after checking I was okay. I continued onwards as dawn slowly came along with the mist. I was gradually slowing now and things were beginning to ache when a welcome sight appeared in the distance. It was the two men who I had seen at Goathland. I had a target now and wanted to get back to them, but they were well aware I was on their tails and kept looking back – they knew to look back as my little red van with Bill in it supporting me was telling them how close I was. I closed the gap between us but I was never quite strong enough to catch them.

Finally I reached Commondale and a fraction over 10 miles to the finish. The wind was picking up and I was feeling quite cold. I had no running left in me as I saw the two runners away in the distance on the skyline. I plodded on now, determined to finish, but my feet were becoming more and more painful. The next checkpoint around 5 miles away took an age to reach; in reality it was around 75 minutes, but I began to get slower and slower and began to wonder if I would ever finish. Tiredness was taking over and it was hard to concentrate. I could barely call this walking pace now; the last 5 miles took around 2 hours to walk and I finished in 25 hours 15 minutes, 1st lady and 5th out of the 499 starters, so not so bad after all.

Later that year I took an hour off my time in the Lyke Wake Race of 42 miles finishing 1st lady in 6 hours 33 minutes and one of my best performances was in the Cleveland Classic. In this local off road race of 56 miles, I absolutely obliterated my personal best and lowered the course record from 11 hours 34 minutes down to 9 hours 11 minutes. I was 5th overall, 28 minutes behind the 1st man. It was at this point with these two cracking performances that I realised I really did have talent for long events. I had heard comments that I was beating international athletes and that these performances were of such a standard that I could be an international athlete, but I had no idea of what races there were at international level above the marathon.

It was as if by chance I then picked up a copy of the Athletics Weekly, and there was the answer. There was a superb article on Carolyn Hunter-Rowe, who had just become the world champion at 100 kilometres, that was just over 62 miles in my language and I just knew I could run this too. I was never quite sure how fast, but I was certainly going to rise to the challenge.

Chapter 6

University and New Direction

I had my goal now and knew what I wanted to do. But how did I find out more? How to find out about international events? What were the selection times and procedures? Were there selection races? What events were there in Great Britain? What training should I be doing? So many questions! This was a big new exciting goal. This was just unbelievable, that I, who a few years ago could barely run a mile and felt pretty useless at everything, was trying to become an international athlete. I began reading here, there and everywhere, trying to gather information. I sent off a letter to John Foden, who was mentioned in the article with Carolyn Hunter-Rowe. A letter did arrive back saying my letter had been passed on to Tony Jones, who was cited as being coach to Carolyn, but that was as far as things went for the time being.

I had been in the local papers on a regular basis as I was winning most of the local off road marathons and broke seven course records that year and even won one race outright! Mike Amos of the Northern Echo had given me a double page centre piece spread titled "Wicked Witch on the Run". I think he always knew I would turn out to be someone special. The title being due to the fact that Bill called me the "Wicked Witch of the South" and I probably don't have to mention a certain birthday in October that justifies his comments.

My marathon time had come down to 3 hours 23 minutes in Paris earlier on that year and knew that in order to become a good athlete I needed some advice. It was almost as if a second stroke of luck happened. In the local Evening Gazette there was an article about a new Bachelor of Science degree in Sport Science available at Teesside University. I enquired about the course and it looked exactly what I needed to teach myself not only how to train but more about my body. The only problem was that I had no qualifications to get me into university.

So next on the list was enquiring at the local colleges to see what they had to offer, and another stroke of luck. The Longlands College, a short

3 miles down the road from where I was living, was offering an Access course for mature students. That was a one year course that gained "Access to University" and was all that was needed to qualify; I didn't have to go through the usual Advanced level route. So it was in September that year that I enrolled. I had no idea how I would do academically, but I had always wanted to go to university, so that was another potential dream that could come true. I knew in my early years at school I was quite academic, but in later years at school I had underperformed due to the worries of my home life.

So back to education it was and I started a science based Access course. The course consisted of five subjects: maths, physics, chemistry, biology and environmental studies. It became evident from the first set of exams that I was reasonably academic in certain subjects. I struggled with the chemistry and some of the biology but easily excelled and made up for it in maths and physics. The course work was all easy, I was never under any pressure and I found it easy to gain marks, but exams were another thing. I was very nervous going into my first exams since leaving school – after all I was now thirty years of age, but I need not have worried as I shocked both myself and some of the lecturers with the results, a staggering one hundred percent in both physics and maths! I was then asked if I would like to do "further maths" up to university level, which was only available to the top students. It could do me no harm to see what university level was like; so I went on for more studies and nearly always came out with one hundred percent. I even enjoyed my time there. All the students were mature and it was very friendly. I got on really well with all the lecturers, especially one in chemistry and physics who was also a member of my running club of Mandale Harriers (Mike Kaiser) and Barry who took a vested interest in my application to university and taught biology and environmental studies.

That year of 1993, as well as excelling in some major ultra distance races, I also gained an elite time for the NutraSweet London Marathon, the race I had vowed never to run again after such a nightmare experience of being tripped over twice. However running with the elite start was a different thing – I could have all the experience of the race and the supporting crowds but without the thousands of runners to trip me over. Now that was something I relished. My time in the Paris Marathon in April was a new personal best at 3 hours 23 minutes. The elite London Marathon time was sub 3 hours 15 minutes; so I needed to improve by another 8 minutes.

At the end of October I had decided to run the local Langbaurgh Marathon. This marathon had been publicised well and attracted a lot of top runners; in particular it was interesting to see a couple of ultra runners I was now following who were 1st and 2nd in the race: Carolyn Hunter-Rowe (2 hours 44 minutes) and Eleanor Robinson (2 hours 49 minutes). As for me, training had been going well and I finally dipped in under the 90 minutes mark for the half marathon the previous week at Bridlington; so all was in place for a sub 3 hours 15 minute clocking. The gun sounded and I shot off at a speed which gave me 6 minutes 15 seconds for the first mile, far too fast as excitement got the better of me. I settled in, but was probably running far too fast in the early stages. By the half way mark I had settled down and managed it in 1 hour 37 minutes; so I did not allow myself to slow down at all now. I knew the course well and just had to keep the pace going, but at 20 miles my time was 2 hours 30 minutes. I began to doubt that I could maintain a time of less than 7 minutes 30 seconds for each of the remaining 6 miles, not including the 385 yards. However, I dug deep. It was a big goal to achieve and it began to happen; I was overtaking and getting more adrenalin all the time. It was possible, but I just had to keep it up. I was checking my watch every mile and at 25 miles I had to run past the finish line with the last mile out and back through the woods. I was giving everything I had now, as I was in line to get my time, but I knew that the extra 385 yards would add a couple of minutes. I came back sprinting for the line and eyes fixed on the clock for the time – it was ticking but not too fast as I crossed the line an ecstatic 3 hours 14 minutes and 50 seconds for 8th place in the ladies race. I had achieved my goal by a mere 10 seconds. I would now be in the elite women's line up at the NutraSweet London Marathon in 1994.

The only down side was seeing just how far I really had to go to be good enough to make it to the top in ultras, as both Carolyn and Eleanor were still so far ahead in terms of their speed, but this was the next step and I had improved dramatically in just twelve months.

It was just before Christmas and very late one night (in fact it was probably the very early hours of the morning) when the phone rang. I was in bed and puzzled by who would ring me at this time of night. It was Tony Jones, coach to Carolyn. Carolyn had reported back to Tony my time at the Langbaurgh Marathon and he thought I might have some potential and said that he would coach me. I was absolutely thrilled. I thought Tony must be a top coach to have such athletes on his books and felt very privileged that he would coach me.

The race I was to aim at was the British 100 Kilometres Championships race to be held at Sutcliffe Park in London on 8th May 1994, but before that I was to run the Barry 40 track race on 6th March 1994 as a mental test.

65

I had never run on a track and could not envisage going round and round in circles for just over one hundred and sixty laps that were needed for that race. The venue at Barry also doubled up as a squad weekend for the international athletes and, although I would not get invited officially, I was allowed access to attend the meeting at my own expense and meet the official selector, John Legge, and a few other important people, as well as getting to know some of the athletes. It was beginning to happen; my dream of becoming an international athlete was starting to become a reality.

The target time for the 100 kilometres at Sutcliffe Park was sub 9 hours and I now knew where I had to run and that this would be another lapped event, hence the mental test at Barry on the track. At first Tony's advice was, "Miles, miles and more miles". I never had a structured training schedule. I just ran when and where I felt like it; it was pretty much hit and miss. My mileage did vary a lot. I had weeks where I ran 30 miles per week and others where I managed up to 50 miles per week, probably depending on how far my weekend races were, but according to Tony I needed to get that up as high as possible as I should be running over 100 miles per week on a regular basis. So I did dramatically increase my mileage.

By the time of the Barry 40, the first weekend in March, I was up to an average of 80 miles per week and was very excited at the thought of attending the race. I met John Legge, the main selection man, and what a nice person he was. John came over for a quick chat to introduce himself and more than welcomed me to the squad as a potential future athlete. It was obvious to me that he had been a runner in his time and it didn't take much research to discover that he was a good ultra runner himself for many years and was one of the London Marathon "ever presents" who had run all the London Marathons. I guess he was well into his sixties at that point. Race organiser Mick McGeoch was also another "ever present". I sat at the back of the room somewhat in disbelief that I was really here with all these athletes who had only been names in the past. It was great seeing them in the flesh, but I didn't really talk to any of them. This was after all a meeting and I didn't have any experience to be part of the "input", just an observer.

The next day was race day. Carolyn was apparently going for a national record for 20 miles plus intermediate distances, which she did achieve. Eleanor Robinson was also there and she went on to win the ladies race. Hilary Walker, another big name, was recovering from a broken tibia and fibula sustained in a race in January. Marianne Savage was also a very good 24 hour runner who was competing. Tony Jones was there and it was the first time we actually met. He was a very "large" man, not quite what I had expected, and certainly not the most welcoming to Bill. Tony said that there might not be room in the squad meeting for Bill and he might have to wait outside. John, by contrast, had welcomed Bill in with me to attend the meeting. I thought it strange that he should not be allowed to be with me.

The race set off and my race plan was to do 2 minutes per lap which was 8 minute miles and to maintain this. Right from the gun I was being shouted at to, "Slow down!" My first couple of laps were only: 1 minute 55 seconds, 1 minute 51 seconds, then 1 minute 58 seconds and 1 minute 58 seconds making 7 minutes 42 seconds for the first mile. By the end of the first 5 miles at 39 minutes 48 seconds I was last of the athletes who were to finish. It was very demoralising. I was much stronger and felt very restricted. At 10 miles my time was 79 minutes 51 seconds, even splits for each 5 miles but I was still last. At 20 miles I was trailing the entire field by over 11 minutes and Carolyn had already broken the UK record and was to retire as planned. Tony was now confusing me; was he telling me to pull out? "What is he on about?" I questioned Bill who was supporting me with drinks. "What is he saying?" The answer came back that I could do what I wanted now that I had done 20 miles, I could pull out, I could slow down or I could speed up. Now that I was half way I was on my own to do what I wanted. Totally baffled by this confusing situation and adamant that I was here to run the 40 mile race I relaxed and began to run how I felt, which was more comfortable at a slightly faster pace. By 30 miles I was 3rd in the ladies race, just catching Marianne Savage and I did the third 10 miles in 77 minutes compared to the 80 minutes for the first two sets of 10 miles. At one stage I was running faster than Eleanor, but she had a massive lead over me and there was no way I could catch her. I finished as 2nd lady with 5 hours 14 minutes compared to Eleanor's 4 hours 50 minutes and I was 18th of the 23 finishers. In the results list I was the only athlete to run a negative split. That is to run the second half in a faster pace than the first half.

After the race I showered and finally found a chance to talk to Eleanor. I was quite shocked to find that she had followed my progress for some time and wondered why I had not tried the top ultra scene earlier. She also had a word of warning for me about Tony to the effect that he was only an "advisor" to Carolyn and she questioned his actual qualifications to coach.

Back at home the next week I knew I had run a race and I felt quite stiff for a few days, probably because I had never run a flat race on the track. My local training ground over the hills was certainly not flat. But Tony did not allow me any rest. This was just a training race and his instructions were to carry on as normal and be back doing my next half marathon a couple of weeks later. By April I had a new personal best in a 10 mile race at Hartlepool in 67 minutes and was nearing the 100 miles a week mark in training, but I had one great disappointment: Tony would not let me run as an elite athlete in the London Marathon, as it was three weeks before my debut in the 100 kilometres event. I conceded but went to the race with Bill and had a walk around the Sutcliffe Park course that I was to race on in three weeks time. The course consisted of a lap of the track, followed by a lap of Sutcliffe Park that surrounds the track. Although I had not been allowed to run in the London Marathon, I was still doing 100 miles a week and was pleased to maintain reasonable speed. I did the Penrith Half Marathon in 90 minutes and 1 second despite my watch saying a full 10 seconds faster! Now I knew why David had been so disappointed not to break 90 minutes all those years ago, for the sake of a second or two that clock that keeps ticking can be a hard task master.

The day of my debut arrived and I was an absolute bag of nerves. I had no idea what time I could really achieve, as I had never run further than the marathon on tarmac. I had done loads of off road ultras, but this was much harder on the legs and I would just have to see what happened. As it was a national championship I really wanted a championship medal. Some of the big names were absent as they already had selection times for championship races; so they did not have to compete here. The plan was to set off at 8 minutes per mile, similar to the Barry 40, but to maintain this speed for 100 kilometres (or just over 62 miles). This would bring me home in around 8 hours 20 minutes but I guessed that something would happen to slow me down. My goal was therefore a sub 9 hour performance so in the program the predicted time was 8 hours 30 minutes to 8 hours 45 minutes.

It was a big race program with eighty-two starters; I thought this was a good field for such a race. The first four laps were on the track so it was easy to gauge my pace before heading out around the park for the fifty-two circuits that followed. I tried to run steadily but was very excited and guess that I probably started a bit too fast. It was annoying being target practice for the local kids in the park playing football and I was not amused at nearly being tripped over twice in the first few laps by dogs that were not on leads. The park was open to the public and they had absolutely no respect for the runners and all the hard work we had put in leading up to that race. It would have been devastating to have fallen and hurt ourselves through members of the public not respecting us. I soon settled into the lead, a bit surprised to be leading, but that was probably the way I wanted it and I felt comfortable with my pace.

Much of the pre-race hype had been on Fraser Clyne, a world class marathoner with a time of 2 hours 11 minutes for the marathon. He eventually faded and pulled out of the race. After half way I began to struggle. I had not taken much of a taper for this race on instructions and was now beginning to feel the effects. Tapering involves cutting back on the high mileage in order to feel fresh and recovered from the hard training for an important race. This would usually be over a period of two to three weeks for a big event. I reached half way (50 kilometres, around 31 miles) in 3 hours 55 minutes and felt much worse at that point than I did at 30 miles into the Barry 40, but it was a race I had to finish and I wanted to make my mark in my debut. I still had a reasonable lead over the 2nd place lady, who I think was Great Britain international athlete Sue Ashley who was to retire.

Tony had now arrived and was beginning to annoy me, jumping out from behind trees and bellowing at me. This was not my style and I chose to ignore him. I was beginning to struggle and could not calculate finishing times, as I was not really that used to this. I had got my drinks bottles organised a bit better than the Barry 40 where I had five hundred millilitre bottles that Bill gave me and I had to throw them down for him to collect. Having watched everyone else there, I now knew that three hundred and thirty millilitre bottles were best as I could carry them for a lap and hand them back again. Bill was having a drink of coke when I next passed him. It was just what I fancied, having never drunk this before in a race, and I proceeded to finish off the bottle for him! I got slower and slower, but the finish was getting closer and closer and I was still in the lead for a gold medal. With just a couple of laps to go, a grey haired Geoff Oliver overtook me. I remembered him from the Barry 40 where I had just pipped him at the finish by a few seconds. Here the situation was reversed and he stormed by me to finish in 8 hours 39 minutes and I finished in 8 hours 40 minutes, well within the 9 hour selection time for the international championships that were being held in September. The clock had ticked well that day.

I remember finishing in somewhat of a daze. I had struggled on in so much pain for the last few hours, paying the price for a fast start and I was just so relieved to finish and achieve my target time. I didn't really know what to expect as it was such a different race from what I was used to. Bill came over and almost immediately John Legge was there. He congratulated me on my performance and asked if I would be interested in representing Great Britain at the forth coming European Championships 100 Kilometres that were being held in September in Holland. I was stunned! My dream had come true! It had happened: I was the British champion at 100 kilometres and was standing there seconds after the race being invited to compete for my country. I would have jumped for joy if I was capable, but I just smiled and politely accepted, trying not to react like an excited kid, although deep down inside my stomach was churning with excitement. The pain of the race had gone and excitement had taken over. How could this have happened to me? This latecomer to running who hated sport at school and who could barely run a mile a few years ago and yet here I was being invited to represent my country! It had been an amazing year. I had set out my plan after my superb performance in the Long Distance Walkers Association 100 miles last year and just twelve months later achieved my goal. I had won my first national championships gold medal.

I had the news plastered all over the local newspapers and everyone at college read about me and congratulated me. It was an amazing experience and took some time to really sink in. As for Tony, well he expected me to be back up to full distance within a week and out there doing speed-work. He had no chance; I was so stiff it was impossible to run and I just wanted to wallow in self satisfaction for a bit. I did, however, run the annual Long Distance Walkers Association 100 miles event three weeks later. This was on Dartmoor and I had no idea of the route, unlike the Cleveland 100 miles where I had gone over it all and still managed to lose my way. After a few miles I found myself running with a good running friend, Gerry Orchard. Although we had not planned to run together, we happened to be running at the same pace and ended up running the entire event together, which made for really good company as there were a few navigational hiccups en route again. It's always easier to navigate when there is more than one of you. I was again the 1ˢᵗ lady home.

After this I trained like crazy. Tony's instructions were, "Miles, miles and more miles". But the speed-work sessions were becoming a real chore. He sent me out on some really difficult sessions sometimes that were absolutely impossible to achieve and when I reported back that I couldn't do them the answer was, "What did you learn from that?" My only thought was that he didn't understand me and didn't have a clue how to train me. I was exhausted and it ruined the training session. I then found out that the sessions were what the Kenyan 10 kilometres runners were doing and I could not see the relevance. "Well," explained Tony, "To run faster 100 kilometres races you need to run faster marathons, to run faster marathons you need to run faster 10 kilometres races, and so on.....". I was becoming more and more disheartened. Some sessions were really frustrating and I was running tired. I was not a Kenyan 10 kilometre runner!

70

The only bit of news to report was that as a result of the 100 kilometres race I was invited to run in a 50 kilometres uphill only road race in Granada, Spain in July. I had not realised at the time of my selection, but the World Challenge 100 Kilometres was being held before the European Championships 100 Kilometres but I had not been selected to run in that race. It was interesting to see that Hilary Walker had been selected despite her broken leg in January and I thought I would have surely been a much better prospect. I believe she ran around 10 hours 30 minutes by comparison.

The race in Spain was hard work right from the word go. I met up with athlete Dave Kelly at Manchester Airport and flew via Heathrow to Malaga. We joined Doina Nugent and Eric Seedhouse at Heathrow. Eric was our best 100 kilometres runner but he had chosen not to compete at the international events. I had to share a room with Doina, which was not the best partnership, as she wanted to share with her partner Eric and I hated my time spent there. Doina won and I was 2nd lady but later that year I heard she had been suspended for a positive drugs test in an event she took part in shortly before this Spanish event. Being new to the system Tony just knew I lived "up North" and the flight from Manchester was because he thought this was where I lived when there was a perfectly serviceable airport 2 hours closer to home at Teesside.

For our holidays that year the backpacking had to take a back seat, as the running was now more important and I could not afford to take three weeks off training. Instead we went for a running and cycling holiday in the Outer Hebrides. We took our Nissan Vanette which had been converted into a campervan and started with the Isle of Harris Half Marathon where I was 1st lady and then ran and cycled around nearly all the Islands. It was fantastic; every island was so different and each had its own character. We both came back fitter than ever.

The selection papers came through and with only a month to go I was beginning to break down. I was always running tired, 130 miles per week now and I was starting to have problems. The tendons on the front of my shins were inflamed and red and giving cause for concern. "Go and see a physiotherapist and get it fixed" was the answer from Tony. So I asked around and came up with two – Pip Chinn from Redcar and Julie Sparrow who was working at the local hospital. Pip was great and instantly gave me treatment for free when he found out what I was doing. I went on to see him several times.

Julie was a bit more difficult to access, but came highly recommended (she went to the Olympics with the gymnastic team). She also gave me free treatment. This was great sponsorship, as treatment was never cheap and with not working now and living off one wage money was getting tight. The diagnosis was that I had over-trained, picked up the mileage far too quickly and was heading towards a stress fracture in my shins. I had to stop running and there was no quick solution. I was fit enough with all the running; so had to rest and run very lightly on soft surfaces. I could cross train on the bike and swim. Tony was not best pleased and told me to continue training. "Who is your coach? Who tells you what to run, your physiotherapist or me?" I was not happy with his advice. Surely professionals should work together? Both physiotherapists were more than happy to communicate with Tony and give him the information on my injury but he was not interested.

I followed the advice of the physiotherapist and ignored Tony. A week before my big debut Tony told me to go out and run 20 miles. If I could get through this then I was fit to compete, if not I was to be withdrawn from the team. I was gobsmacked! I was fit enough to compete, but if I ran 20 miles then I could endanger my performance and I would never run 20 miles just days before a 100 kilometres race. I told him that I did it and had no problems, but in reality I had done just 3 miles going at an easy pace on grass. The other big issue was kit. I had been waiting for weeks to get my Great Britain kit, but, when it came, it was such a disappointment. I was sent a vest and shorts and a jacket that fitted Bill! I saw others wearing tracksuits, t-shirts, sweat tops and tights; but all I got were the bare minimum to run in and it arrived the day before I left home!

As the athletes all lived in different parts of the United Kingdom the plan was to take various local flights and meet up at the De Klinker Stadium in Winschoten, Holland. Bill was travelling with me, as it was so nerve racking I needed him by my side. The event was to be ten laps of 10 kilometres so it was easy for Bill to be at one feed station per lap. We flew out from Teesside to Amsterdam and were then to take the train to Winschoten. This was our first error; we got on the wrong train and as we were seated Bill spotted John Legge standing on the platform. Why wasn't he getting on the train? We got up again and were told we were on the wrong train; so we made a quick exit as the train was about to leave. Seconds later the correct train arrived in the same place.

It was a stress free journey to Winschoten after that and it was good as we now had company to show us the way to the stadium. Here we were to be taken to host families who provided our accommodation. We had been told that all the host families were extremely friendly and we were picked up and taken to their homes. Although excited about the event, we were all split up and I didn't feel like part of a team. The instructions were to meet up again the next day. One of the other team members, Sylvia Watson, was staying with a host family in the same road as us, so she was a good guide for me. When we met up there was a team meeting and the itinerary for the event was planned. Everyone was wearing Great Britain kit apart from me. I had none, only my vest, shorts and big jacket. The parade was discussed and what to wear for it. I had no choice. I had no kit; so it was decided the team would all wear the jacket similar to mine rather than track suits as I didn't have one.

The parade was quite exciting in some ways, but I still felt like an outcast as I had still hardly spoken to any of the other athletes in the team. We had a very late meal that night in a local Italian restaurant.

The next day was my big debut for Great Britain. I had hoped for a big improvement from my 100 kilometres time back in May, but did have a few shadows cast over this due to my shin trouble and poor training in the last few weeks. I need not have worried though, as I was easily the 1st home of the three Great Britain athletes selected (the others being Hilary Walker and Sylvia Watson). I improved my time by 12 minutes to 8 hours 28 minutes and was 6th lady home in the European Championships 100 Kilometres.

My shins had been great and I had had no problems at all, but it had been a long hard race. It was so exciting competing with athletes all wearing their national kit and I was quite impressed with my 6th position. The team position was out of the medals, unfortunately, after initially being told by Tony that we were in bronze medal position. The closing ceremony was the next day and immediately afterwards we went back to the train station for the trip home. On reflection I had been disappointed with the whole "team event". I still hardly knew any athletes, had been really pleased that I had paid for Bill to come with me and was even more despondent with Tony after what he had told me to do before this race.

From my debut back in May up to September, although I had trained hard, done lots of miles and done speed-work, my training regime was still very "unstructured" in the real sense and had very little recovery planned in any of the weeks. I had been reading up so much prior to starting university and could see no benefit in taking instructions from Tony. His advice had all been about miles and speed-work and my last injury incident had shown that he really knew nothing about me, about recovery or how to treat an athlete. Nor would he listen to other professional helpers. I felt that I had reached this position with almost no help anyway, so did I really need him? Communication had broken down significantly since our last conversation before Winschoten and as I was about to embark on my BSc Sport Science course I thought that it would be best to train myself for a bit. The next championship race was not until May next year so I had time to think and time to look over my training to see what had worked and what had not!

I could never rest for long though, as I really did love running and I was soon out racing again. On looking through the Road Runners Club yearly race guide I found a race that was also a championship race – Sri Chinmoy Amateur Athletics Association (AAA) of England 24 Hour Championships. Now there was a new challenge! I had run for 24 hours over rough terrain in the 100 miles events but how far could I run when the hills, navigation and carrying of compulsory kit were taken out of the equation? The date was close, the next month, 22nd and 23rd October 1994. I put my race entry in. I was too late. The closing date had passed and I received a wonderful polite letter back from the late Tony Smith (stuck in my scrap book still) explaining that he would dearly love me to take part in the race, but it was already oversubscribed. The entry limit had been reached and being a track event was restricted to just forty athletes: so I was put on a reserve list in case anyone pulled out. There were usually athletes who did have to withdraw, but I was bottom of the list and didn't rate my chances. The fact that I had just run for Great Britain in the 100 kilometres race obviously stood for nothing and gave me no special entry here. I was just on the list the same as any other athlete.

Back to the drawing board and back to the local marathons. Three weeks after my international race I took part in the Cleveland Classic again, 56 miles. The next week it was October and the calendar read like this: 1st October, Falcon Flyer, 26 miles and 1st lady, 8th October, Pathfinder 25 miles, where I badly sprained my ankle very early on overtaking a walker in the deep heather and 2nd lady, 15th October, a cautious Throgger Thriller, 24 miles with a strapped up ankle that was still very bruised and swollen and 1st lady, 20th October, telephone call from Tony Smith, organiser of the 24 hour race to say that an athlete had dropped out and that at this late stage (Thursday before Saturday race) nobody wanted to accept the late call up, so did I want to run? My reply was, "Well, er, yes, I think I would like to run but I haven't exactly tapered (eased back on mileage for recovery) for the event, having run marathons every weekend for the last four weeks and I don't exactly know how to approach such a race. What happens?" Tony responded, "Your support crew can set up a tent and table alongside the grass verge on the back straight of the track and we will provide additional refreshments. Come and enjoy it and run as many laps as you can. A lap recorder will manually record your lap time each time you pass."

Bill came home and I dropped the surprise: "We are away this weekend, what do you think I should take?" I had no idea. This was so different from the Long Distance Walkers Association events where you had time at the checkpoints to refill bottles and stop and rest and eat; this would be similar to the 100 kilometres events where you don't have time to stop. Whereas I didn't eat anything in the 100 kilometres events, I knew I would have to eat in this event; so I took a few "snack things". As I had now started university the first instruction I had been given was to measure and record everything I ate and drank. I thought that was a good idea and would be useful to analyse for future events. So the next day it was off to the supermarket and down to London.

The day dawned and another new experience awaited. I collected a starting list and there were many faces and names here that I recognised: Don Ritchie, Mick Francis, James Zarie, Geoff Oliver, Stephen Till, Dave Cooper, Hilary Walker, Richard Puckrin and Marianne Savage to name just a few. The previous year's winner was Alan Young, again in the field and someone I was about to get to know a lot better in future years. Each one had a paragraph written about them in the program and it was daunting, facing a real world class field of just forty athletes. I wasn't even included as a very late entrant, but guessed a few would know who I was. But more daunting was how little I knew about the event. Exactly how do you run a race like this? How do you pace yourself? How much do you eat and drink? What do you eat and drink? Do you ever stop and rest? Do you plan to walk or continuously run? How are your laps counted for 24 continuous hours? How monotonous is it? Do you get bored just running around a track for so long? So many questions, but this was the challenge again, something I had never done before. A new challenge, but what was my goal? I had barely had any time to think about this one. Would my sprained ankle from two weeks ago hold up? I had nothing to lose but everything to gain. It was new to me, whatever I did would be a new personal best, and like the 100 kilometres, would give me a target to improve on. So it was: experience, learn and improve.

Midday was the start time. Bill was set up with our little Nissan Vanette, basic but it had an awning attached for extra space, a cooker, a bed and all that was needed for Bill to look after himself while he looked after me.

A quick briefing by Tony; and off we went. I settled in behind Hilary Walker, who was extremely experienced, and although I had taken her scalp at Winschoten in the 100 kilometres, this was different and I knew not to go ahead. I kept my distance, but she knew I was there. Hilary settled me in nicely, just the odd comment here and there but basically silence, how I guess we both wanted it. Once settled it was easy to maintain the same rhythm and pace and when we each did our individual bits, such as popping to the toilet or taking refreshments after a few hours, we soon split up and progressed individually. Hilary now seemed to be speeding up and starting lapping me. I was content as the newcomer to settle into the starting pace. I then heard the announcement that Hilary was off on another world record attempt - this time the "World Best 40-44 Performance" for women for 50 miles, which she easily achieved with 6 hours 37 minutes and 6 seconds. My 50 mile time by comparison was 7 hours 15 minutes. But the big difference was that Hilary set this world record, then slowed down significantly with her goal achieved and I continued to progress to achieve the 24 hours.

It wasn't long after the start that the rain began, and it rained and it rained and it rained, torrential for some of the time, but on and on and on, round and round and round. I might add that we did change direction every 4 hours which was a really weird experience. Strange, but after running for so long in one direction it suddenly felt like a completely different race going the opposite way and initially it was hard to keep to the inside of the track. The other thing with changing direction which many spectators didn't realise was that athletes didn't ever see people's faces, only their behinds, so it was good to put a face to the style which could be recognised for just a quick glimpse.

The night progressed and Bill decided to go to sleep for a couple of hours. It was a miserable night but he left a few drinks and snacks on my table for me and disappeared. I was unaware of it at this point, but I had started to speed up and was taking very few walking breaks, but I was being closely watched and monitored by officials and Andy Milroy, a great ultra distance statistics man. It was easy running on the track, nothing to think about in terms of navigation; so I could simply focus on running and on what I wanted to eat and drink. I also thought about the clock quite a lot, it was easier to break this race down into segments of time rather than checkpoint to checkpoint or 10 kilometres segments. Here the clock was in your face all the time, ticking away. At times I was content to just watch it and look for the 4 hour segments to change direction again, at other times it was looking to see exactly what the time was.

I changed clothes several times as it was so cold and wet. It rained all night long. Eventually I overtook Hilary again and reached 100 miles in 16 hours 26 minutes. This was quite amazing compared to a 100 miles in the hills at around 25 hours. But the race was about to get to me and my good spell had ended. Bill appeared again I got slower and slower and walked more and more, the next 10 miles taking around 2 hours 30 minutes and then 3 hours for another 10 miles. I was walking completely now, my shins were very sore and bruised and my feet throbbing and blistered from constantly being wet. The clock was ticking incredibly slowly now, I wished it would speed up as my pain would be over once the clock reached 24 hours.

I eventually finished and reached my target of 127 miles (204 kilometres) and I was the 1st lady and 5th overall. Not a bad debut, but a lot of lessons learnt. I received a huge trophy, but I could hardly walk to collect it. Not a bad year: debut at 100 kilometres and 24 hours, national champion at both and my international debut. What a year in fact! And to round it off I appeared on the front page of the Road Runners Club news magazine, the only person to ever win both national titles in the same year – and I still remain the only person to ever do this!

That event took some recovering from, but I was ranked very highly in the world rankings. I did another couple of off-road ultras to finish off the year. These were some reasonably local events where I won the Darlington Dash 40 miles and the Rowbotham's Round Rotherham 50 miles. By the end of that year, my big debut year of 1994, I had run forty-seven races, a total of 1100 miles of racing. I had also achieved seventeen race wins and been placed in the top three on twenty-five occasions. It was quite a progression for me, as eight of these races had been in excess of 30 miles.

The clock had been on my side all year, ticking perfectly in all races; achieving far more than I thought was possible. The year had gone in a flash and in some ways I just wanted to sit and savour the highlights, but this was just the beginning, there was still far more to achieve. My times had been established. I now needed to improve and beat the clock to faster times and further distances.

Chapter 7

International Medals
and Learning More

The year of 1994 was just the start of my career in all senses, my first international vest and the start of my Sport Science degree. I went to university to learn how to coach myself, how my body responded and adapted to training, training techniques, and a whole range of subjects that were on offer, the best module for me being the long-winded "Personal Development in Relation to Sport." This was a subject personal to me and how I developed and put the information I was learning into my sport. I built a massive portfolio for this and had monthly meetings with my mentor or lecturer for the subject.

Although I wasn't that keen on the psychology side of the course, as it felt like a load of theories and waffle at the time, it was to end up shaping the way I thought and was the key to finally conquering that last 4 hours of my 24 hour races as you will see. As part of my degree I can always remember learning about goal setting, something I had been doing all along but not realising it. Now it was here in black and white, short term goals, long terms goals and steps to achieve these goals. As part of the exercises in one lesson I had to write down the main goal for the next year and for a long term goal what I would like to achieve in several years time – what would be my ultimate dream as an ultra distance runner. Well that was quite easy, next year I wanted to bring home a medal from an international event and my ultimate dream – I did think for a little while but it was obvious what this would be for me. Being a world champion was one thing, every year there would be a world champion, but to break a world record was the ultimate dream for me. This was making your mark in the history and development of your sport and this was what I wanted. But what distance? Should I run 100 kilometres or 24 hours? Neither, I wanted to set a world record on home soil for the longest thing I could do in Great Britain; that happened to be running from one end of the country to the other – Land's End to John O'Groats. I put this in writing in 1994, although I had no idea of the distance or the world record at that time.

University for me was a new challenge. Having been a bus driver for nearly eight years it was a big change. I really enjoyed my time at Longlands College, but the subjects and course work were very light compared to university. I now had to get to grips with learning how to use a computer, as all of the assignments had to be typed or word processed. This was a challenge in itself but would prove very useful. I put all my efforts into university, the same as any other challenge. Most of the students were straight out from the school, college and A level route; there were few mature students and at the age of thirty I was the oldest of the lot. The only pleasing thing was that I was also the highest ranked athlete and the only current international standard athlete. There was a good swimmer who had been to the Olympics but had retired from the sport. The course was also quite new, into its second year at that point and still developing in terms of the staff and equipment.

I felt I had a lot to prove here. I had come back to university for a reason. I had a real desire to learn and a hunger for knowledge to satisfy. My aim was to use the knowledge gained so that I had all the tools to make me the best athlete possible and achieve my goals and dreams. I think some students and certainly non-sports students think that Sport Science is an easy degree and all about playing sport. None of the lessons are given to practising sport; they are all structural lessons like all other science courses. Of all the lessons, I really did enjoy the exercise physiology side, using the specialised equipment in the laboratories and seeing how the use of equipment could measure specific factors of fitness.

I found the first semester reasonably easy. I did not do the normal student thing of going out and drinking heavily. I was married, had a mortgage to pay and many miles to run. I attended nearly all my lectures. If I skipped a lesson it was because I was away and racing. I had sacrificed a lot to come here and I had no wages now. I had to apply for a student loan to help the finances just the same as many other students. I was fascinated by many of the subjects and in the coaching module came some of the structure I strived for. Although it was a coaching module, it meant I could coach myself and prepare my own programs based on what I was learning.

In 1995 I wrote my first training program based on what I was learning and the lessons from the previous year. No, "Miles, miles and more miles", as Tony Jones had instructed, but a structured program around periodisation, three progressively harder weeks followed by an easier, recovery week. Within each week there were specific sessions; speed-work, hill repetitions, sustained runs and races. I knew from the previous year the highest mileage hit was 130 miles; so I based my highest week of mileage on this to build me up for the next international race in May, which was the European Championships 100 Kilometres in Chavagnes-en-Paillers, France.

The program started well, I achieved a new personal best time in the Malta Marathon in February with 3 hours 7 minutes and even came home in 3rd place with a massive trophy, presented by Emil Zatopak. The mileage was still too much though and, although I didn't break down this time, I was constantly running tired. The program was "tweaked" and in that next international 100 kilometres, race I stood on the podium alongside Eleanor Robinson and Lynn Harding to collect my first international silver team medal with my new personal best time of 8 hours 21 minutes. My written goal had been achieved. As Lynn had taken the individual silver medal and Eleanor a veterans' trophy, the team trophy was given to me. The trophy was a gorgeous blue china souvenir that I cherish as my first international award. As we had driven there and this was a breakable item I also had the best chance of getting it home in one piece.

We drove home and stopped off in Cambridge on the journey to show off the silver medal and team trophy. I was still wearing my kit as a great big box full of kit had arrived this time; track suit, t-shirts, tights, sweat-top

First international medal and trophy, Chavagnes-en-Paillers, France
(team silver, with Eleanor Robinson and Lynn Harding).

and back-pack. The response was, "Here she is again showing off" and I was given quite a cold reception before John promptly went up the pub. Quite upset by this, it was the last time I ever mentioned running to them unless they brought up the subject and I vowed never to show them another trophy or medal unless they asked to see it.

I finished my first year at university in fine style. I got excellent grades in most of my subjects, the only exception being psychology. I could never quite get to grips with all the theories and essay writing that felt like waffle compared to laboratory reports and assignments. I had no fear now that I wasn't good enough to gain a degree. I had the ability but it did take time to keep on top of all the work and I looked forward to a few months off over the summer. The course to me was like a full time job, hours to attend at university, and many hours planned at home to keep on top of all the study involved and writing of assignments. Many students had part-time jobs. I don't think I could have coped with working as well; my work would not have been up to scratch.

During the summer months we had a little break and experienced Land's End to John O'Groats. After our wonderful cycling trip the previous year that saw excellent results we put panniers on our bikes to carry the camping equipment, took the train to Penzance and cycled to Land's End. Not used to the bikes, it was an eventful trip. We travelled the scenic route by the coast initially, went over the high passes in the Lake District, visited Fort William and after ten days of cycling and nearly 1,000 miles we finished at a wild and windy John O'Groats. It was hard to visualise running this amount of miles but it was an excellent holiday.

Later that year I went on to improve my 100 kilometres time, down to 8 hours 12 minutes in the World Challenge 100 Kilometres held in Winschoten, Holland, achieving sub 8 minute miles for 62 miles. To finish off 1995 I came 3rd in the Lanzarote Marathon, having run the Lanzarote Challenge of four events in the week before – oh, and set a course record in the Round Rotherham 50 miles event a week after. In 1995 I had run fifty races, done over 1,000 miles in racing for the year and came in the top three positions in twenty-five of these races. I was learning more all the time now. In the second year you could choose more specific modules. The anatomy and physiology done, it was now onto exercise physiology, biomechanics, sport psychology, motor control, sports injury, sports coaching and nutrition. I still put a massive amount of work into all my assignments and Bill was often tucked up in bed while I was still studying away. Even though I was an international standard athlete this counted for nothing in terms of study at university. When I went to Lanzarote for training and racing for two weeks I was given an assignment on the Monday before departing with three weeks to complete it. I realised that I would be away on the due in date and asked for an extension. The response was, "You have five days to complete that assignment this week; that is enough time", and no allowance was made for my being away. So when others think university was an easy life for elite athletes, the only concession given was authorised absence for important training and competitions, but no extra time for assignments. I was also to miss an exam during this trip. I was prepared for the same response and having to take the exam before I went, but this was relaxed until I returned. I didn't think at the time but it would have been good for the others should I have seen the exam before they took it. Unfortunately I didn't get to know what was on the exam before I took it, but still did well.

One of my other frustrations at university was working with others. I was a rare breed of student who did all my reading and got on with assignments the minute I was given them as I soon learnt that at the end of each semester there would be a mountain of work to do and lots of assignments and exams due all at the same time. But others were not so keen. When doing group work it was always last minute stuff, no time to adjust and research more and although I mainly got grade A's with individual assignments, group assignments tended to pull me down. There was even

Celebrating with cocktails after a podium place in the Lanzarote Marathon.

an occasion where I got dumped with two students who failed to attend lessons for one group assignment. It was while I was away in Lanzarote that groups were formed for a poster presentation. Not being aware of this until my return I was grouped with two others who had not attended that week (and many other weeks). I did the work on my own as the others either made up excuses and could not meet up or else made a meeting time and never turned up. The week before I saw the tutor to inform him of the situation and he agreed that I could present my work alone. One of the students then frantically tried to contact me the day before the presentation. Bill was on the other end of the telephone as I was away racing and Bill told him the work had been completed. He turned up expecting to present something that I had done and he had no knowledge of. Needless to say the next day at university was the last time I was ever to see him.

Although I could work in groups, you can't when they fail to meet up. The only way forward for me was to do the work myself as at least it all got done and I was in control, but it did annoy me that others could go out and enjoy themselves while I slaved away. I still personally disagree with this policy as it is an individual degree, not a group degree. Working with others is fine during lessons when the students are there, but their commitment outside of lessons was hard to come by. The only positive lesson was that I was the real one who was learning; they were just there for the ride.

Nutrition was also one of my great interests with running such long distances. I knew this would hold the key to a lot of my performances too and I had a good rapport with Claire Harrison, the lecturer for this module. I always remember researching a cyclist who was cycling from Land's End to John O'Groats for an assignment that I was given. I obviously tackled this job with great enthusiasm.

In 1996 there was a surprise award at the Teesside Women of Achievement event. I had been nominated by Liz Barnes from the university for my world class ultra distance debuts, not that I knew it at the time, and made it through to make the three finalists. Allison Curbishley, a 400 metre hurdler at the time and then 400 metre runner picked up the main award, hot on the heels of Sally Gunnell retiring. I was to learn that younger track stars would always have an advantage over older ultra distance runners.

My first big disaster also happened that year. I had been progressing steadily, improving all the time, but university was time consuming and mentally quite draining. I worked hard on all my assignments. It was not easy making the transition from being a bus driver to a student and despite writing my programs and reducing the mileage to a maximum of 110 miles a week, the World Challenge 100 Kilometres in Moscow was a nightmare. I struggled from 50 kilometres onwards, slower and slower, but the team around me also suffered. Hilary Walker failed to get to the start line, Carolyn Hunter-Rowe conceded to an injury and withdrew and it left just three athletes to record a team finish. I finished behind fellow Great Britain athlete Sylvia Watson, with 9 hours 36 minutes. It had been a long, hard slog to finish and decided I had just overcooked things a bit before that race; it was time for a break and, with assignments heaped up, I took a month off running to catch up.

But sitting down to complete my assignments created other problems. My hamstrings were getting stiffer and stiffer with just sitting and reading and writing and by the time I started again I struggled to return to form. By the time of the European Championships 100 Kilometres in Cleder, France in August I was running reasonably well, but psychologically I lost it. The route was four laps of approximately 25 kilometres and after reaching 50 kilometres 4th of the Great Britain athletes I pulled out of the race. It was my first "did not finish" and it upset me immensely. I was a proud runner and didn't do my country proud on that occasion. The only good news about withdrawing was watching the finish of the race; Carolyn Hunter-Rowe had come back strongly after injury to take the gold medal and it was an honour to see her win the title.

It was a hard learning curve that year, but I still had one more race to perform, the second 24 hour race of my career just four weeks later. In some ways this had been the reason for my withdrawal. I was performing below par; the team was performing strongly ahead of me, and with another race so close I withdrew to hold myself together for the next one. In that event, the European Challenge 24 Hours, Courcon, France in September my performance wasn't great. I struggled on, ate far too much, again learnt a great many lessons about the event, but again stood on the podium with Eleanor Robinson and Sandra Brown to collect another team silver medal. As we had driven to the event, yet again we called in at Cambridge on the way home. We were given the usual reception and left the silver medal in the van, only to be shown if they asked to see it. Needless to say it remained in the van. It did not surprise me that there was no request and my parents have never seen anything else I have ever won.

Of note here is Sandra Brown. The previous year Sandra and husband Richard, both very renowned world record holders of events longer than

24 hours and the "World's Best Race Walking Couple", independently set their respective world records for Land's End to John O'Groats. Sandra had set the record of 13 days, 10 hours and 1 minute for the distance of just over 830 miles. So then I knew what I had to do to achieve the dream goal I had written down at university in 1994. Richard also wrote a book, "The Winning Experience," which referred to their world record breaking run along with other factors, but it was not a highly detailed book on the event, more about "winning in life", an excellent read, no daily distances to copy, just references.

As part of my studies I had had to research the history of my events, which I had found fascinating and went back years to a time when ultra distance walkers raced for big wagers and it was a very popular sport. The names of Sandra and Richard in more recent times had highlighted their performances to me. Eleanor Robinson, who I knew very well by now as she was always my room-mate at events held one of the best records for me; she held so many ultra distance world records that she actually held the record for holding the most athletic records. Then of course there was Hilary Walker, met in my first ever ultra distance race, still a formidable force. Between Hilary and Eleanor they had pushed each other to more and more records, world records and now veteran's records. Following in their footsteps was not an easy process; to break any national records meant breaking the world record. Not to forget the great Don Ritchie and the amazing performances and world records that he still holds. Don's world record of 100 kilometres on a track of 6 hours 10 minutes and 20 seconds set in 1978 is just an amazing feat that has still yet to be bettered.

I finished 1996 a wreck. I had run continuously on damaged hamstrings and my stride length was getting shorter and shorter, not to mention how painful it had actually been to run. I finally succumbed to injury and sought help. Julie Sparrow, the physiotherapist, reduced me to tears by telling me I would need a year out to fix myself, as I was far too over-trained, running on injuries and ignoring and abusing my body. It was a hard lesson to learn, but being a stubborn athlete I guess that was the only way she could get the message over to me of how serious my injury had become. If I didn't stop and kept on running the result would probably be carry on running for a year or two and then never run again! Running was now a way of life and as far as I was concerned I was not finished with it yet. Eleanor and Hilary had long careers in running and I wanted the same. I finally admitted defeat and stopped running on the 10th November after one last ultra run in the Darlington Dash 36 miles, in a disgraceful 6 hours 5 minutes.

The scare that Julie had given me worked and made me stop running. I followed her advice religiously, steadily progressing under her guidance and luckily didn't need a full year out. I was starting to run again six months later. The time out from running also put paid to my big dissertation. I had been planning a 24 hour treadmill run in the laboratory as a case study project. The injury meant that I had to change the entire dissertation and think up something new. I changed to carry out a diet analysis of the Great Britain squad of about thirty athletes. Most did respond with great detail of everything they had consumed over a seven day period along with training completed. They were all rewarded with a detailed printout including carbohydrate, fat and protein content and percentages along with all their vitamin and mineral content and the calories consumed. From studies it was evident that a diet high in carbohydrate favoured ultra distance runners, but a good percentage of protein was also important. The analysis revealed much information. It was clear that the better athletes also knew how to eat well; the lower end of the squad appeared to have less adequate diets. I was lucky having access to the software for performing the analysis; so my diet was good as I had done several weeks of diet analysis on my own diet to improve it.

The big issue this new dissertation left me with was time to complete it. I had to completely review all the literature again and was running out of time to finish the dissertation in the allotted time frame to the desired level of my ability. Despite getting many grade A's, enough to finish with a first class degree, my final dissertation only reached fifty-six percent and was awarded a grade C. Had this reached sixty percent, enough for a grade B, I would have been awarded a first class degree. Instead, that small four percent from the dissertation knocked the final result to an upper class second degree. The rules are that the final dissertation must not be more than one grade below the final classification, not that I was aware of this until after my results came out. I had assumed I would get a first class degree and was bitterly disappointed with the results. As with most things in my life, I had set my goals high.

I started late in 1997 due to the injury and my first marathon back was in Leeds with 3 hours 17 minutes. I was content with this race just two weeks before the next international event in May, the European Championships 100 Kilometres, Florence, Italy. I was not too sure what my performance would be, but I was confident of running injury free and achieving a sub 9 hour performance were it to be a selection race. John Legge had been instrumental here as a selector. He had intermittently spoken to me all through my injury to see how I was and when I was back running. He was aware that I might not be back to full fitness but that I was capable of a strong performance and I was selected very late on with the blessing of Julie.

The race was horrendous for many reasons. Bill's mother had suddenly died the week of the event and her funeral was to be on the day of the race. Bill had lost his father just six months earlier after a long illness. I was prepared not to go to the race to support Bill and pay my respects to his mother. Bill was quite insistent that his mother would have wanted me to continue to race. Bill's family were always so proud when they saw the Gayter name in the paper for all the right reasons. Although they never understood my running, they knew I ran well and were pleased for me and always wanted to see my medals and trophies. This was the complete opposite to my parents.

The route was the famous "100 Kilometres del Passatore", or "Firenze to Faenza", basically around 50 kilometres uphill and 50 kilometres downhill, so not a fast course. The race started in the heat of the afternoon after a long bus journey from the finish to the start of the race. I had prepared drinks for every 5 kilometres during the race as usual, but these nearly all disappeared in the race and the few that did appear were completely muddled up. By the time I had reached 50 kilometres I was getting dehydrated. I had struggled to get anything to drink, the crews were having problems accessing the feed stations and although the top Great Britain runners and those behind me were getting support, I had nothing, stuck in the middle of the field. At the 50 kilometres point at the top of the steep climb the crew were finally there. It was no surprise that my drinks were missing, but in need of a drink I was handed a drink belonging to a man who had already gone through. Yuk! It was disgusting and I spat out the only mouthful I took. It later transpired to be Isostar with salt added. Isostar is a carbohydrate drink with additional nutrients such as sodium. The person whose drink that was failed to finish!

The route then hair-pinned very steeply down and my own worries just paled into insignificance beside what I then heard. Eleanor Robinson had been leading the ladies race, running extremely well and with a point to prove in that event, as a few questions had been raised over her age, when she was knocked down from behind by a cyclist. Eleanor was taken to hospital with concussion along with many bad bruises and cuts. The cyclist fared even worse with broken bones. I finally managed to get some drink and a banana from Sylvia's partner Geoff, who had been cycling the course where possible to support us.

Darkness fell and I completely ran out of energy. I was struggling and getting slower and slower, in need of food, but I had none. The feed stations were hard to find in the dark with all the villagers out and blocking our views, although they were out to support us. I drifted further and further back in the field. It was the early hours of the morning, there had now been a few showers and it was getting cold. Finally I heard the noise of the finish line, a little kind of ramped stage to run up. There was a great roar from the crowd; I thought it was for me until I nearly got bowled off the ramp by a blind runner and his helper. Obviously this was whom the crowd were cheering for. The time was 9 hours 14 minutes. I was cold, tired and hungry and had to sit around for ages until transport was organised. I was not alone. There were many of us in the same boat. Dave Walsh, the men's team manager managed to get me a sausage kebab to keep me quiet.

Back at the hotel room it was hard. It was so quiet without my room-mate Eleanor and I had little news on how she was. I so enjoyed Eleanor's company. She was such a vastly experienced athlete and I was always honoured to share a room with her and hear the many stories of her long career. I didn't sleep well.

The next day was the awards ceremony. The Great Britain women had won the bronze medal (as did the Great Britain men), although we didn't get medals! I stood on the podium with Hilary Walker and Helene Diamantides and we got a team trophy and no bronze medal. It was the same for all the medallists. On top of that I really didn't feel part of the Great Britain team due to our kit. Reebok had taken over as kit sponsors from View From and had no kit for us. As usual another big event was taking place and there was no kit left. The rules were that we all had to wear the same kit, so we had a flashy green and black vest and shorts, and a long sleeved white t-shirt with a black tracksuit to wear. Eleanor was brought to the ceremony after her night in hospital and given a bouquet of flowers, still rather concussed and unwell, but she wanted to go home. Not an event I want to remember.

At the World Challenge 100 Kilometres in Winschoten, Holland I performed abysmally yet again, despite a really good build-up. Having never eaten food much in 100 kilometres races I now needed food to get through these long races. I had a couple of practice events in the 24 hours too. In July I had practiced a strategy of running with planned walking breaks from early on in a local event at Hull. This practice works for many athletes, but just didn't work for me. I found it frustrating walking, continually clock watching to plan the walk, and having to eat when I had

Flashy kit (green and black) worn for European 100 kilometres, shown here running in the Tour of Tameside, a double marathon over 6 stages.

to walk rather than when I felt like it. Later in the year I used my sport science knowledge to have a practice with my food. Having eaten very little in my first 24 hour event, and too much in my second, I was now to try eating fifty grams of carbohydrate per hour as recommended to sustain energy for the event at Tooting Bec. By 8 hours into the event I found this was also too much and went back to eating when I felt I needed it. This event also doubled up as the Amateur Athletics Association of England Championships and I brought home the gold medal yet again. My distance wasn't fantastic at 193 kilometres (120 miles) but somehow got ranked as Great Britain's number one for the year.

I had now finished my BSc Sport Science and needed to pick up the finances again. The student loans had increased and our finances had decreased. My sister Julie was very proud of my achievement of gaining a degree, a first for our family. Julie had ended up working in a supermarket, big brother Paul was fitting windows and step-sister Melanie had taken an office job for an insurance company. Julie wanted to see the graduation ceremony and made the big journey from Cambridge just for the occasion. My mother tagged on, but she probably felt this was more like an obligation and due to a sense of duty rather than her desire to see my achievement, but it was nice to have some family support. Deep down, although I did grumble at my upper second class degree, I don't suppose it was a bad transformation from having been a bus driver with no A levels to my name and in addition being a rather mature student in a young student's subject.

Bill was so proud of my achievement. He wanted the biggest photograph possible of me collecting my scroll in the academic robes (still very prominently displayed in our house). There were no members from Bill's family who had gone to university. Bill had a twin sister and was the youngest of five children. But having been in the Army he had little contact with his brothers and sisters, two had moved out of the region and he had a brother and sister living close to Middlesbrough. Bill had supported me every step of the way. He always had belief in everything I did and encouraged me though my "down times", when the studies got on top of me. He never grumbled at having to take out the loan to complete my studies and encouraged me in every way possible. Bill did have an ulterior motive to support me though my degree. In his eyes Bill thought that by getting a degree I would get a top job that would more than support us both and he could take a back seat. He is still waiting!

We were now living in Guisborough and the house needed quite a bit of upgrading. To open the back door we took out some nails and the door fell off. We opened a couple of metal framed windows and they were so buckled they would not close again. So spending money on the house was vitally needed, but it was in a great place. I loved the little town of Guisborough, nestled beneath the woods on the North York Moors, the tops of the moors just a short run from the house.

The first job I took was delivering sandwiches to service stations, shops and other businesses. It was nothing special, but it brought in a wage. I really struggled with the early mornings and was constantly tired. University had been great for my running, allowing me sociable daylight hours to run, time to plan my assignments in my head and drift away with the world. Although running was strenuous work, it was my relaxation and relief from the toils of the day. I really did love running. But very early mornings combined with concentrating on driving long distances every day, was detrimental to my running and pleasure time. I was never a day time sleeper who could go for a nap (unlike Bill who can drift off at the drop of a hat!) and had to go running the minute I arrived home. I was in bed so early that poor Bill never had company in the evenings.

After about a year or so I progressed to work for Securicor, driving again but much more sociable hours for me and I quite enjoyed my time there. Bill also changed jobs. He too became a victim of the local thugs on the buses, a scar is still prominent on his face as a result of that assault, and I was now the one who didn't want him back on the buses, as he used to come home so wound up when incidents happened and it was not a pleasant job. He started work for a local vacuum tanker company, Central Industrial Services at Redcar. Rather dirty work at times, but regular hours and weekends off which worked well for us.

Bill had now become addicted to running too. For him it kept his weight under control and he could eat almost what he wanted. He also still had a great love of football. I guess this was always his passion. His claim to fame was having a trial for his beloved Boro Boys. Although he was good at football, so were all the other lads that were having trials that day and there was nothing to distinguish Bill from the other enthusiastic young boys. He made it through to the final selection and that was as far as he went. He never pursued his football; so he never really found out how good he could have been. The main sports he enjoyed in the Army were football and boxing and he has a few trophies to show for his efforts. Bill also ran and improved significantly at the marathon and trained quite seriously to run a spring and autumn marathon most years. Like me, he shared a great love of the hills and in reality was a far better fell runner

91

Bill on his way to his marathon best at the Robin Hood Marathon.

than me, always able to bound down the hills compared to my tiptoeing, but it made for a good partnership. On some of our longer trail races Bill would always start with me, I would do all the navigating and when he started to tire I would continue alone and he would drop back and try to tag onto runners behind for navigation. This was never one of his strong points. The Robin Hood Marathon in 1997 was to be Bill's best; his time was 3 hours 10 minutes. He tried hard for the sub 3 hour marathon but it never came.

Bill had tried ultras. His first attempt was also his last. A local event called the Darlington Dash was his big debut, 36 miles. He ran well for the first 26 miles and then walked the final 10 miles. We both accepted quite early on that Bill was never cut out to run ultra distance races. He tired easily, stiffened up and gained no pleasure from this. I was not going to encourage him into the sport, as it worked well for him to support me at ultras now, but his understanding of running probably helped our communication of the highs and lows that were experienced during such events.

I was glad to see the back of 1997 to start a new year afresh and get some good performances to my name. There had been many prominent family issues that year. Leaving Cambridge I had cut regular contact with my mother, just the odd telephone call now and then, but back in Cambridge there were some serious conflicts. Older sister Julie had now completed her family, Emily and Joshua making the final five. Step-sister Melanie had also got married, separated, had a baby girl Summer to another man, and that relationship had failed too. But step-father John's first official granddaughter was always more important than any of the other grandchildren and family conflicts continued. Julie had sought help from a counsellor; she never had guidance in all these years and the scars were still very raw. It was while at one of the counselling sessions that she was asked, "When all this was going on with John, what did your mother do?" It was not until that point that it dawned on Julie just how little our own mother had done to stop such happenings, how little she really cared. I am sure if her husband David had done anything beyond normal parenting to their children she would have defended them. So the demons did not all stem from John, but our own mother too, in not protecting us from his outbursts. Julie was encouraged to confront our parents about the past to have it openly admitted and "put to bed". But this just opened a can of worms and I will not repeat what was said at their final communication, other than to say that it was the last time they spoke to each other.

Even though I had often acted as go-between, there were a few more telephone calls from my mother where I only spoke the truth and defended Julie. Soon these phone calls stopped and Melanie never rang again either. So I have never had a falling out with my parents or step sister and yet have not spoken to them since. I have no regrets and no desire to make contact. I have not lost my parents; it is they who have lost me. The first year after this big bust up was difficult for Julie; it was a kind of grieving period, but never had Julie been so content and happy in her life. No more pretending all was happy, bowing to John's every whim, keeping the peace, yet secretly screaming inside, often tearful when alone and often upset when I talked to her. Time now began to heal the wounds for Julie and she finally got on with her life.

My life had been healed by running, leaving Cambridge and finding Bill who had brought me to normality. Running was my sanctuary, it was my escape from life and gave me time to think, be free and see my beloved hills. Moving away from Cambridge I never had pressures to visit the family anymore and keep in contact and finally Bill was my rock, he was everything I could ever have wanted: a carer, a listener, a supporter, an adviser. He oozed love and affection and took pride in every single achievement in my life. I don't think it was any one thing that sorted me out, but the combination of these three things together that gave me a life. I no longer felt like an outcast in society, not worthy to talk anymore. On the contrary, I had many great things to talk about. I will always remain an introvert in a crowd, always retreat if I feel threatened; I still hate violence and abusive language, but know this is not how I have to live my life. My home life is stable and I was now happy that Julie could also try and find her peace.

My first major event for 1998 was a new local event that was only ever held the once; a 12 hour track race at Catterick Garrison. I had never done a 12 hour race and looked up the records for this. The 12 hour world track record was held by Ann Trason from the United States of America, second on the list was Eleanor Robinson, who held the 12 hour British and European track record at 134.8 kilometres, with Hilary Walker close behind at 134.1 kilometres. Based on running 100 kilometres in around 8 hours 30 minutes, if I could run 35 kilometres in the last 3 hours 30 minutes I thought I could have a bash at the record. The race started well and I set off in the lead, followed by a number of men, who one by one dropped back, but I hit problems early on with a problem in my foot that eased with taking my shoe off and massaging it. I ran well, much better than the previous year and maintained my pace well. I had started to get faster and just began to get excited about the prospects for this race when I had an asthma attack and was forced off the track for a while, the record now out of reach completely. I got back on the track but finished with another big lesson learnt and 128 kilometres, that put me third best ever on the British rankings. My only consolation was that I beat all the men!

But I was back and running well and felt I deserved my vest when the selection came through, but my next event was to prove yet another disaster and not to do with my fitness. The event was the European Championships 100 Kilometres, Night of Flanders event in Torhout, Belgium, a night race that started at 8pm. Due to the darkness and the route not being lit in places, we were allowed to be accompanied by a cyclist to light the way. I was allowed Bill to follow me, which also meant he could carry all my food and drinks in a basket. This was great news and I arrived at the event with confidence. The event started well and darkness soon fell. However, running along the coast near the ferry port I started to feel sick and dizzy. The railings that we ran alongside were creating a flashing effect, made by the light the opposite side of the railings with the shadow it cast. I had to walk a couple of times and was glad to turn inland again. I soon began to feel better and get back into my rhythm again. On past 85 kilometres and all was going incredibly well. I was easily going to break the 8 hours 30 minutes mark when we turned left following a sign and the markers disappeared. I was being followed by other athletes, but began to think I might be off-course, as we had not seen any signs for some significant time. We had gone off-route. But how were we to find the way back? Where was the route? How far had I run? I stood frustrated in the road and could hear angry voices all around me. It wasn't my fault the runners had followed me; the route just wasn't marked clearly enough. A car then found us and led us back to the course. Apparently the path had been taken "left" across an unlit field and not "left" on the road. Well how could I have known that, running a road race? Frustrated and upset I lost all momentum. I had been reasonably high up in the positions judging by the finishing times, but with so much time lost and so much extra distance run (approximately another 5 kilometres) I jogged to the finish just outside 9 hours and finished 18th lady. Katie Todd was the only other British female to finish that day in 9 hours 30 minutes. The only consolation was the excellent performance by the men. Stephen Moore was Great Britain's first man home, followed by Simon Pride, both under 7 hours, William Sichel was the 3rd counter for the team in 7 hours 21 minutes.

That put behind me, there were still another couple of international events to compete in. In August we travelled to Lille, France for the European

*Leading the Great Britain team to a silver medal and
a personal best in the European 24 hours alongside Eleanor Robinson.*

Championships 24 Hours. Having done a couple of practice runs at this and widening my knowledge of the event all the time I finally achieved a new personal best of 212 kilometres (132 miles) and led my team home to a team silver medal, Sandra Brown and Hilary Walker making the rest of the team on the podium.

The last event of that year was another very special event, the World Challenge 100 Kilometres. This followed the banks of the River Shimanto, Japan in October. This was the purest river in the world and a real experience. It was not going to be a fast event, far from it with the heat and hills we were expecting, but we had a strong team in both the women's and men's event. As it was a long way to travel we were allowed to fly out a week before the event and had some time to acclimatise in Osaka before taking a tiny plane to the remote part of the island where we were to compete. We were welcomed so well and the whole experience of this part of the world was fantastic. It was my first big adventure outside of Europe. As for the event, well it nearly didn't happen after a typhoon the day before the race where we were all confined to the hotel with the shutters firmly closed and not supposed to venture out. It wasn't until late into the evening that the race got the all clear to go ahead after a day of thinking it was cancelled. We had to leave early in the morning and the race was delayed a little but it went ahead through the mountains.

The downside to the typhoon was some of the devastation it had left behind and a few lives had been lost. For us there was intense heat and humidity left in its wake, I heard reports of up to thirty-five degrees Celsius and one hundred percent humidity. After 5 kilometres of running I thought there was an insect crawling down my leg. On trying to brush it off I realised it was sweat dripping from my shorts. I never normally sweat this heavily but it was quite a steady climb and the heat and humidity were having an effect. I continued cautiously after that and drank well. There was quite a climb for many kilometres and finally after around half way the downhill started, but this was where I hit a problem. It was the foot problem that had caused some grief in the 12 hours race earlier in the year. It had intermittently given me problems, but was to slow me down significantly in this race and I even stopped a couple of times to take my shoe off and massage my foot. The heat and course made this a slow race and Carolyn Hunter-Rowe probably performed a personal worst time in winning the gold medal in 8 hours 16 minutes, another outstanding performance. Behind her the team was 4th and I finished in a very slow 11 hours 3 minutes.

I didn't start too well in 1999. While driving to a race across the North York Moors in early January in heavy snow the van rolled off the road, landing on the roof before crashing on its side. Although I was not seriously hurt, it affected a few races with some rib and back pain and we were down a vehicle. I was now riding a 125cc scooter as our second vehicle, cheap and easy with our finances still being in recovery mode. Bill had now gone through a variety of jobs, I think he was jinxed, as every job he seemed to get was doomed to failure: lost contracts, company went bust, company closed down. He got through five jobs in the space of around twelve months and it was a very depressing time. Bill was a very proud man, his aim in life was to care and look after me; the same way as his father had done for his family. He was a hard worker and like me enjoyed life to the full. We had an incredibly active life, very little time for sitting around and were out and about nearly every weekend with racing and other commitments.

Bill needed a job where he could be in control, something that was more secure and could in some ways control our destination. With having my foot problem and trying to massage it, it was obvious the benefits that

97

sports massage could bring to athletes. My only token gesture for being an international athlete was that for the first time I was presented with some vouchers that would pay for either physiotherapy or sports massage, but I was limited where I could use them. There were no suitably qualified masseurs that lived near Middlesbrough and I thought this would be a good start for any potential business to use these vouchers to massage international athletes that lived in the region.

So to take control we decided to take a sports massage course, useful for ourselves for running and also useful for a future job. I researched the courses well and also got advice from our governing body as to what qualifications were needed. We had to travel to Birmingham nearly every other weekend for about six months for a full weekend of theory and practice. The course had a syllabus that was one of only three courses then recognised as being of a standard to treat international athletes. Bill had not been confident enough to do this on his own, but it worked well for both of us as we could get good feedback on the treatment we gave to each other. It was a hard six months though, as I finally took the frightening step of becoming a lecturer. It was not that easy stepping straight from being a student to lecture at the University of Sunderland and do a few hours at Middlesbrough College too.

If Bill thought it was nerve-wracking training on the sports massage course he should have tried being in my shoes. My first lecture at the University of Sunderland was in one of the biggest classes with several different degrees courses all taking the same kinesiology lecture. I was nervous and it probably showed; I dared not hold a piece of paper in my hand as it would have shown how much I was trembling with fear. The smaller classes for the seminars were much more relaxed and I began to enjoy these lessons. My confidence and lecturing ability grew with time and by the end of term I could look back and laugh at my first shaky lectures.

By comparison the lower level A level (soon to become AS and A2 level) and BTEC classes that I taught at Middlesbrough College were far easier; much smaller classes and a much lower level of work where text books could be used with the very structured syllabus to guide the lessons. The only problem there was that half the lesson was taken up trying to keep the students in order. The couple of year's difference in age seemed to make a massive difference in levels of maturity. The college also had a football academy and with the class heavily biased towards male footballers this didn't help the balance. Most of these students only wanted to do their football and it was hard getting them to focus on lessons.

I had been seeking a solution to my foot problem and had various diagnostic tests; one of the bones in my forefoot was pushing upwards and physically leaving a bruise on my foot. Having struggled for nearly a year with this problem, it was finally diagnosed with various operations prescribed to stabilise the bone. A much easier solution was eventually suggested with a very simple taping technique to stop the toe from moving. I tested the strapping in a small 100 kilometres event in France early on in March, the L'Aunis 100 kilometres, a superb loop of 25 kilometres and Bill could again cycle alongside me to carry drinks. I ran well but poor Bill suffered. The chain broke on the bike and he had to scoot the final 50 kilometres to give me drinks. I think he finished in a worse state than me! I was over the moon to finish free from pain in my foot. The problem was cured with just a little piece of tape – the result was 8 hours 54 minutes which I knew I could improve on.

We were both working so hard now, me holding down a couple of lecturing contracts, trying to run and doing lots of travelling to Sunderland every day and Birmingham nearly every fortnight. I was trying to fit my training in where-ever possible: early morning, between lectures, late in the evening and not all the best quality sessions. Preparing new lectures was mentally draining; I longed to be back out in my hills around Guisborough. At the weekends in Birmingham we also had to fit in training around the course, going out running the minute the course finished around 5pm. We had dinner in a local pub and then slept in the car. We did another run the following morning and finally had a shower in the Birmingham Alexander Stadium where the course was being held. Then the long drive home after the course finished and the cycle started all over again.

Bill now had another job driving mainly nights, as the job dictated, but the lure of a new job nearly proved fatal. Having come back from Birmingham in the clapped-out car we had purchased after the Nissan Vanette was written off in the snow; Bill went straight into a night shift. Just a couple of hours after finishing he had to travel to Manchester for a medical for a superb new job he had just been offered. Tired from the weekend and driving all night he had another accident, potentially far more serious, as he fell asleep at the wheel and clipped the back of a lorry sending him out of control, crashing into the barriers on the motorway that ripped the wheel off the car and wrote that off too. The engine came through the dash-board and stopped just short of breaking his legs. The only good news was that he passed the medical and secured a new job with a fixed salary, far bigger than any previous wage. The bad news was that he had the accident on Monday and on Wednesday we were driving to France for the next World Challenge 100 Kilometres at Chavagnes-en-Paillers, again.

Luck was on our side. Ian Johnson, our mechanic from Marske, was about to go on a motorbike trip and loaned us his car. What generosity! All we had to do was insure it. Fantastic! Problem solved. It was off to France again. The result this time was a marginal improvement from March, the time 8 hours 42 minutes. There was no team finish for Great Britain in the race as only two athletes were competing, Hilary Walker being the other athlete selected. The men were a different case. Just after crossing the line for the third time on this four lap course of 25 kilometres the leading men were about to finish and I was lucky enough to hear who was finishing. Simon Pride from Great Britain and Thierry Guichard from France were battling it out together and I turned to watch as Simon Pride took the gold medal in 6 hours 24 minutes and 5 seconds, just 21 seconds ahead of Thierry. The men's team ran well, Stephen Moore (6 hours 54 minutes) and Mikk Bradley (7 hours 12 minutes) completing the team that took the bronze medal.

It was to be a busy year. Three weeks later I took a bronze veteran's medal at the British Trail Running Championships in Nottingham and two weeks after that ran in my first English vest at the Anglo Celtic Plate 100 Kilometres in Dublin, Ireland. I was first lady in 8 hours 27 minutes and together with Eleanor Robinson took the team gold medal too, also an English team record.

Bill now had his new job and had been settled for a few weeks. We desperately needed another vehicle to go with the scooter so made a brave decision and took out a £10,000 loan to buy a shining new silver Fiat Ducato van. It felt like a hotel compared to our Nissan Vanette, as we could stand up in the back and it had space for much more equipment and even had the luxury of a toilet. But no sooner did we collect our vehicle than Bill dropped the bombshell: the company he had been with and the nice big salary had gone. Overnight it had gone into liquidation and there was no job and instantly no money again. For me it was now the summer holidays and no lecturing hours. I was just hoping that come September I would get another contract. What to do? No money coming in, a big loan to pay, a mortgage to pay and two very tired people. We had nearly completed the sport massage course now, just the exams and course work to complete.

I took the bull by the horns and made the decision to have a cheap holiday, get away from everything in our new "hotel on wheels". With so many changes of jobs we had not been away in ages; so we went camping and training at Font Romeu, France. We had three superb weeks, cycling, training at altitude, massaging, resting, reading and preparing our work for the Sports Massage Diploma. We came back fully revived and eager to get back on track. I fell straight into a permanent lecturing post at Middlesbrough College and Bill got a job with Express Dairies delivering milk to supermarkets. Now how could he lose a job like that!

Having come back super fit, I had high hopes of a really good performance at the European Championships 100 Kilometres being held in Holland again at Winschoten, but an inflamed shin just above my ankle saw a below par performance again. The only consolation to my 8 hours 51 minutes was the fact that I stood on the podium to collect a bronze medal in the veteran 35-39 category and I was the only British female to finish the race. The only man to excel was stalwart Stephen Moore, 8th man with a cracking performance of 7 hours 2 minutes for the 1st veteran 50-54 age category, even beating the 1st veteran 40-44, not that he was impressed with going over 7 hours. He was a true gentleman and dedicated athlete; I hold Stephen in the highest regard.

There was one last championship race for the year, the British National and Amateur Athletic Association of England Championships at the Sri Chinmoy 24 hours track race at Tooting Bec, London. This was again a gold medal and a steady performance of 201 kilometres (125 miles).

Chapter 8

A New Millennium and New Sports

There were high hopes for the new year and new millennium, but they began with even worse events than in 1999. This time it was being knocked off the scooter on the way home from Middlesbrough College. Not that being hit by the taxi was the problem; it was the scooter landing on my left ankle. When the scooter was lifted off my foot, the foot was facing the wrong way. The telephone call Bill received from the attending policeman was that it was the worst broken ankle he had ever seen. However, after being dosed up with morphine and splinted, the ankle returned to position and the policeman and Bill could not believe it when they saw me in hospital. But significant soft tissue damage resulted which was to change my year completely and I doubted that I would ever be an ultra runner again.

For the initial recovery I could do nothing. There was neck and shoulder damage and I had a large wound on my ankle where it had been scraped along the ground. It hurt my shoulder to use the crutches and I was pretty immobile for some time. To add insult to this, I also had the knock at the door for an out of competition drugs test. Unable to even walk and having been injected with morphine from the accident, I was more worried about a positive drugs test than the injury. The timing just could not have been worse. But I declared what had happened and how and why the morphine had been administered, but was still relieved when the negative result came through.

Psychologically this was the most draining position ever. I had assignments to mark, but could not get my head into study mode. I struggled with everything I did and could barely move my ankle. The only other news which for me came at the wrong time was my first potential sponsor for nutritional products from Mannatech. Who would want to sponsor an athlete who was crippled? For several years now I had tried to get a sponsor. I was an international athlete, representing my country, but I still had to work for a living and pay all my own running expenses.

Fran, an associate from Mannatech, gave me some products and I had nothing to lose in taking the supplements, after all they were supposed to support the body and help it heal. Week by week went by with guidance from Julie Sparrow again and I was soon back walking, but running was another thing. There was little I could do during this time but sit and watch television, a real rarity for me. I have never been a great watcher of the television, often there were other more pressing and important things to do or read. In general I did try to have one day a week where I would sit down and relax with Bill in the evening (often on a Sunday after racing). I would have a night off from cooking, Bill would collect a take-away and watch a film and eat chocolate and popcorn. Bill by contrast loves watching films and television. He likes a real mixture of stuff from sci-fi, war and history, to Walt Disney films, comedies and thrillers. In fact there is little that he doesn't like, and of course there is his beloved football and sport which is compulsory viewing for him and compulsory non-viewing for me. I will agree to watch most athletics sport and championship events and I do become engrossed in this along with all top class athletic type events. I enjoy watching tennis, triathlons, cycling and ice-skating, but hate watching football and cricket, but am always interested in the results and like to see England and Great Britain do well in all events.

During the time I was injured, having physiotherapy took up many of my hours. I visited the currently named James Cook University Hospital in Middlesbrough most weekdays where Julie would send me upstairs into the gym to carry out rehabilitation work. Initially this was learning to flex my toes and then the ankle and progressed slowly to walking. By the time I took the bus from Guisborough to the hospital, did the work allocated and made my way home, this took up a considerable chunk of the day and it would be lunch time. After eating, Bill would be home after his early starts and I did very little else. I longed to be out running again. If the weather was good it frustrated me all the more. Some weekends when the weather was foul I could sit at home glad not to be battling the elements in races I was due to compete in, but if the weather was pleasant I would be jealous and get very down-hearted at my continued non-running.

Bill did his best to support me and keep me amused at weekends. If I didn't race he didn't want to race. I hate watching races when I am injured and can't be part of it. I get little pleasure from watching others when I feel I should be out there and it can depress me even more to see what I am missing. If I am tired from having done a big event my outlook was very different. I have a reason for watching and excuse for being on the side-lines if I have done my specified event and can wallow in self satisfaction watching others achieving their goals having successfully completed mine. Bill liked to have the challenge of me in the race; we never raced with each other, always against each other. We would set little goals against each other, have handicaps based on who was best. In fell and trail races the loser always had to clean the muddy shoes, in road races it was often who had to make the tea on our return home. You will never have seen such amazing rivalry and performances to beat each other so that one of us could gloat at the losing partner.

I did initially get back running only to stop again because I seemed to be getting blisters on my feet in strange places compared to normal and I guessed I wasn't running normally. Time off again to retrain the foot to move correctly meant that I missed my first international race since 1994. I know Hilary Walker ran but I'm not sure that any other athletes were even sent after our previous performance.

My next big race was the 24 hour race at Apeldoorn, Holland. This was such an excellent event, a wonderful loop of about a mile in distance through a park with no sharp corners. The weather was good, there was a relay race at the same time with tremendous supporters and we were able to camp right on the course. The result was not good. I was still struggling with the ankle and ended up walking to finish the event. Somehow I managed to be the 1st lady with 191 kilometres (118 miles), but deep down I knew the ankle was still far too weak and in reality the swelling had never returned to normal since the accident.

Next up was my second vest for England in the Anglo Celtic Plate 100 Kilometres again, this time at Edinburgh. Although the ankle could not do 24 hours, I thought it would hold up to 100 kilometres. My left ankle still measured three centimetres bigger than my right. The weather was awful in Edinburgh that day and in the first 3 miles I took a heavy fall on a corner, not realising how slippery drain covers were in the rain on a downhill section. Badly winded, badly grazed and with a sprained thumb I walked for a bit. I managed to get going again and caught up with the lead ladies but then began to struggle, nothing to do with the ankle this time. With everything hurting I finally came in to get my bloodied grazes patched up and a quick look at my right ankle that was giving some grief. I got very cold and wrapped up to continue in the rain, but it wasn't to be. The fall had taken its toll and I just could not pick up the pace. With the team now performing well, it was my turn to retire from the race feeling battered and bruised with just 33 kilometres run. It still upset me to withdraw and I felt I had failed, but at least it hadn't been the original ankle that had caused me to fail.

Onwards and upwards though, and I was pleased to hear I had gained selection for the World Challenge 100 Kilometres in Winschoten,

Holland yet again. This time it was the turn of Jackie Leak to take a tumble and sprain her ankle. With the team destroyed early on, there was only Hilary Walker and myself to finish. Even with no team at stake, I struggled and could only achieve a disappointing 9 hours 44 minutes, some 40 minutes behind Hilary. Stephen Moore was again the first British man home and again 1st veteran 50-54.

There was one last event to conclude a disastrous year, another "did not finish" in the European Challenge 24 Hours in Uden, Holland. I had pulled a muscle in my buttock running the Manchester Marathon on a bitterly cold morning earlier in the month. The organised buses were late, so I ran to the start line the minute the bus arrived at the start, still very cold and shivering and then sustained the injury. I had to pull out at 6 miles not wanting to risk further damage. There were only three women in the team and if I did not compete there was no one to replace me, so I took my place in the team. Hilary was the first to drop out and with no team at stake yet again and struggling with more than one problem I quit after 90 kilometres. Sandra Brown battled on to achieve 176 kilometres. The men were the saviours of the day, with a cracking performance of 230 kilometres from Adrian Stott, Don Ritchie 220 kilometres and Walter Hill 216 kilometres and a team bronze medal.

It was always at the end of the year that I would sit down and reflect and plan the next year. 2000 had been taken out of my control with the accident early on in the year and I struggled to know where to go next. I still had a great desire to compete, still thought my best was yet to come but wondered how to get over the injury with the ankle that would not let me go the full distance. I decided I would have one last crack and wrote a program to build me up for the Intemelia 100 Kilometres Track Race, Italy. I had a wonderful trip being spoilt by Franco Ranciaffi, transporting me and providing accommodation and food. My performance was a mediocre 9 hours 22 minutes for 3rd lady. I was satisfied with this. It was a steady run, an improvement on my last performance as well as something to build on and my ankle had not given me too much grief.

John Legge, who had stepped down as a selector some time ago, sadly died earlier in the year. He had been one of the London Marathon "ever presents" (an ever decreasing band of runners who had competed in every London Marathon). The bombshell was then dropped. I had not been selected to run for Great Britain in the European Challenge 24 Hours to be held in Apeldoorn, Holland in May. Why? Sandra Brown was selected after her 176 kilometres and I had run 191 kilometres in Apeldoorn just a few months earlier. Hilary Walker was now apparently involved in selection and I was deemed not fit enough after my 100 kilometres race. I would concede that my last year had been bad, 191 kilometres was not a good performance but it was still the best female British performance and I would agree that I had run much faster, but then we all have bad years.

I entered the open race that ran alongside the international event anyway, determined to do my best. Sandra opted to run in another 24 hour race in Great Britain I believe. I ran well for the first 12 hours but then the ankle began to bruise and swell again. I ran for another 2 hours and then talked to Bill as to what I should do. In an instant I was out of the race. I wasn't so bad that I still could not run, but was concerned that continuously running on the ankle might cause more damage. Could I have continued for another 10 hours? I had not pushed myself to my limits, which was to be a big mistake, but another lesson to learn from, as my next event showed. The bronze medallists of 2000 also failed to perform well here, recording a team 10th. It was bad news all round for ultra distance.

I came home so disheartened. Where did I go from here? No longer good enough to represent my country, no longer able to finish 24 hour races, 100 kilometre times an hour behind my best. I gave up. My ultra distance career was over. I had been defeated by an accident and an ankle that refused to let me perform. I still loved running. I still loved exercising. I would have to change sports. I had already started quite a bit of cycling when my ankle had been bad, so I thought I might try and swim a bit better and try long distance triathlons, as I had dabbled in this many years ago. The other sport I was to try was race walking. This puts the ankle through a wide range of motion due to the specific technique of keeping in contact with the ground.

John Paddick was a member of my running club, New Marske Harriers and an Olympian (he had represented Great Britain in the 20 kilometres walk at the Olympics). I had been with this club a couple of years now as my previous club, Mandale Harriers, had so few female athletes that competed in races that I took part in. John was keen to encourage me into race walking. I had always had the dream that I wanted to be a Centurion (walk 100 miles in 24 hours). John had a small group of runners that he was now training in race walking. I joined that group and regularly started walking with them, usually twice a week. I also began swimming lessons and cycling, along with a little running. If I wasn't to be an ultra distance runner then I was going to try to excel at something else.

A strange thing then happened. I had already had a few "snippets" on television on my running exploits when the BBC rang up and wanted to follow me on what had been my next planned ultra distance race in Great Britain, the West Highland Way: 95 miles from Milngavie to Fort William. I wasn't quite sure what to do. I had not entered the race, as I had no intentions of running it after my decision to withdraw from the 24 hour race, but pondered whether to run this one and try to finish because of the publicity it would generate? It would be good for the West Highland Way race and as I enjoy these long off-road events anyway, much more than the road events, I agreed to run it. The next obstacle was getting into the event, as it was only a week or two away and I would have to run this off general fitness. Initially I was rejected by the organiser, not realising I had run this race before and was a previous winner (in 1997 I was 3rd person overall in 21 hours 3 minutes, three weeks after an international 100 kilometres event). On explaining my background and the coverage the race could get I heaved a great sigh of relief to be entered, only to realise that the start time had changed, from 3am to 1am!

The journey up was fraught. Bill finished work late. We got no rest and drove non-stop to Glasgow, on a very busy Friday evening. Not long after we arrived it was time to check in for the race, and after a quick interview for the BBC we were on our way. In the rush I had forgotten to put my head torch on and together with a small group proceeded to get lost before the first checkpoint. Not good news. But Bill got my head torch and step by step I continued, just hoping to get as far as I could before the ankle would force me to stop. The cameraman was excellent; he popped up in all sorts of places and I was told to ignore him as if he wasn't there. He got a great shot just after sun-rise looking back to Loch Lomond and with a cyclist bivouacking in his sleeping bag; he slept through us all running by him!

Rowardennan was 26 miles into the race and where I started to feel the ankle. I discretely took a pain relief patch from Bill to put on when out of sight and a couple of ibuprofen. The next section was along the loch side and we would have no contact until Inverarnan at approximately 40 miles. I guessed it might be here that I might have to quit. The patch and tablets worked well and I progressed steadily. I was surprised to reach 40 miles still in reasonable shape and not in too much pain. The decision to carry on was easy; I would take it checkpoint by checkpoint and go as far as I could. And so it continued, checkpoint after checkpoint after checkpoint, until I reached Kingshouse at around 72 miles with just 23 miles to go. It was at this point that I knew I would finish. The ankle had given me grief, but it was tolerable and was not progressively getting worse – had I continued on in that 24 hour race in Apeldoorn just maybe I could have finished. I had pulled out while feeling the ankle in that race, but it had still been "runnable" and within my pain tolerance. The fact that the BBC was here and I was trying not to look stupid and pull out with an injury had pushed me further and began to realise that it was possible I could still be an ultra distance runner. I continued running to the finish and achieved a time of 21 hours 10 minutes, only 7 minutes slower than four years ago, and was again 1st lady and 3rd overall. Not a bad performance! I even surprised myself with this one, got myself on television and the West Highland Way a bit of publicity.

I came home with mixed emotions. I had been totally unprepared for this race. I had not rested or slept a wink beforehand with all the travelling and was now preparing for my debut in a half ironman event (an ironman triathlon is a 2.4 mile swim, 112 mile bike and 26.2 mile run, a half ironman is half the distances) and had plans to compete in several duathlons (run, bike, run). I continued with my schedule. I had been cycling and swimming and still wanted to have a crack at the triathlon, but did alter my plans slightly to include an easy run out for enjoyment in the World Championships 100 Kilometres in Cleder, France. This was the event where I recorded my first "did not finish" way back in 1996, so I had to come and correct this issue and run the race. Selection had changed dramatically now and only one athlete was representing Great Britain. This was Danielle Sanderson, new to the 100 kilometres scene after a good international career in the marathon.

It was an excellent race. The French always seem to put on a good show and we weren't let down. Bill was allowed to cycle with me from the 20 kilometres mark, as I was in the open race, which also added to the pleasure of the race for me. I camped with a few other British men that I knew very well who were also running in the open race, Roy Bainbridge (and wife Marie), Brian Harney and Kerry Booth. We enjoyed the whole trip and, given my level of fitness, I was pleased to run this easily with no discomfort in 9 hours 11 minutes for 37th lady.

Two weeks later it was the Bluesure Half Ironman UK Triathlon 2001, Llanberis. I stood at the edge of the lake below Snowdon just after dawn on a cold, windy September morning. The temperature of the water was reported to be one degree above the point where the race would have been called off. I was dressed in my wetsuit shivering, contemplating the race ahead. Did I really want to do this? Could I really do this? I was freezing and wasn't going to get any warmer on entering the water. It was the closest I ever came to chickening out and not starting the race. I think the only thing that made me get into the freezing water was the cost of the event and the fact that we had travelled a long way to come and do the race.

I held my breath as I eased into the water, took one last deep breath and dived into the water once and for all. Heck, it really was cold as I spluttered about a bit and tried to acclimatise. It took a while to get my breath back and the race had not even started yet. The start was strange, no direct start line as for running races; instead we were just treading water in the lake waiting for the siren to sound. I started with the front crawl but found myself zigzagging all over. I kept looking up and thought I was heading in the right direction but the field in front soon splashed away. I was happy with this, as it gave me my own space not being the best of swimmers. It was when the second wave of swimmers stormed up and nearly drowned me that I started to panic. I gave up and clung onto one of the many rescue canoes hovering while the main bulk of the field passed and then did a lot of breast stroke to keep in line and see what was around. In the final section I started front crawl again but it was a relief to exit the water.

I got out nearly last with a lady much older than me. My goal had been to break the hour in the 1.9 kilometres swim. The lady told me the swim had taken 56 minutes, and asked what had gone wrong? "Absolutely nothing", was the reply. That was fantastic - I had achieved my goal! I promptly stripped off the wetsuit, changed into dry clothes, got on my bike and left the field in my wake. I progressed well on the 56 mile bike ride, still not proficient, but compared to those at the back of the swimmers I was much stronger. The weather made life difficult. It was a cold, blustery day for September and on one hill section I had battled so hard to get to the top of the pass I was looking forward to freewheeling down the other side, but no such luck, the wind was so strong now I had to cycle downhill. It was draining and, by the time of the last transition to running, I could barely feel my hands and feet. My legs were like lead and just would not run. They were still in cycling mode but I needed to keep moving to try and generate some heat. Eventually I began to warm up and the legs began to respond and soon I was in overtaking mode again. The coastal section was another big battle against the wind and I was extremely relieved to finish. It had not been the best experience, as the weather had made the race so hard and running 100 kilometres just two weeks earlier probably didn't help. It had been a new experience and worth a try, but I doubted I would ever do well at the event.

I was still ticking over and doing some road racing, but I was soon to try the other sport that was new to me, race walking. I had been training a few months now and was brave enough to enter my first race, the Yorkshire Winter League 10 Kilometres Race Walk. The field was supposedly good for race walking, but for me it was the smallest field I had ever been in and I was the only female. I could not fail; I was either first or last lady however you looked at it. My time was 63 minutes 24 seconds, 12th of the 18 competitors. It was nothing spectacular but a start.

My first love always had been and always would be ultra distance running. I had dabbled in a couple of sports now and had a taste of them, but it was the race walking that kept drawing me back. When I first started training my shins and buttocks really ached from the training. Different muscles were needed for the style of walking and it also put my ankle through a good range of motion and I began to wonder how it would be affecting my damaged ankle. I had tried all sorts of strengthening techniques but it never held out without pain over longer distances. My last gentle 100 kilometres run had seen the ankle finish in the best shape ever. Was this race walking improving my ankle? Would my ankle now last out if I ran 24 hours? I just had to try one more time this year.

I had tried my new sports and was to travel to the 24 Hours du Cher in France. My only goal here was to finish the race running and free from pain in my ankle. I did not have a great fitness level this year and the goal was a small one. The weather was damp and drizzly and it was not the best of courses, as there were lots of sharp corners to really test the ankle, but it was the clock that I needed the challenge with, just to finish running 24 hours.

I remained happy throughout the race and finally achieved my goal. I ran the whole race and finished the race running. The ankle had finally held out. The result was a reasonable 191 kilometres, 1st lady in the race and the best performance by a British female for the year yet again. I still strongly believe it was the race walking that strengthened the ankle to allow me to run again and it would always now be part of my training routine. Race walking was also very good for complementing ultra distance running. Sandra Brown is an immensely strong race walker and can walk further than many can run in 24 hours.

At the usual end of year reflections I felt that the year had finished with a high yet again. I could still be an ultra distance runner. It had been an unusual year. I had enjoyed much of the year, done some really different things, kept in reasonable shape and could now seriously start preparing my big comeback. I had always achieved a higher ranking at 24 hours than I had at 100 kilometres and with the state of affairs with UK Athletics it was best to concentrate on this event for the time being. The European 24 hours and 100 kilometres events were just one week apart in September and so I had to choose. I had loved the event in Apeldoorn, Holland, the weather had been good, the support good, the travelling easy, the camping superb and it was a wonderful course. This was in May; so I planned my training around this. There were a couple of important preparation races to lead up to this, the Doncaster Doddle 40 miles and the National Championships 100 Kilometres in April.

The new year also brought some other challenges back into our lives. Bill, who had nicely settled down with his work at Express Dairies for over two years appeared to be jinxed again. The dairy was a thriving company in the middle of a built up area and the wagons were restricted with the neighbouring schools. So the dairy was to close with the loss of many jobs. The onus was back on me. I was still lecturing with a point five lecturing post (half the hours of a full time lecturer) at Middlesbrough College but had set up Mobile Massage, a sport and remedial massage business in any spare hours I had. Bill got a good redundancy package for his two years in the job that afforded us a small hatchback car for the business, an upgrade on the scooter that had been deferred to Bill since my accident. He had also had a couple of minor scrapes on this lethal machine, one on ice where the ditch got the better of him and another toppling-over accident when a taxi did a u-turn into him. Bill's next employer was David Fox Transport doing road haulage.

Training was spot on. I had my programs down to a fine art now and improved my time in the Doncaster Doddle by roughly an hour, finishing in 6 hours 36 minutes, breaking Eleanor Robinson's course record and finishing 3rd overall. At the National Championships at Moreton-in-Marsh, Gloucester I brought home the gold medal in the 100 kilometres yet again and the steady run that I had planned for 9 hours was done in 8 hours 53 minutes. The reports all said I would have been disappointed with this performance as it was 3 minutes outside of the qualifying time for the European Challenge 100 Kilometres, but I had no intention of running that event and just did the race as a training run. Had I wanted to have run 3 minutes faster I could easily have put some effort into the last 10 kilometres of the race to have achieved this. I was back racing again the following weekend.

The goal was obtaining a distance that would qualify me for the European Challenge 24 Hours that was to take place in September. This result gave me the confidence that my fitness was good and I could perform well in Apeldoorn. I was to be proved right; the result was an astounding new personal best of 217 kilometres (135 miles). The ankle was well and truly fixed. At the time of running it was the best performance in the world that year, but on the same day in Russia my performance had been eclipsed by a mere 200 metres and so I was now number two in the world. Surely that was good enough to win back my vest?

Three weeks later I competed in the Hundredth Bradford 50 Kilometres Walk, not my best of performances with 6 hours 6 minutes, but a good step towards eventually attempting to become a Centurion. My selection came through; that year only Danielle Sanderson was selected for the 100 kilometres; Stuart Buchan and myself were the only two representatives for the 24 hours in Gravigny, France. We both performed abysmally. Nothing to do with my fitness, I had cut my shoes to try to reduce the blisters which was my main stumbling block in Apeldoorn, only for this to cause major problems with both my feet in this race and I was forced to abandon the race after around 16 hours with 158 kilometres completed. I had come with such high hopes, just to slump away defeated again. It was another hard lesson to learn.

I attempted one last event that year, a special celebration event dedicated to Donald Ritchie MBE. The Road Runners Club 100 Mile Track Race was to promote Don's twenty-five year old record of 11 hours 30 minutes and 1 second. It was only a month after my aborted 24 hours and my feet were not fully recovered and I had hardly been able to train at all, but it was a privilege to run at Crystal Palace in honour of Don and I duly completed 50 miles on the track before retiring. The race was an epic, with two Russian athletes Kharitonov and Jalybin both narrowly breaking the world record, 11 hours 28 minutes and 3 seconds and 11 hours 29 minutes and 32 seconds respectively. William Sichel and Walter Hill were the only other two athletes to finish the 100 miles that day.

One different highlight of 2002 was winning "Juggler of the Year" at the North East Women in Business Awards. This was for managing to run a successful business; hold down a job with Middlesbrough College, study for my PGCE (Post Graduate Certificate in Education) and continue my athletics career. The inspirational guest speaker happened to be one of my favourite customers, the great Paralympian, Dame Tanni Grey-Thompson, who also awarded me the trophy.

For me this was a strange award to win as I had not completed something specific to win it, but if I did take a step backwards and look at the life I was leading it should have highlighted why I won this award. My sports massage business was called Mobile Massage. After completing our training we had continued to practice our massage techniques on the runners at our running club, New Marske Harriers. These were a great group of runners who supported us well, let us practice and improve and they were so resolute on supporting our efforts they set up a donation box insisting that all runners who got treatment should respect us. We gained confidence in treating a variety of people and as I had a bit more time with having a point five lecturing post it was easier for me to set up the business. With having a Sport Science degree to back up my massage skills also helped. For one year only I advertised in the Yellow Pages. There was never any need after this as word of mouth got round and I never needed to advertise again.

The hardest part of the business was actually finding time for myself and I rarely managed to get a massage from Bill as I was never home. The goal was eventually to become a team with Bill and become self employed. A day in the life of this "Juggler of the Year" typically consisted of running to Middlesbrough College and back when I only worked the mornings (approximately 10 miles each way and getting up around 6am), running in my lunch hour when I was at college all day, and all other hours were spent driving around to different people's homes to fit in the Mobile Massage business. I had a variety of customers, those that wanted day-time hours, those that wanted treatment in their lunch hour, and those who worked days and only wanted evenings. I had some customers who were athletes, but more needed remedial massage for ongoing problems or were people whom I saw intermittently for various ailments. I soon had a good rapport with some regular clients who had treatment every week and developed some employment stability with these great people. All my clients were really friendly people and it was a superb job to do, but it was extremely hard work, being on my feet most of the day, running when not working, lifting and carrying a heavy massage table around and at times barely having time to eat. Most evenings I had to work and rarely got a chance to see Bill. What time we did have together at weekends was racing and the business also encroached on our weekends too. I rarely went to bed before 11pm, my eating patterns were erratic and I snatched food whenever I could. On many evenings I could not plan a meal to eat with Bill and somehow I managed to fit in preparing my lessons and even studying for a PGCE along with everything else. This involved attending lessons for 3 hours once a week plus various assignments and lesson observations.

I had a few very high profile customers. I did get some international athletes, professional sports people, Premier League footballers, but the bad news was; the vouchers for sports massage were soon to be ditched. Tanni Grey-Thompson was one of the athletes who did have a few to use up still and as my service was so convenient for her with having a young daughter to look after. Tanni, along with husband Ian, continued with my services after the vouchers stopped and we became the best of friends. I also won a cracking contract at a local castle that was used for a couple of months leading up to Christmas. This was treating extremely high profile people from all walks of life – supermodels, royalty, actors and actresses, singers, designers, authors, lords and high flying business people. This paid well but it was unsocial hours on Friday and Saturday evenings but it was inspiring to meet so many well known people.

One very high profile customer at the castle was also to fully sponsor my next year of training, Elle MacPherson. Arki Busson, father of their two sons, had picked up a copy of the Daily Mail with a double page spread on my next big challenge, the Flora 1000 Mile Challenge, and like most people asked, "Who sponsors you?" The difference being that they actually did something very positive about it. They were a very generous couple and Elle did quite a bit of running too. Arki was a very astute business-man, a devoted father to his sons, an impressive philanthropist and such an easy person to communicate with.

This generous sponsorship now meant that I was able to give up my employment at Middlesbrough College, as the Flora 1000 Mile Challenge needed a couple of months off work. I could squeeze the odd week off here and there for an important event, but this was too much time to take off without affecting the students. I always knew deep down that I would come back to teaching, as I had so much knowledge to give back and this was a great way of staying involved in the giving back part to sport. I now had a Post Graduate Certificate in Education for teaching post sixteen. I found it unbelievable that I could take up such a post without any formal teaching qualification, so as part of my development plan I had studied this qualification part time alongside all my other commitments to become more professional at my job.

The Flora 1000 Mile Challenge had now been on the cards for over twelve months. I was the original athlete selected to take part and I was used in the publicity to advertise for the other five people to apply to be involved in this challenge. This was a really unique event based on Captain Barclay. Professor Peter Radford had just written a biography on Captain Barclay and together with Dave Bedford from the Flora London Marathon had concocted the idea to replicate Captain Barclay's feat. This was to complete on foot 1,000 miles in 1,000 hours and only 1 mile could be done in any hour. So in 24 hours, 24 miles would be completed. The 1,000 hours added up to just short of six weeks. Captain Barclay had the luxury of the wonderful green Newmarket Heath for his challenge; we had the route of the Flora London Marathon. We were to travel some thirty-eight times up and down the route, using a tour bus for living, eating and sleeping.

Immediately after Christmas that year after the annual trip to my sister's in Cambridge I began a trial. For five days I was to run 1.5 miles every hour. Similar to the challenge I was to run 1.5 miles at the back end of one hour, then 1.5 miles to start the next hour, leaving nearly 90 minutes for a break between miles. I started the trial very tired having deliberately gone to bed late each night sleeping at my sister's in Cambridge. The challenge was to run 1 mile per hour, but for training I was to run 1.5 miles per hour to replicate being further into the challenge. I completed the challenge but not without feeling acutely tired. I was unable to concentrate or read, just do the essential jobs every day. I was continuously clockwatching for fear of not getting out in time. By the end of the trial I had had enough. I struggled to run and was now walking the miles. My legs were stiff and I could not concentrate. I was constantly eating and drinking, but losing weight. I knew if I ran all the miles in the challenge I was going to suffer. The only answer was to do a lot more walking. This was far less strenuous and tiring than running, but meant I would be on my feet a lot longer. However, the lessons were heeded. It was going to be one of those immense feelings of going into the unknown again. Could I complete it? Could anyone complete it?

The five people chosen were from a diverse selection which made the challenge all the more interesting. There were to be six challengers in all, two women and four men. The men were Lloyd Scott, Paul Selby, Rory Coleman and David Lake, the other female was Shona Crombie-Hicks. Lloyd was more famously known for his charity fundraising events and being the slowest ever competitor in the Flora London Marathon completing it in a diving suit. Paul now lived in South Africa, was the oldest competitor but a very experienced ultra distance runner and had famously run the Comrades Marathon back to back along with many marathons. Rory was a veteran of many "Rory marathons". I call these "Rory marathons" as they are just that, marathons that Rory has run as training, but not all actual marathon races, not events open to the general public. His latest blog claims "630 marathons in 14 years". It was the first point that confused me about Rory. I thought he must travel the world every week looking for marathons to compete like this, but obviously the answer was they were not competitions. I'm not sure how many marathons I have run in training. What I can tell you is that I have run over 900 races, accumulating in excess of 19,000 miles of racing, each one recorded with results where available and race number glued into thirty-seven scrapbooks.

I guess as this event was up and down the London Marathon route thirty-eight times Rory would class this as thirty-eight marathons. For me personally, this was one ultra distance event – and a marathon to finish with. David Lake was an Army lad, from the same regiment as Captain Barclay – the Royal Welsh Fusiliers, a fit lad, but a novice to running marathons. Shona was the best marathon runner of the lot, not an ultra distance runner but she boasted a fantastic marathon time of 2 hours 40 minutes.

There was a fair bit of publicity around the Flora 1000 Mile Challenge and in preparation for this we decided to go away warm weather training. Where better than the other side of the world in Australia where my sponsor Elle MacPherson Intimates came from. We had three glorious weeks training hard, living in a campervan and touring from Sydney to Melbourne and back via Canberra. I had intended running one last race there, a 100 kilometres race, but this was not the best organised on the day. It started late (well very early in the morning after the midnight start was delayed) and running in the dark with little light and on a short section of cycle track with u-turns and overhanging trees I only ran 25 kilometres before I withdrew rather than cause an injury on such a course.

We did manage a few days with our friend Graham Ives while in Melbourne and I came third in a race of the unusual distance of 15 kilometres. Graham had been the organiser of my first 100 kilometres race in Sutcliffe Park back in 1994. He had emigrated to live in South Africa, married and then settled in Australia. He had had bowel cancer in South Africa and was in remission from that, but was now in the "finishing straight" having been diagnosed with lung cancer and wanting to live his life happily without further treatment. He had a great positive outlook and I felt privileged to spend a few days at his house. He accompanied us on a couple of training runs, still looking extremely fit and well, Graham on his bike and us running.

The big event started at 4pm on 2nd March 2003 and was to finish 1,000 hours later at 9am on 13th April 2003, in time to set off on the Flora

116

London Marathon to decide a winner if we all made it that far. Sadly Chris Brasher, founder of the London Marathon, had died shortly before and we had a minute silence in his honour before Prince Andrew, the Duke of York, set us on our way. The first problems were to hit one competitor and several partners very early on: a bout of food poisoning. The egg sandwiches provided at lunch time looked like the culprit. Fortunately I avoided these, Bill fell victim to them. Late into the night, trying to keep me company, he was very ill from both ends, not easy when there are no toilets around. Lloyd was the unlucky competitor. It was a particularly vicious bug, as Bill had a strong stomach, but it completely wiped him out for a few weeks and he ended up the thinnest I had ever seen him.

Our tour bus had six sets of three bunks. Each competitor had a set of three bunks each, all on top of each other. The two girls were at the front of the bus and the four boys, separated by a single curtain, all behind. I used the top bunk for kit, the middle bunk for sleeping and the bottom bunk for food and supplies. We were given a daily allowance for food and were each allowed a single support crew at any one time. Support crew were given 12 hour shifts starting or finishing at 8am. We all allocated our own support crew. Bill did all the day shifts, which included all the shopping and cooking and I had several different night time crew. At night between the hours of 10pm and 7am the "silence rule" applied, meaning that anyone such as crew or competitors on the bus must respect the others and not just be quiet, but "silent". The only person who continually broke this rule was Shona, along with her crew breaking "the toilet rule". Lots of little rules that may appear petty, but for the sake of everyone aboard they were essential for the smooth running of the event.

The rest of the bus had six coach style seats at the front, known as the "quiet area". To the rear were a big sofa, table and television for relaxing. This was quite a "loud area", as the television always seemed to be on and very loud, so much so that you could hear it at the front of the bus. Downstairs was a small kitchen area that had a kettle, microwave and toaster, a few seats and a table. This area was mainly for the referees. The driver also had to stay with the bus continuously. Mark was the driver mostly on duty and did a fantastic job keeping the bus clean and tidy, emptying the toilet, refilling the water and keeping the electric charged where possible, so much so you really noticed when he wasn't there and he was a great independent support to us all. The engine was quite noisy when we were trying to sleep; so it was always turned off for the "silent time", but on for most of the day when the power was constantly being used.

117

The first week was pretty easy, just getting used to the routine and figuring out how and where to get food quickly. I often settled for microwave meals from Marks and Spencer's which was on the route, but you had to catch it during opening hours at the time it was passed. McDonalds also came quite high on the list for being convenient and quick. We were all weighed on a daily basis, as during Captain Barclay's original feat he lost a significant amount of weight and I knew just from my trial that constant food was important. Shona weighed in almost the same as me at fifty kilograms and the men all significantly more.

The first week was also finding out about each other and how we got along, or didn't, as the case may be. We were six strangers who all had a common interest in the event, all had a diverse background and fitness levels and all had different reasons for being part of the challenge. For me it was something new. Six weeks felt like a really long time. The 24 miles a day bit I knew I could do with ease, but trying to sleep on a bus in the middle of London with five others and function on continuously broken sleep was the challenge. I also liked the figure of 1,000 miles; I still dream that one day I will set a world record for this distance; so it was an easy way of experiencing such a long event. Eleanor Robinson had retired from competing at international events with a bang by breaking the world record at this distance, a record I believe Sandra Brown held before her.

I only had one hiccup and that was with navigation. It sounds a bit stupid really, but going along the Flora London Marathon route when it is not marathon day throws up its own challenges. Detailed maps were provided to navigate the streets. After several trips up and down the route it did become easier, but to start with, especially during darkness hours, the maps were needed. It was while I was with Ramona that the map was mis-read and we went off route and it was during the "time restricted mile". The bus moved 2 miles along the route at a time. After the last competitor got off, the bus would move 2 miles to its next allotted parking area. We would all do a mile shortly before the hour was up; wait with the referee until the hour ticked by, then complete the next mile right at the start of the hour as planned. I always worried about something happening and not making the hour; so always allowed extra time for some "mishap" to happen and it did. Strolling along during the early hours one morning it dawned on me that my surroundings were not familiar. I stepped on a grass verge crossing the road and immediately suspected we were not on route, I could not remember ever stepping on grass before. Ramona was my supporter that night; she was diligently doing her task but had mistaken a right turn for a right bend in the road. Once I looked at the map I knew what had happened. Frantic, I tore back down the road and it was possibly the only significantly uphill mile on the whole route that I sped along probably at sub 6 minute mile pace, fearing my challenge was over. One second over the hour and it would be immediate disqualification. Those were the rules and I would be taken off the bus in an instant. It was with great relief and breathlessness that I finally spotted Lloyd looming in the darkness ahead, plodding along unaware of the sprint to finish behind him, I could ease back at last, the adrenalin rush over, with a big sigh of relief that I "was still in".

Bill had taken unpaid leave to come with me on this trip; so he had made a big sacrifice and would not have been best pleased to have seen it end this way and I must confess I would have been distraught had this happened. It was an "eye opener" and was to awaken me to be more vigilant from this point onwards. The only other significant event of the first week was a quick meeting to discuss David's feeding strategy. He cleverly had meals on wheels delivered by the Army, very ingenious, but it caused jealously amongst others so a meeting was held to discuss whether he should be allowed to continue. When the challenge had first been discussed I had thought Bill might possibly follow and sleep in a campervan to assist and cook food, but this had been dismissed early on and David's meals were to go the same way. All six were in on the open discussion along with the referee and David Bedford to find a fair solution. From that point onwards David had to fend for food the same as the rest of us.

The second week saw a few happenings, including another quick meeting, as the other competitors all wanted massage, as Captain Barclay had this at his service. I had planned well and Bill was my masseur, but I guess again that jealousy came into it and others wanted the same. David Bedford originally said that it was up to us to get our own masseurs, the same as I had done, but did eventually relent if we were all in agreement. I could have twisted the knife here, as it was something we all had to agree to. I had my own personal masseur with me daily so I did not require such service. It was agreed though and a daily rota system was made up for access to a variety of therapists. I did use the service occasionally to give Bill a break, as he was still quite ill from his food poisoning. Also, it was better having a table to be massaged on rather than "make do" wherever we were.

The saddest part of the week was when we said goodbye to Lloyd. It wasn't that he was injured or not fit or able enough to complete the challenge. He had a few personal issues that were vital to solve here and now and would

119

not wait another four weeks. It was an incredibly hard decision for him to make and a few tears were shed as he departed. For me Lloyd had been an unknown quantity, well famous for his diving suit marathon, but such a nice character. It's one thing to see someone on television and make up an opinion, but another to live with the guy on the bus. He was a really great character, one of the best. He made a point of making conversation with me every day which I liked. It was just general "chit chat", as I have never been an easy conversationalist in a crowd and often retreat into my own quiet world again. I was and still very much am an introverted person. I enjoy small groups, but am always the quiet one in a big group and this was to be no different. Others were to see me differently. I missed Lloyd greatly and the mood on the bus changed instantly. We all missed the big guy's presence.

By the third week it was very much "groundhog day", repeatedly being woken hour by hour, competing mile after mile. My website was now up and running. It had been started late the previous year. My friend Ella was studying website design and wanted a few websites to set up as a portfolio. She had already done a marvellous job for my business site and thought it would be good for supporters to follow my progress. I took a bit of persuading at the time, but again was most impressed with what she and friend Vicky delivered and it was good to have an outlet for the many

Flora 1000 Mile Challenge with supporters, Ella, Bill, Sharon, Vicky and Geoff.

frustrations on the bus. We were encouraged to write a daily blog on the official website for the event. Rory was best at this, as he always does a daily blog on his life and is the complete opposite to me. Call it a clash of personalities, but I found him an extremely ignorant, arrogant character. However, he certainly had the gift of the gab and came across well. I always did my best to avoid him rather than cause conflict, but this in itself became a big cause of a rift on the bus. From the start Shona had always been an elusive character with me. She got on well with everyone but completely ignored me, only speaking to me when she had to, but no problem, I could cope with that. We all had helpers and this used to make me laugh, that although these two competitors were not that easy to get on with, their helpers and all the other support crew were all amazingly happy, supportive people.

Rory's routine seemed to be to do the utmost to upset me, but I could deal with him. I had a routine of sleeping and eating and was easily getting six broken hours of sleep per night and could cope with that. In reality I was rarely tired and during the day all we did was sit around between the miles. At home I was always rushing around for things to do, so it was quite restful by comparison. As I regularly ate my main microwave meal in the evening slot with Bill, Rory then decided his helper should heat his microwave meal up at the same time as me. I had Bill plan ahead to heat the meal while I was walking a couple of miles while everyone was off the bus, so it didn't disrupt the others too much, but Rory insisted that his helper cook his meal first, even though I was a faster walker and would return to the bus first, just little games he liked to play, but in reality he probably disrupted himself more. He was always an intimidating character, would lounge full length on the sofa, even fall asleep on it and, far from being polite and just moving if you came to sit down you would have to ask him to move. Of course he would move if asked but in a confined space did you really have to ask? Well that is just Rory.

At one stage driver Mark caught an intruder on the bus, rifling through our possessions while we were out. When the two laptops provided went missing one morning I thought they may have been stolen. But no, Rory had hidden them in his bunk so that I could not use one to do my blog, just pettiness yet again. I always did my blog first thing in the morning when the others were having breakfast and they would not be in use. Rory obviously didn't like this; so tried to disrupt the routine again. He had tried by putting the lap top in front of Shona one morning; she was obviously still eating her breakfast, very bleary eyed, but was doing as Rory said. Rory seemed to hijack one laptop just for his own personal use and the rest of us made do with the second laptop. Bill handled these situations far better than me and I don't think I could have coped with such antics without him to keep me stable and prevent me from getting upset.

Shona only once "blew up" in my face, upset that my helper had asked the referee to re-iterate the rules that Shona's crew liked to ignore. The referee on duty at the time was Hugh Jones, previous London Marathon winner. There was one toilet on the bus, for "peeing" only, as it was hard to empty on the streets of London. The toilet was restricted to competitors only and female crew as it was tricky for them to find private places, but Shona's crew still used the toilet and right in front of me when I wanted to go. At night the toilet was the first or last thing to do on waking or going to sleep. She may not have thought that both her and her male helper going immediately on return to the bus was important, but by the time I waited for them both it meant the rest of the men had arrived back on the bus for sleeping and I had to walk through a corridor of men stripping off for bed and it was not exactly courteous to them in what little privacy we already had.

Shona was always the one to wake me during the "silent hours" and was never silent. She slept little and my routine of being awoken at 35 minutes past the hour, to get dressed and out of the bus by 40 minutes past gave me 15 minutes walking time and 5 minutes waiting time, just in case a road was difficult to cross or some other event happened. Shona was nearly always up before me sitting at the front of the bus and talking quietly. In the same way as after the night miles, I would always be back in my bunk and have to listen to her talking with her helper or rustling and eating bags of crisps. She often liked to re-shuffle the whole of her bunk on my first sleep stint of the night when she was still not sleeping. I told Bill of her antics every night and he was amused to "catch her in the act" one night. The car that delivered the shift change supporters was occasionally late due to London being London. That night I had just shut my curtain to sleep when Bill heard some tins rattling and plastic bags rustling. From the front of the bus he watched as Shona repeatedly picked up and moved most items in her bunk for no apparent reason. Only on realising Bill was watching did she "scupper away" the rear of the bus. But thankfully for me she rarely did it again after that.

At half way through the challenge there was a big celebration. We all wore different brightly coloured tabards, labelled with the four big charities that were being supported by this challenge. They all had plastic pockets on to hold mile numbers. Every mile the helpers changed the numbers to indicate to the public how many miles we had completed. It was a good guide for us too, so that we knew how many miles we had done, as it was a pretty monotonous challenge. So all wearing "number 500" was special. There was a celebration cake, champagne, pub meal and a visit from ex-boxer Mike Watson, who was making a fight back to fitness by walking the Flora London Marathon over several days. Over the six weeks there were to be a number of celebrity visits and Hazel Irvine visited quite regularly for BBC updates and filming.

It was to be a busy day, as next up was a surprise drugs test. We had been warned beforehand it was likely we would be tested. No problem for me being an international athlete, but it was new to many, if not all of the others. Next up was another medical and blood test. I was now beginning to have problems. In the second week I had become quite croaky from chatting with my crew so much and had resorted to being quiet during the night phase. I also think this helped me to get to sleep better by not waking up completely and being "chirpy", but it was now the asthma that was plugging away at me and my breathing and coughing were becoming more obvious. I was taking medication, but it was progressively getting worse and was beginning to worry me. I got no joy from the doctor other than to double my dose of medication. I knew it was from the continuous pollution and exhaust fumes from the capital city. I did find a solution to this, but it was much to the amusement of others and was the focus of the next BBC visit.

Many of the cyclists in London wore face masks to fight the pollution and so I gave one of these a try to see if it helped my asthma. I was astounded from the first hour of wearing it, as there was an amazing difference to my breathing and I had not expected such a dramatic change; it was just unfortunate that my nickname became "Hannibal Gayter". It didn't bother me. It just meant I slept better, could breathe better, knew I could finish in good shape and it was probably far healthier to remove the dirt rather than take more mediation for it.

It was around this stage that we all began to realise that we were not going to dramatically break down with sleep deprivation. Shona had been the first to wear flip flops with her blisters in the first week, nothing in comparison to what I have suffered, but a big commotion was made. Rory, by comparison, had major blisters and even got the doctor out for these, not that the doctor was particularly impressed. As an experienced runner I would have thought he could have dealt with them himself. I had the odd tiny one, but nothing that even bothered me. Walking quite a bit, as opposed to running, had put pressure on slightly different places on my

Wearing a mask to combat the pollution causing my asthma at 600 miles into the Flora 1000 Mile Challenge, with David Lake.

feet, but only completing 2 miles at a time was nothing severe or strenuous. Most of the competitors had a stable daily weight. By the fourth week I had lost around two kilograms in weight although I was eating masses; Creme Eggs were high on the menu and I was getting a daily dose of two to three along with lots of Mars Bars.

Focus was now turning to the end. The real competition. The finale was to run the Flora London Marathon to determine a winner. There was money at stake. Like Captain Barclay years ago, the bookies had odds on to win. Initially I had been at 9/2, Shona and David at 10/1, Rory 7/4 and Paul 5/2, but by the start of the challenge Shona was now 3/1. I had placed a £500 bet on myself to win, confident I could do the 1,000 miles, knowing I could run a marathon in a tired state. Shona had bet £3,000 at 7/1, so had a considerable stake to win or lose. She was easily the fastest marathon runner, but how would her marathon stand up after 1,000 miles of the challenge?

Now that I could breathe a bit better I started running the odd mile. Shona had done various bits of running and strength work throughout, but was the only one to get help for injuries, supposedly Achilles and other shin trouble. After the palaver of her first blister I could never quite be sure with Shona who played all sorts of tactics, some most unsportsmanlike, and I had absolutely no respect for this. I like a fair and square fight. Tactics are fine, but I like sportsmanship too.

A week before the finale I decided to get my real running legs back and ran the 2 miles of the challenge, then ran a loop around Docklands several times during the "break" before completing the next 2 miles of the challenge. I ran a distance of 18 miles and judging by how I felt and the pace I ran I could make a good judgement of what my fitness was like and what my predicted time would be. This helped me to know what pace to set off at. Paul was doing the odd bit of training and David also started running some of the miles. Rory had run a couple early on, but as his feet were probably the worst of all of us he continued to walk.

In reality each night, getting up at 35 minutes past the hour, taking roughly 15 minutes to walk the mile back to the bus, 5 minutes for a quick pee and shoes off, I managed 70 minutes in my bunk. When you multiply this 70 minutes by the five overnight breaks I was getting nearly 6 hours of sleep per night and with most of the miles early on being at walking pace the major stiffness and tiredness experienced in the trial never materialised in the event. It was far easier. The challenge never came to the heights of sleep deprivation expected. I have always been a light sleeper and just the slight noise of the curtain drawing that closed me in my bunk was usually enough to wake me. I was never annoyed or hit back at any of my supporters, as many expected would happen. The challenge was what I wanted to do and I wanted to be woken to complete the challenge; so I had reassured them there was no violent behaviour or words of abuse that would come from me.

It was no longer a major challenge, just ticking the miles off until home and a normal life could resume. I would not exactly call it boring, but I was getting fed up with the same routine day after day and felt a bit like a fish in a goldfish bowl. We were all living on this bus for observers to come and see. Drivers often beeped their horns, the likes of Rory and Shona loving it, the likes of me hating it, jumping every time a horn beeped, waking me up at night, and being stared at by passers-by. I had to switch off from this and be oblivious, very much like at international events where I knew there were crowds of supporters watching and cheering, but I just had tunnel vision in my own little world, focussing on the task in hand. I couldn't wait for the last week, to be at the marathon exhibition and see all the other marathon runners and have something different to look at.

It took an age for the last week to arrive, I wished the clock would hurry up and tick, but I loved being at the exhibition. Although the music played over and over again, I was at least meeting other people. Having been cocooned on a bus in central London for over five weeks some familiar faces appeared. I had seen the odd friend come and visit, Ella Towers and Vicky who were keeping the website updated daily, and husband Geoff Towers, Mike Amos from the Northern Echo walked a few miles, Pam Storey paid weekly visits to keep up morale as well as a few others. Many running friends, runners from the North East and ultra runners gave me a look in while walking the miles at the exhibition and the general atmosphere changed. There were no longer just the five of us on the bus with the support crew.

My own crew had changed over the weeks too, Bill remaining the only constant during the day. Nanette Cross did three individual weeks of night shift interspersed with Andy and Ramona Thevenet-Smith on two different weeks and local New Marske Harrier and ultra runner of many years ago, Mike Harper, helping out on one of the middle weeks. The referees also had a lot of shift work to cover. Brian Webber was the main project manager, amusing and diligent, Dave Walsh from the ultra distance management, Hugh Jones, highly proclaimed course measurer and Ian Champion, organiser of the London to Brighton ultra distance race for many years and extremely experienced referee, all rotated with the long shifts. All of these were great characters who were a pleasure to work with, all so understanding and tolerant.

But the great day of reckoning was closing in and the end of this repetitive daily routine, a change at last and escape back to my own world. The night before the race preparations were in place, most of our belongings were to be removed to the hotel for post race and just a bag of essential kit left on the bus overnight, so that Mark could take his bus back for a break from the monotony too. I had really enjoyed the last few days. The routine had been changed slightly with staying at the exhibition; so we walked out for a mile and back for a mile to complete the distance. It was much easier staying put and much easier to find food too. We also had a room at the exhibition to escape from the bus and have "our own space".

It was a nervous night, but I still slept reasonably well. The last few miles were highly public, with lots of media interviews. I might comment that for the first time in my life I had media training. This was fun and I gained so many useful lessons that I could use for all future interviews, some very valuable tips on how to stay in control and get your point across.

Our final 1,000th mile in 1,000 hours was filmed in its entirety. Half way through that mile Tanni Grey-Thompson was completing her warm up training in the opposite direction. We exchanged pleasantries, but, as always, she needed to be focussed as her marathon event was first for the off. Some more interviews and finally time to change into racing kit. We all wore our individual 1,000 numbers with our names on, not that it would make life that easy to pick us out from the thousands of runners and we started on the green celebrity start line. I was never that nervous, just very excited. I so much wanted this challenge to come to an end, to have a change of lifestyle and some decent food and sleep without being continuously woken during the night.

Bill was a spectator and was to move around the course and possibly see how the others were running. I was confident that my time was good enough to beat all the men, Shona was the unknown quantity. Her marathon best was far superior to mine and I was not the best of marathon runners anyway, due to my ultra running. An average marathon for me nowadays was around the 3 hours 20 minutes mark compared to Shona's very recent 2 hours 40 minutes. The challenge would obviously have some impact on our times. I am used to running on tired legs and predicted my time to be 3 hours 40 minutes based on the 18 miles I had run the week previously. Shona was still getting ultrasound treatment for her Achilles tendon, but I never took much notice of this, as I had got used to her "tactics" now.

I had a runner with me who was to report back every 6 miles or so on my progress times. He was an Army friend of David's who had supported him during the event. He had never run a marathon, but was fit and eager and really wanted to run the event. I had no issues. Bill was originally going to run with me, but a series of injuries that had been plaguing him since Australia had crippled him even more during the event, even to the extent of not always walking all the miles with me, as he had been hobbling badly. He had also been asked to run with Sir Steve Redgrave's wife who would be slower than me, but he was not even capable of running, full stop.

It was finally time to line up. It was a gorgeous day; the sun was shining, predicted to be warm and my favourite conditions prevailed. We all got placed at the front of the start line. For us this was a race against each other. For me personally a race against Shona, but also against the clock, there was no point shooting off and running for running's sake. I knew my ability. My last training run had indicated my fitness and what I should aim at. The goal was 3 hours 40 minutes and around 8 minutes per mile the initial pace. The gun sounded and we were off. I saw Shona speed off in the distance but didn't notice anyone else, it was more a case of look where you are going and don't get tripped over. It was far more crowded than I had ever remembered the race being and, despite having been up and down this route some thirty-eight times, it felt so different now. Instead of walking along the pavements, crossing roads, it was straight down the middle of the roads and it now felt like the Flora London Marathon that it was.

I settled down and never saw any other of the Flora 1000 Mile Challenge competitors again during the race, although the feedback was that I was in 4th place at Cutty Sark, only Rory supposedly behind me. It was shortly after that first feedback that I lost my running partner, very easy to do in the crowds but not important to me; it just meant that there would be no direct feedback on how I was progressing, as I didn't take a mobile phone and had no intentions of ringing someone while running the event. Over Tower Bridge and half way and I was making nice and steady progress. Bill had shouted that Shona was well in front; this still didn't bother me as it was a marathon and pace judgement was vital. I was a fraction ahead of my schedule by half way, a little bit quicker than 1 hour 45 minutes. I reached the Isle of Dogs and the familiar surroundings. It was on leaving here that I heard more news that Shona was now looking really tired and her pace had dropped significantly; there was hope.

Shortly after 20 miles and I was now beginning to feel the effect myself, not of tired legs but of energy loss. I had been constantly losing small amounts of weight throughout the challenge and with walking all through the night it had been difficult to build up carbohydrate stores. They were being constantly depleted with all the miles during the night. By 22 miles I was beginning to struggle and my pace was dropping. I had thought that the adrenalin on race day was going to see me run sub 3 hours 30 minutes but it was a struggle to continue. I faltered a couple of times, having a short walking break, but then got dug in again; this was a race and I still wanted my best performance. At 23 miles it was obvious that Shona was still well out in front and too far ahead to catch, but I still wanted the best time possible and dug deep and eventually the finish came into sight. Many familiar faces appeared and I could hear the commentary reporting my arrival, 3 hours 34 minutes for the marathon and I finally finished the challenge. It was over. I was 2nd finisher; Shona had run 3 hours 8 minutes. I took my hat off to her and was magnanimous in defeat. That was an amazing time after such a challenge, but although I greatly respect her performance and athleticism I still have no respect for her unsportsmanlike behaviour and personally could not have treated her in the same way I was treated. Paul Selby won the men's race in 3 hours 44 minutes, David Lake ran his first marathon in a fantastic 4 hours 15 minutes and Rory ran a recorded marathon in 4 hours 21 minutes.

I ran as hard as I could and was supported well at the finish I but really wanted my own space again, to get away from everyone and retreated to the sanctuary of the bus. I finally burst into tears and poor driver Mark was there with a cuddle, not part of his duties but he had become an integral part of the whole event. I was now hungry and Nannette came back with the only food available – a Whopper from Burger King. But it went down nicely and I was very grateful. Finally back to the hotel and the event was over, no more clock watching and miles to walk, just me and Bill now. Last of all I enjoyed a shower in my room, as during the event showers had been limited to fire stations, sports clubs and health clubs that fell close to the course and you didn't always hit these at a convenient hour to use.

That evening was the presentation for the winners. Paula Radcliffe had an astounding run breaking the world record in 2 hours 15 minutes. We all got a mention and as part of the publicity had a photograph with Paula the next day. We had another couple of nights in London before returning to Cambridge for a final scan. There had been many tests done on the competitors, various medicals, psychological questionnaires and a DEXA scan that determines body fat, lean tissue and bone density among other things. Even though I had eaten very well since the challenge I was now three kilograms lighter than before the start. I had only lost a small percentage of fat but was well aware that I had lost significant muscle from my quadriceps muscles, which was proved by the scans.

While completing the challenge my support crew had recorded all the food and drink consumed. There were some very amusing facts! Many thought I had eaten loads of Cadbury's Creme Eggs, as a regular supply came in from my supporters and yes, I do love chocolate. On counting the ones recorded I had eaten fifty-two of them, but more surprising was the fact that I had eaten ninety-five Mars Bars. Bill also laid claim to the fact that he made nearly all of the four hundred and eleven cups of tea that I drank!

We spent the night with my sister Julie in Cambridge, who cooked a superb roast dinner. How different freshly cooked vegetables tasted after weeks of microwave food. There was one last journey to my safe haven. I couldn't wait to get home to our little dogs that must have been missing us so much and the fresh hills and moors around Guisborough. The street was out to welcome us home, banners, balloons, flowers, friends and neighbours. All had been following my progress. Ann and Tony Tansley who lived opposite had been looking after our dogs; they had even sent a photograph of them to me, comfily settled on the sofa in their house! They had been very well looked after as usual.

But it was time to reflect and get life back to normal. It had been a long couple of months, barely at home since February and now it was mid-way through April. Just being back in my home environment, with home cooking and over-active little dogs and my own bed again and sleeping all night and life was back to normal. The Flora London Marathon had been on 13th April 2003. My next race, my local club race, was the Bydales 10 miles race on Good Friday, 18th April only five days later. The result was a nice steady 74 minutes and I even picked up a veterans 35-44 prize. The Monday after was the Easter Egg 10 kilometres at Hartlepool. I was back to normal, running and racing the way I liked it. I really didn't need any adjustment after this event. I had enjoyed the challenge to start with, but towards the end it did start to grind me down a bit, not the physical part, not sleep deprivation but living in close quarters with others whom I found difficult to get on with. I knew from the start the biggest challenge would be getting on with the others and being in the public eye all the time where any "spats" would be highly publicised. In some ways I think this was expected and people thought that we would all be at each other's throats by the end of it. I personally always shied away from any conflict. If I didn't like something I just walked away from it. I hated the loud noise of the television all the time and the presence of Rory sprawled the length of the sofa, so kept to the relative quiet of the front of the bus. Although I caused no conflict by sitting at the opposite end of the bus, not "mixing in" was seen as conflict and created its own problems, problems that the others liked to highlight very publicly on the event blog. To me this was just victimisation and ganging up on one person. I had tremendous support from "others" at this stage and chose to ignore their comments. I think they expected some big "bust up or outcry" from me. But this is not me, the mental torture I endured as a child taught me the way through was to lay low and wait for the clock to tick by. In the same way in this event, I knew that the clock was ticking and soon enough that 1,000 hours would be over and never again would I have to conform to what they wanted on this bus.

A couple of journalists visited after the others made their "statement", but they could not justify their words in any way. I had done nothing to them except go on my way in my own manner and that was what they didn't like. I was organised, planned ahead and preferred my own company. I asked the journalists what they said I had done and there was nothing to answer to. One of the programs on ITV which had been following Shona and David thought it was time to pull me in on the act to see if the conflict was sorted. To me there had been no conflict. Not one of the competitors had been brave enough to say one word to me, just sneakily wrote the statement on the blog to the world as if it was all me doing nasty things to them. If they had a problem all they had to do was ask, but not one did, so what was I supposed to do? Apologise for sitting at the quiet end of the bus? Apologise because I didn't like the television? I had done nothing wrong and had nothing to apologise for, so not a word was ever said. The only person I spoke to on the matter was David. I was very surprised that he joined in with the statement and he personally apologised to me and said he did not agree with it, but I assume he was just bullied into it and I could make a pretty good guess as to who the ring leader had been. But this was all behind me now; in time it would be forgotten and listed as another challenge completed.

The only urge it did ignite for me was that deep down desire to be better than them all and go and get that dream world record that I had written down many years ago. I had now done 1,000 miles very slowly. Land's End to John O'Groats was around the 840 miles mark. This had been a long, slow, relentless event and the miles had been covered. I had grown as a person, strengthened in many ways, now highly motivated and very goal driven. I was an international athlete, currently Great Britain's best 24 hour runner, ranked number five in the world for the previous year, so could I go one better and achieve a world record and mark my name in history? The flame flickered slowly and was soon to glow stronger as my desire to run the ultimate challenge began to take shape.

Chapter 9

My Strength and Desire
to Achieve My Goal

My next marathon was four weeks after the Flora London Marathon, the local undulating Leeds Marathon; an average performance in 3 hours 18 minutes and 4th lady. The following week I ran the National Championships 50 Kilometres at Sutton Coldfield and two weeks later the Apeldoorn 24 hour race again in Holland. This had probably been just a little too much though and I pulled out quite early on with a couple of "niggles". I came back to get selection for England for the Anglo Celtic Plate 100 Kilometres that was being held in Edinburgh in July. Again, not my best of performances, as I pulled one of my buttock muscles turning a sharp corner and hitting a ramp. It was something I could run with but it was uncomfortable. At the time the team ahead were going well. Siri Terjesen was in the lead but Isobel Partridge in 2nd place was going through a bad spell and was unsure if she was going to finish. Had this been an event I had entered, I would have withdrawn at this stage but I was wearing an England vest and the team placing was important; so I continued because I was able to, but I was not running fluently. It was not until quite a late stage in the event that it became clear that Isobel was going to finish, but at this stage I only had about 15 kilometres to make the finish line myself; so having run this far I continued to claim the bronze medal as this was doubling up as the National Championships 100 Kilometres. I finished with the agonising time of 9 hours 47 minutes.

In August we had our annual holidays and raced at "Race the Train" in Tywyn, Wales, an unusual off-road race. This event was notable for Bill. He had been struggling with injury for some time and was unable to pinpoint the exact cause. It was shortly after this race that he was screaming in agony, rolling on the floor in the tent with pain in his leg. I didn't know what to do. Get an ambulance? Get a doctor? He needed some pain relief, but it looked like some form of cramp and took some time to ease. Ibuprofen was all we had. He hardly dared to move and I dared not let him drive in case it returned, far worse than cramp. It was to be the last time he ran for some very significant time to come, but the diagnosis of his problem was not obvious and took some time to confirm.

I had returned to fitness again, got over my little niggles of the year and was looking forward to one last performance for my country this year, the inaugural World and European 24 Hour Challenge in October. The status of the event had increased and this was the first global event for the 24 hours. The European event had been the highest level at which the event was recognised. My selection came through with a list of strings attached, which eventually boiled down to having a blood test at a specific hospital. Shona had struggled to recover from the Flora 1000 Mile Challenge and blood tests had shown up some overtraining aspects for her, but she was a marathon runner and not an ultra distance runner. However, the 1,000 miles had not been overtraining for me.

There were major difficulties in getting the test and the person involved was reluctant to return my calls and make an appointment. It was not until the Monday before the event that I travelled to Nottingham to have the blood test carried out. Psychologically this was destroying me, as my training and performances counted for nothing, it was a blood test that would confirm if I would go and it was left until very late in the day before the person in charge would make the appointment. Even then I don't think he really understood how important it was to me. I had to ring for the results on Tuesday; I was travelling on Wednesday. I was asked to leave it until late in the day and rang around 4:30pm, only to be told I was not top priority; he had other people to see to and should get around to my results the next day. I was fuming and asked exactly what I needed to do to be "top priority". I had waited weeks for him to oblige me with an appointment, I was travelling the very next day to the event and the results of this determined whether I would travel or not. How much more priority did other athletes have? Did they have an international event that weekend? I think the message finally got through and he went in search of them. It didn't take long and around 20 minutes later I got the all clear to travel, but all he told me was that my iron levels were good! What? I travelled all this way and waited this long just to be told you were looking at my iron levels? Couldn't my local doctor have done this? Did UK Athletics really want to get the best out of their athletes by making them travel this distance in the week of an event and not know whether they would be withdrawn? Was this the best way to prepare mentally for what has to be the toughest and longest event of all races that UK Athletics support? But problem solved and it was off to Holland again, the town of Uden this time.

We travelled across in our Transit van, bought with the proceeds of the Flora 1000 Mile Challenge. Our Fiat Ducato had given up the ghost long ago. It had had three new engines and was so unreliable. It had first blown on a trip back from France, then again on the way to the Abingdon

Marathon and never made it. Finally it had blown up driving home from the Round Rotherham 50 miles race and this made for a very long, tiring day. The van was returned and the loan along with it. We had taken unpaid leave for the entire time from February through to the end of April, but the £6 per hour for the challenge, plus £1,000 for completing the challenge, plus £1,000 for completing the marathon added up to a nice £8,000 that was just the fee we paid for a year old Transit van from an auction. Now all kitted out inside we were to camp in this for the 24 hours.

The ferry from Hull to Rotterdam gave us a restful journey, with hardly any driving and we arrived in good shape for the race. We slept at the track side in the park in our campervan and I had my own space and food whenever and whatever I wanted. I was the only female selected. The four men were Walter Hill, William Sichel, Adrian Stott and Stuart Buchan. Performances were good for this first world event, standards very high, my performance was a creditable 205 kilometres, 15th in the world. The men did not perform so well, only Walter Hill was to finish in front of me. The event had moved on and I needed to move on with it. I had one reflection on this event where I made a crucial error. Because of all the worry beforehand about whether or not to compete, whether I was still fit enough and had the Flora 1000 Mile Challenge had any effect? I had set a lowly goal of just 200 kilometres that was above the selection criteria and would confirm my British dominance in the event and prove that I had justified selection. But once I reached this goal with ease I found it hard to continue in the last 4 hours. I had set my goal too low. Had I set a higher one I could probably have fought harder to achieve a better result. But more lessons were learned and I would move on just as the event had done.

I had one last event for the year, one to enjoy. It was the World Challenge 100 Kilometres in Taiwan in November. I was not representing my country on this occasion. My last 100 kilometres race in Edinburgh in July had been a poor performance and not worthy of selection on the basis of this, but UK Athletics were now imposing new rules. I must specialise. I could not run both events. I could not run an ultra event within eight weeks of a competition. The World Challenge 100 Kilometres was five weeks after the World and European 24 Hour Challenge. On this occasion I was content with this, I did not feel in the form of my life. Taiwan was a new country. The course was a challenging one and the heat, humidity and hills sure to throw up some interesting results. I also still had sponsorship to pay for this event from Elle MacPherson Intimates and wore my camouflage kit personally designed by Elle MacPherson.

I didn't have the best of runs. The course was steep, especially in darkness hours when the lights gave way and a few athletes fell in the snake pits that lined the road. Luckily there were no snakes to bite but plenty of other injuries occurred. I struggled with my breathing, had an asthma attack shortly after half way and walked a significant amount of distance after that. I finished as 38th lady in 11 hour 49 minutes – a new personal worst!

Bill brought the usual "sinking feeling" of news for the start of 2004; his job was to disappear yet again. After the Flora 1000 Mile Challenge, David Fox Transport had held his job open but could only offer the night shift on his return. I was reluctant for him to take this after a previous night time collision where I am sure night time work had played its role. I had now given up my lecturing and had taken on the Mobile Massage business full time. It was good to have one job again and my running. I could plan my day a bit better and had a little more time on my hands. I did most of my running in the mornings and massaged in the afternoons and evenings, but the hours were much easier and I had more time to rest and eat between appointments and training sessions and had more flexibility built in. It was now the ideal time for Bill to come into the business with me and help with my workload, but in reality it was difficult to shift my regular customers with whom I had built a good rapport to be treated by Bill. For some there was the issue that Bill was male and for others they wanted continuity. It was obvious Bill would have to build his own client base and I could not transfer the people I treated across to him. Bill was very reluctant and still preferred his driving. We did a little promotion locally to generate some customers for Bill but it wasn't to be. He had waited a while and then got a job driving long distance with Wrights. He was away from home a lot sleeping in his cab with this job, but they closed down and Bill was lucky enough to be taken on by Bulmers Logistics, more or less doing the same work and the company took on the contract that had been left by Wrights departure.

The World and European 24 Hour Challenge was not until the end of the year, October in Brno, Czech Republic. With Land's End to John O'Groats now firmly in my mind I began my quest for multi-stage racing. I had run things like the Tour of Tameside a few times, a double marathon over a week, stages run over six days and a few other races back to back, but this year's challenge was to be the Moravian Ultra Marathon, seven marathons in seven days. I was not going to just run these; I was going to race these. If I wanted to train a marathon every day I would go and do just that, but I wanted to know what it felt like to really push hard and drain yourself every day and get up again the next day and do the same all over again, and then again and again for seven marathons. I had some good build-up races and several months of hard training, the longest event being the Woldsman at 50 miles. I set a new course record for this in 8 hours 36 minutes and had not really been pushing hard.

July was the big month, a couple of days in Prague to start with and then off to the classroom which was to be home for the event. I was supplied with an airbed and used my own sleeping bag. My room-mate was German athlete Anke Molkenthin, previous winner of the Marathon des Sables. There were a few good female runners here, Irina Koval of the Russian team and Nina Mitrofanova of Ukraine, both of whom had superior 24 hour performances to me and both had run this event before, so would know what to expect and how to pace themselves. The whole trip was such a joy to compete in. Based in the school at Lomnice in Brno we had all our evening meals and breakfast here. Each morning we were to be taken on a short sight-seeing tour, have lunch out and then run back to base every afternoon. Every day was to be so different. Every route was a challenge. Every day was a race to the finish.

For the start of the first marathon, a circular route starting and finishing in Lomnice, there was an opening ceremony by the Mayor at the local Town Hall and the first mile we all ran together through the village. On the climb out was where the race began. Most of the routes were off-road and we were given some black and white photocopied maps which were not the best; the route was also marked with tape. We climbed steadily from Lomnice and soon hit the trails and that was where I took up the race and led the ladies, initially weaving around in the forest looking for tags and following runners, getting used to the way the race was marked. Suddenly I came to a t-junction in the woods. Where to go? Left or right? No tags. I could not see where we were on the maps. I had been following the runner in front rather than reading the maps and was now lost. Funny how I only thought left or right, whereas, in reality, having lost the tape I should have thought to return to the last piece of tape. There was also the problem of the language barrier. Those around me mumbled in their respective language, English not understood. A couple went left, I went right and another man followed. Eventually we came out of the woods to a road. I stopped again and tried to make sense of the map, the fellow runner doing the same. We shrugged shoulders as communication, but neither of us knew where to go. A cyclist appeared, help at last. He still spoke no English, but with a glance at the map he seemed to recognise where we were and indicated on the map where to go. We had actually run further than the map had copied but followed the road close to the railway line to the next crossing where we appeared back on the map. We found the checkpoint and were now back on course, nearly last at this point. As devastated as I was not to be in a position to win the race; this had not been the object of the exercise. The goal was to run hard marathons every day, so off in pursuit of running hard I went. I closely followed the maps now and a few road sections where I made up good ground; I stormed through the field and "picked" runners off one by one. The good thing about being at the back of the field was that there were more runners to follow. By the end of the first day I made it back to 3rd place in the ladies race, 4 hours 41 minutes compared to Irina Koval at 4 hours 9 minutes and Anke in 4 hours 27 minutes. Vladimir Bychkov from Russia was the 1st man in 3 hours 44 minutes.

For the second marathon I had to claw back the deficit of 32 minutes. I had run further on day one than the others, was it possible to do this over six marathons? It could possibly be done but I had to work hard. The routes were tough ones, very hilly, rough in places too, but I enjoyed them. We started the day touring Lomnice, the church and the castle and were then driven to Kunstat. The first three men and women were presented with pottery vases at the Town Hall and all got certificates with individual times and positions. Today the slower runners started at 2pm, the faster runners at 3pm. Having run a slow time I was placed in the 2pm start, which I was happy with. Irina had been placed in the 3pm start but requested to be in the 2pm start and that just helped me to have her as a target in the same race. She knew I had gone off route and knew I would be a force to be reckoned with. At the start I knew I had run hard the previous day and could feel the stiffness. The weather was hot again and there was a fair bit of road to start with. Most days there were around six checkpoints on the route for re-filling bottles and light snacks. Irina set off well with me in 2nd place and chasing, it was around half way through the marathon between checkpoints three and four that I got glimpses of Irina up ahead and knew I was closing her down. The route then went steeply down in the woods and it became apparent that Irina was not so good on this terrain, picking her way down. My many days spent running the North York Moors were to pay off and I took advantage of this section, gaining momentum and overtaking her with renewed confidence. I deliberately put an extra spurt on to pull away and was quite surprised looking back on reaching checkpoint four that she was not in sight. I stormed into Lomnice strongly and after a shower looked at the results. I had finished in 4 hours 10 minutes; Irina was 2nd with 4 hours 34 minutes; Anke 3rd with 4 hours 35 minutes. I had clawed back 24 minutes and was now in 2nd place in the women's results. Vladimir was 1st man again with 3 hours 24 minutes.

Day three was an early start with breakfast at 6:45am. By 8:15am we were on our way to Nedvedice, it was cold and raining. The castle here was said to be one of the finest in the Czech Republic, it certainly was superb but quite tiring climbing the many steps and being on the 2 hour guided tour with no sitting down. The presentation was at a fair ground today; everyone went on stage for a pen and postcard along with certificates. By the time the race started I was unsure what to wear. It was still raining, but quite cool. I guessed I might be a bit slower today with two days of hard running in my legs; so opted for a long sleeved shirt under my vest. The start was hard, uphill running through the grounds of the castle, but the rain was beginning to ease. There was another long climb on the road to checkpoint two and I finally warmed up and was down to vest and shorts again as the sun came out. Shortly after checkpoint two the trails appeared and I immediately overtook Irina who had not got out of visual distance that day. I finished the day fastest so far with 4 hours 7 minutes, Irina 2nd in 4 hours 23 minutes. This now meant I was 1st lady on aggregate times by 7 minutes, not a confident lead, but I was pleased to be challenging Irina. Vladimir was 1st man again with 3 hours 17 minutes.

The next day there was a trip to a museum and monastery at Tisnov and the usual presentation of certificates at the Town Hall from the previous day's race. The first three athletes received a pottery mug and a t-shirt. The weather was sweltering again, but I really didn't feel any worse than I did on day two. I took Irina even earlier today between checkpoints one and two, but it was not to be a good day. Soon after entering the woods I found myself off-route again and alone this time. Heeding the lessons of the first day I retraced my steps and struggled to find the path between two bushes and I was back in 3rd place. I increased my pace and was soon in the lead again and running very hard. The route marking was different today. I guessed someone else had marked this and between checkpoints five and six I went off route yet again. Re-tracing my steps I found the arrows pointing me into the woods, only for the same to happen yet again. Re-tracing my steps this time I bumped into Irina coming the opposite way. I ran even harder to stay in front, joined the familiar road section back to Lomnice and had a narrow victory of 4 hours 38 minutes to Irina's 4 hours 44 minutes. Vladimir's winning time was 3 hours 28 minutes.

We had another early start to visit the castle that was being restored in Veverska Bityska. I had a couple of blisters now from having wet feet in the trails' they were painful to start with, more so on running downhill. For the first time I took the lead from the start, through the grounds of the castle and down to a bridge. It was to be a really tough course today, very long with many steeps climbs. The seven checkpoints should have fore-warned me. I had no problems with navigation, but finished with 5 hours 6 minutes, my slowest so far. I had started to tire after running for the usual 4 hours and realised from the maps this was going to be a long day. Irina finished in 5 hours 23 minutes. Rainer, one of the German runners wearing a global positioning system (GPS) said the route was 47 kilometres (a marathon is 42 kilometres). Vladimir finished in a creditable 3 hours 41 minutes.

Just two more marathons to go now and I was extending my lead over Irina by a few minutes every day. The next day dawned with really heavy rain and the excursion for the day was cancelled. This was a relief; as much as I liked visiting the region it was extremely tiring and I was grateful for a morning of rest. The presentation and start of the race was at Boskovice, with a gift of a candle in a glass and picture of Boskovice. The sun finally started to break through the clouds for the start of marathon number six. The route felt so much easier after yesterday's long hard route and I finished strongly with 4 hours 20 minutes. Irina was 2nd again in 4 hours 41 minutes and Vladimir finished in 3 hours 10 minutes.

For the last day there was a staggered start and a circular route from Lomnice, similar to the first day. It was a kind of handicap race, slowest runners first, fastest last. My start time was 10:50am, Irina 10:40am. It was also to be a two lap course today, but I could not find the way out of Lomnice. It was not marked and after running up and down three different roads I returned to Lomnice to ask directions. It had been one of the routes we had finished with, but running in reverse felt different. Eventually I got it right and had no more problems that day, but I had given Irina a good head start. It took until shortly before the end of the first lap to catch Irina and I finished the seventh marathon in 4 hours 9 minutes, Irina in 4 hours 24 minutes. Vladimir won in 3 hours 3 minutes.

There was a big buffet dinner and presentation that evening and we watched the race on local television. Vladimir and myself both won a real silver medal. Vladimir's finishing time was 23 hours 50 minutes. My time was 31 hours 13 minutes, Irina 32 hours 20 minutes and 3rd lady was Anke with 33 hours 20 minutes. I was elated just to finish and could not believe I had really won this top class event. I was surprised by how strong I remained throughout the race. I had envisaged getting slower and slower as the race progressed. As I didn't come here to pace myself for a week of marathons, I had run each marathon as an individual marathon race and put the effort in accordingly, as that had been the plan. Only seventeen

athletes finished all seven marathons, six of these were females. I finished
8th overall. It had been one of those "new experiences into the unknown"
that I loved to do. The event, the organisation, the many friends I made,
the whole experience was one that was hard to forget. Both Irina and Anke
spoke English and were to become firm friends in the many future events
where we were to see each other.

Back home again and I felt none the worse for the long hard week. By the
Wednesday I ran the Croft Circuit 10 kilometres and the day after the
Hummersnott 5 kilometres trail race. I thought all was well but I had
begun to have an ache in my groin. It progressively got worse and I didn't
realise it was to do with my running. I had no signs of this in the Moravian
Ultra Marathon and even went to the doctors to see if they could find the
source of the problem. It was difficult for them to diagnose and after a
visit from my friends Marie and Roy Bainbridge, Roy suggested a sports
medicine doctor whom he occasionally visited. Dr Martyn Speight was
based at the Wharfedale Clinic in Otley, nearly 90 minutes away, but his
expertise was supreme and I got an instant diagnosis that proved correct.
I was heading towards a stress fracture in the neck of my femur. A bone
scan eventually revealed the stress reaction that had just stopped short of
cracking the bone. One more race and the outcome could have been far
worse and needed a much longer recovery. So, after all that fitness gained,
it was onto the bike to maintain fitness as best I could while taking the
compulsory six weeks of non-weight bearing exercise to repair the bone.

The other news that was finally revealed that July was the problem with
Bill. Since last year's "Race the Train" event he had still not run and was
progressively getting worse. It was not until he visited local Osteopath
Simon Barnard who suggested getting an x-ray that the real problem came
to light. He had osteoarthritis in both hips. I was absolutely gob-smacked
and had not realised that arthritis could get this bad at such an age. Bill
was just forty-three years old. I read about this in depth, got him several
supplements and he also got medication from the doctor to ease the pain.
We now did a lot more cycling together.

On return to weight bearing exercise I returned to lots of miles of walking
and a few miles running and was to fulfil another ambition of mine, to
become a Centurion. That was to walk 100 miles in 24 hours. John
Paddick had encouraged a fair few athletes to take up the sport of race
walking now and had set up a local club called Redcar Race Walking Club,
of which I was now a member. Dave Jones, a New Marske Harrier who
had turned to race walking after knee problems, had successfully become

a Centurion and was now aiming at an England vest in the sport. I loved this tiny individually numbered badge that he received for his achievement and I wanted one. The race walking community had watched the Flora 1000 Mile Challenge with interest, as Captain Barclay had walked all his miles. There had not been a race walker contestant in the challenge despite former Olympian Chris Maddocks making the final selection, but I was a race walker occasionally and I entered the National Long Distance Championships that were being held in Colchester. It was a very long night compared to running. The miles ticked off so slowly. It was not as demanding or as much hard work as running, but it required endurance and that clock just ticked so slowly. I finished with 22 hours 41 minutes to become Centurion Number 1006 (shame I wasn't number 1000) and 2nd lady in the championships behind the formidable Sandra Brown. Sandra dominated these events and was 1st person home in 19 hours 17 minutes; such was her supremacy at race walking. Dave Jones was to finish 2nd man with 20 hours 57 minutes and went on to earn his English vest at future events.

Bill was now earning a reasonable wage and I was struggling with the massage. The long hours on deep tissue work were taking their toll and I needed to reduce my hours as my wrists were creaking and cracking. I was contemplating going back to Teesside University to study MSc Sport and Exercise when an accident helped my decision. While out cycling with Bill, he was struggling behind and I turned to see how far back he was and fell off my bike. It was a heavy fall and among my injuries I chipped a piece of bone from my thumb and so was unable to massage anyway, I gave up the business and started back as a post-graduate student at Teesside University.

The next day we also realised why Bill struggled and felt a little unwell. After a visit to the doctor with chest pain, Bill was wired up for an electrocardiogram tracing which reported abnormal and he was sent home while the doctor rang a consultant at the hospital. We got home to find the telephone ringing and an ambulance was on its way, blue lights flashing. Not quite an emergency but this was how he needed to be admitted. I would have been quite happy to have taken him, but that was the system. The ambulance staff wired him up to an electrocardiogram monitor again and the information was sent directly to the hospital. It was only an overnight stay but he was sent home with all sorts of medication and given several tests. The diagnosis was Left Bundle Branch Block, something to do with the electrics in his heart. With his parents both dying relatively young and mother dying suddenly of a heart attack his family history was taken into account.

After the poor performances of the 24 hour athletes in recent times there was no funding to send anyone to this year's international 24 hours. The selection policy was changing as were the people at the helm. There was now an Ultra Distance Sub Committee, with several names from the ultra distance running community involved in this. It was Stephen Moore who finally confirmed selection for this event six weeks before. Stephen had retired from international racing and was now supporting fellow athletes. I had personally always targeted this race and had already entered the open race assuming that no athletes were officially going, so it was not an issue to have to change plans at late notice. I had already booked my flights and accommodation. The funding was to come from the Home Counties though, not from UK Athletics, I believe it was the intervention of Norman Wilson at this stage that managed to secure the funding for us to compete. Without this we could not have competed for our country. The three athletes involved were myself, Sandra Brown and Ramona Thevenet-Smith, her first vest for Great Britain. No men were selected.

Many people believe that once you are an international athlete the governing body funds you and you can be a full time athlete. Ultra distance running is not an Olympic sport. Most of the funding on offer is for sports that are in the Olympics; so no funding was available to support athletes. The only funding we received was for expenses to be paid at international events which UK Athletics selected you for, such as travelling, accommodation and food. Our fight as ultra distance runners was just to get the funding to be allowed to compete for our country. Other athletes moan at how little they get, perhaps they should get a taste of what our expectations were, probably running more miles than any other sport and this was our only funding. Nearly all the runners worked, holding down full time jobs and fitting training in around work and using holidays to take time off for international events.

Tomas Rusek was the organiser for the World and European Challenge 24 Hours. A great ultra distance runner himself, he was the person who organised and picked me up from the bus station at the Moravian Ultra Marathon earlier that year. The route was not the best, many very sharp corners and large kerbs, but it was the same for everyone and I just had to get on with the job of performing. On top of this I had a few problems myself. The hiccup in falling off my bike had only just been x-rayed and to attach the piece of bone might need an operation. It was the week of my big race though and I had no intention of putting my performance at risk. I did not want a heavy pot put on my wrist; so it was agreed that a Velcro wrist splint would be used to stop my thumb from moving.

I did not enjoy the course and struggled with the tight corners. I was not happy with my 202 kilometres which placed me 16th in the world. Ramona ran 182 kilometres and Sandra 176 kilometres; the Great Britain team came 6th in the World and 4th in the European event.

It was now 2005 and another year, more new plans. I needed a good performance. I needed to move forward. Being back at university was great for me; it was far less strenuous than working as a massage therapist and I even had time to sit and study in the evenings. This was the ideal scenario to pick myself up again and get back to the performances I expected of myself. I had some funding from Teesside University and wondered how best to put this to good use. I always struggled in the winter months with my breathing. To get a good head start to the year I needed some solid training in the heat; so asked for the funding to be put towards some warm weather training and it was agreed. I found a quiet resort in Portugal, near the coast, for some trail running and a gym to do my weights. For two weeks I could be a full time athlete. It was reasonable weather to wear shorts and t-shirt and there were good hilly trail runs that Bill could follow on the bike. A nice relaxing rest and read in the afternoon before a second session and some weights and a massage every night. It worked a treat and I came back in great shape and full of confidence. Unfortunately the weather was still bitterly cold back here.

I was away the first two weeks in February, building up for the Barry 40 track race and then the Anglo Celtic Plate 100 Kilometres in Dublin a month later. In the Barry 40 the weather was bitterly cold. Although fit, I struggled with my breathing even though I took it very steady to start with and my asthma came on badly around 20 miles into the event. There was no way back with the weather still biting hard with a cold wind; so I was forced to withdraw. I knew my fitness was still good and would not interfere with the next planned 100 kilometres race; the only thing it did interfere with was being selected to run for England in the 100 kilometres race. Sue Bruce had already gained selection on the basis of an earlier race, Lizzy Hawker won the Barry 40 with 5 hours 12 minutes and got selected and Vicky Skelton was selected after a planned withdrawal completing 30 miles at the Barry 40. Vicky was recovering from an injury, so was testing it by only running 30 miles. There was space for a fourth athlete and I also considered myself a better runner than Vicky. She had never beaten me over 100 kilometres, my 100 kilometres time was far superior to Vicky's, but that was Norman Wilson's decision. Withdrawing at 20 miles in Barry somehow rendered me unfit to compete four weeks later.

I entered the race anyway as it was part of my plans and was also the National Championships 100 Kilometres. The games going on at the helm of ultra distance running were a joke. Stephen Moore had now resigned. He had no choice with some of the decisions being made; there was too much fighting and disagreement. Stephen was in the committee at the request of the athletes, as he was such a good ambassador for the sport and had excelled as an athlete. Although extremely upset to see him leave, I understood his decision and I would have done the same in his shoes. As for now, being an athlete I made my own choices. At the start of the year I would decide what races I wanted to do and then just do them, whether selected or not selected. So here was the first race of the year and I was not selected. This was not a problem; there was an open race. We all ran the same course, the same race and I could still go ahead with my plans.

The flights were pretty cheap and Bill accompanied me. Sue Bruce made an excellent debut with 8 hours 14 minutes, Lizzy Hawker was 2nd with 8 hours 40 minutes and I was 3rd with 8 hours 45 minutes, just 5 minutes slower than what I had expected. Vicky Skelton struggled and was the last female with 10 hours 22 minutes and was incredibly ill that night. Norman Wilson did congratulate me to say I had proved my point. I had run the race because it was part of my plans. Yes, I would have preferred to have run it in an English vest rather than my New Marske Harriers vest, but hey, it was part of my plans and nothing was disrupted.

The International Association of Ultrarunners (IAU) had now announced the races for 2006, the 24 hours was early in the year and the 100 kilometres very late. That left the summer months free for the challenge I now felt ready for, my attempt at running from Land's End to John O'Groats. I had planned most of the route but wanted to cycle it again. With Bill's hips deteriorating badly he could only cycle for fitness and even that was limited at times. He was on the waiting list for a hip replacement and just ticking the days off until he could be pain free again. We set off from Land's End with a trailer for the camping equipment. There was a massive difference in our fitness levels now, but with me carrying the equipment it equalled us out a little. The route was horrendous: busy dual carriageways, noisy roads, intricate navigation at times, a struggle to find the best routes through the towns, but a great preparation for what was to come.

After a week of cycling we planned to reach Edinburgh in time for the marathon. My quadriceps were fatigued from the cycling, but it was all good training. We camped and took the bus in to collect my race number on the Saturday. It was here that I bumped into Shona Crombie-Hicks from the Flora 1000 Mile Challenge. It was the first time since the challenge that I had seen any of the competitors. Shona was nice and friendly this time, but it was me who could not be bothered to make an effort. I would not call her a friend, just an acquaintance. On the blog she made a statement about me that was just plain bullying and yet here she was nice as pie. No thanks, I thought, I can walk away. We were not in a confined space living together and forced to spend time with each other and I don't have to be nice. I wasn't rude but I certainly made no effort to make conversation. I achieved a steady 3 hours 35 minutes on my tired legs, similar to what I had done in back in 2003.

After that reconnoitre I sat down and re-did the route. I used maps off the internet to plan the route through towns, used Sustrans to find some cycle paths to avoid some of the road routes and find quieter roads to run along without adding significant distance. I drove three different routes from Carlisle to Edinburgh, measuring the different distances and assessing the traffic, hills and ease of parking to come up with the best route. I then drove the entire route and mapped out the route with written directions to follow, measured off-road sections with a surveyor's wheel and marked every single mile of the route on maps.

Later that year was the World and European Challenge 24 Hours in Worschach, Austria. The same three ladies as last year managed to get selection this time funded by UK Athletics. The weather was hot with some torrential rain showers. I struggled again and was puzzled as to why. I had a tearful session shortly after half way, not understanding why it was such hard work, I still had not realised what was wrong, even though I was frequently visiting the smelly port-a-loos very regularly for a pee, even in the last 20 minutes of the race. I finished 14th with 200 kilometres, Sandra was 26th with 180 kilometres and Ramona 49th with 150 kilometres. The team was 5th in Europe and 7th in the World.

I had been to see my doctor just a couple of weeks earlier, as I had some very swollen glands in my groin, protruding like strawberries, but not really giving me any grief. After the event I returned to my doctor, my glands still swollen and with a little bit of back pain that I guessed could be my kidneys. A water infection was confirmed and antibiotics given. This sorted one problem, but I was referred for a biopsy on the glands which should have gone down long ago. I now had a reason for my poor performance, not an excuse, but it wasn't my training or fitness that let me down, just bad luck having a water infection and swollen glands at the same time. It was still frustrating as the years were ticking by and I was still yet to have that good performance that was waiting to come out.

I eventually had a lymph node removed from my groin as they were so stubborn to retreat and it was not normal for the glands to stay swollen for so long. It was a worrying time, but in the end all came back fit and healthy. Having the operation was not fit and healthy though! I was horrified at the inch long incision left in my groin that took an age to settle down.

It was while recovering from this operation that I got the invitation to run in the inaugural Gore-tex Transalpine Run. This event started in Germany, ran through Austria and Switzerland and finished in Italy. I was covering the event for Running Fitness Magazine, having met Paul Larkins at the Flora 1000 Mile Challenge. It was an incredible event. For the first staging of such an event it was so well organised and really generated a superb atmosphere. I had to find a partner at very short notice; the only partner was an adventure racer, Fiona Paterson. This was not ideal in some ways, as there was a difference in fitness levels, but, not being completely fit as I was recovering from my groin problem, it was a race to enjoy and I could still write a report and witness the event. I was rewarded well, as this was my kind of event: incredible trails, stunning views, stiff climbs with frequent checkpoints, excellent back up staff, mountains of appropriate food, presentations every night with a party atmosphere, footage of the days run in photographs and films and great camaraderie. Writing the report was a joy, recording the experience, the remoteness, the heights, the views, the scary bits with ropes and small ledges, following tracks cut into gorges, wonderful waterfalls, just all around amazing! They certainly knew how to put on an event and organise it in four different countries - just fantastic! If you ever wanted to run a long event in stunning surroundings, this was the one, faultless from start to finish. The only grumble for me was that I didn't sleep well in some of the stuffy gymnasiums. It added to the atmosphere and experience, but personally I would prefer to pay and use hotels. However, as I wasn't running hard on this occasion it was great to soak up the whole of the event. The result: 33 hours 48 minutes of running, 202 kilometres of incredible paths, 9,816 metres of altitude and 4th ladies team.

The following year's events had now been confirmed by the International Association of Ultrarunners. The World Challenge 24 Hours in Taiwan was in February and the World Challenge 100 Kilometres in Korea was in November. Selection had now come out for these events and WOW! I know the athletes had not performed well, but the criteria were way beyond what anyone expected. I know selection should be tough; you have to "earn" the vest rather than be given it, but if every country had the same criteria there would hardly be an athlete in the race.

There were now two levels of selection criteria, as there often has been. "A" standard was for individual athletes, "B" standard was for team athletes. To make a team you need three athletes. For the 24 hours in 2005 the "A" standard for women had been 190 kilometres, the team standard 185 kilometres. The new "A" standard for 2006 was 215 kilometres and 195 kilometres for team standard. That was a massive 25 kilometres extra for individual standard. As an event moves on, you do expect the standards to move on and get tougher relative to performances. The criteria for "A" standard was based on the top ten percent of the results from the previous year's world 24 hour event and the average of the team bronze medallists for the team "B" standard. The excuse given for these new standards, we were told, was that the same standards would now apply across the board for all endurance events. This was not correct and I tried to point this out. Looking back at the results from the previous world event in Austria there was a total of fifty-seven women. Rounding this up to sixty women, the top ten percent would mean the top six women. Sandy Powell was the 6th place woman with 214 kilometres. To compare this with other endurance events I looked at the championships for the marathon that had been held in Helsinki in 2005. In the women's marathon there were fifty-nine runners, just two more than the 24 hours event, so assuming the same top ten percent requirement would mean the 6th place woman in this event. Yumiko Hara was in 6th place with 2 hours 24 minutes – so this should have been the "A" standard for marathon selection. Was it? Definitely not, their standard was considerably less, so we were being treated very harshly by comparison.

The team standard for us was not quite so bad. European team bronze medallists in 2005 had performed 552 kilometres, world team bronze medallists covered 604 kilometres. So I was not quite sure how 195 kilometres was calculated. The next event for us was not a combined event; it was a world challenge only as it was outside of Europe. If other countries followed our lead then there would be only six athletes in the individual competition. Granted that if you took the team scenario into account this could potentially add another six athletes to the field.

There was no budging on the part of the selectors, so it was just get on with the job and try to qualify. The standards were released before the final 24 hour events in England so I had a chance to qualify. The next event was the usual track event at Tooting Bec; so I entered this. For the last week in the build up I had struggled with a stomach problem and felt very sick. I had entered and hoped that I would feel alright on the day, but it was not to be and after running for barely an hour I felt sick and had stomach pains and withdrew. There was another event being held at Hull only three weeks later that had been postponed from July. I went to the doctor who diagnosed a stomach infection as the problem lasted much longer than a normal stomach bug and three weeks later I lined up again. I started well, but had some really dizzy spells late into the event and had to lay down for a bit. With the goal of 215 kilometres gone, there was no incentive to push hard and I walked to finish with 198 kilometres. I had to aim at the "A" standard as there were not three athletes above 195 kilometres to make a team.

Bill's six month wait was finally up and it was at the beginning of November that he had his first "Birmingham Hip Resurfacing" and was to be off work for eight weeks. He recovered well and the whole house got decorated while he was regaining his strength and mobility. He did get one new present on his return from hospital. Bill is the television addict in this household and the television had been on the blink for a while, so we invested in an enormous forty-two inch plasma screen television, much to his delight when he sat in control of the remote for the first few weeks.

This was to be the big year now, 2006. My first goal of the year was to maintain my status as "Great Britain Number 1". I had now done this for the previous nine years and ten was a nice round number to finish on. I wanted to get this out of the way early on to allow me to concentrate on the big one for the year and the attempt at the "End to End" world record. The date had been set in July and I had already recruited some supporters.

As I could find no European 24 hour races in the first couple of months of the year, I planned to run in the open race of the World Challenge 24 Hours in Taiwan. It was a long and expensive trip and, as much of Bill's holidays would be taken up for the Land's End to John O'Groats event, I travelled alone to this distant land. The Elite Athlete Bursary Scheme from Teesside University also helped out with my expenses for this trip. I had not enjoyed my last trip to Taiwan. My memories were of snakes, spiders and earthquakes. There had been two significant earth quakes that were quite frightening and, although the food had been excellent, it was not appropriate for endurance running. This time I was to stay in the Public Training Building which was a bit like a boarding school, basic, but it had everything required and school style dinners which were absolutely fine, with plenty of rice for carbohydrate. As I did not like Taiwan I travelled late. I am not the best of travellers, as I can never sleep while travelling and I left home at 5am on Wednesday and arrived very tired on the Thursday. Friday I went to see the course; the route had now changed. I took note of the area I had for putting my supplies out, a large table covered by a gazebo style tent, and watched the opening ceremony. I bought my water and supplies and relaxed in the evening with everything prepared. As I had no support crew for this one I had prepared most of my supplies in shoe boxes so they didn't fall over and were easy to organise and find.

Start time was 10am, my favourite time, but on 25th February 2006 this was not good. I had not slept a wink all night, the time difference having too much of an effect. Since 2am I had been up making tea. It was now 10am and I was feeling very tired and ready for bed. My training had gone well; the good news about not running for my country was that I was not under any restrictions for my training. In the last two months I had run well in the Round Rotherham 50 miles race, a long muddy run in just less than 8 hours, and two weeks previously had a steady run around the Draycote 35 miles in steady 8 minute miles to finish with 4 hours 46 minutes. The other bit of good news was that Teesside University had let me use the environmental chamber to help acclimatise to the heat and humidity expected in Taiwan.

The weather was humid and sticky, the thermometer now reading twenty-two degrees Celsius and eighty percent humidity. Hilary Walker was here on International Association of Ultrarunners duties. Although unable to support me, she did offer to visit intermittently, as her duties allowed, to mix drinks or refill bottles. I was set up for the first 12 hours, but was grateful for mixing after that. Since my stomach infection last year I had taken to Mannatech's GlycoSlim for my drinks, as they had gone down incredibly well. Mannatech had now supplied my nutritional supplements since 2000 when I had sustained the accident on the scooter. GlycoSlim was a meal replacement milkshake drink and ideal for this type of event and I loved the taste, but with the warm weather I was worried about the drinks going off, so I could not make them up for the whole of the race.

I sat at my table contemplating the task ahead. No Bill by my side. I missed him already. I had never been to a 24 hour race without him. I had done many 100 kilometres races without him but this was to be another challenge. Everything about this race was challenging for me; my personal goals were tough. I was desperate to get back to the "World's Top 10" after being 14th last year. I hoped for a personal best to improve on my 217 kilometres, but the bare minimum was to make 215 kilometres for future selections and this should also place me at the top of the Great Britain rankings for the tenth consecutive year.

I stood on the start line not feeling excited at all, not nervous or hyped up. In fact I just wanted to be back at home and tucked up in bed! This 10am start was actually 2am for me. The gun went and I started the long journey, going through the motions and running on this really twisty course with bad cambers, big curbs, rutted roads and tight, narrow sections. After a couple of hours the temperature was rising, now twenty-five degrees Celsius and I guessed around ninety percent humidity. The traffic was also building up and, smelling the exhaust fumes, I began to worry how my asthma would hold up.

On through the first 4 hours and I could not figure out how far I had run. There was a big plasma screen recording the champion-chips for the international runners. Next to it was a screen for the open race runners, but it was still displaying an earlier relay race. It was around 6 hours into the race that the plasma screen came up with the number of laps completed. It was also around this time that David, a Canadian runner in the open race who had been allocated a space on the supplies table next to me, withdrew. The sharp corners were taking their toll on his knees, creating blisters and it was far too early to have problems. I now knew how many laps I had run, but as the course had changed to a short 730 metres I could not calculate how far I had run.

By the end of 8 hours it was dark and the temperature was dropping slightly. Some of the runners were putting on extra clothes, so after 10 hours I put on a long sleeved top. I was still running blind, not knowing how far I had gone. My drinks were going down well, but my feet were getting tender on the turns and I had stumbled many times on the uneven surface. My left knee had also begun to ache on the twisting course. Shortly after this I noticed Hilary refilling my drinks bottles and mixing milkshakes. I was pleased with this, as it now meant I didn't have to waste time doing this myself. If I had been a little more observant I would have noticed that she left me a note informing me of the top women in the race and that my distance at 11 hours was 109 kilometres which placed me 7th.

It was around this time that I started sinking. All I knew was that I was the 2nd lady in the open race. A Japanese runner was a lap or two in front and I knew from the entry list that her previous distance was 180 kilometres, so was I running really badly or was she running really well? My feet were hurting. I knew I had several blisters already, my knees ached even more and I was becoming very frustrated. I really needed Bill now to snap me out of it. I was thinking, "What would he be telling me to do now if I was going through a rough patch?" Well, I knew I would get though it and come out the other side, so I just had to persevere and get on with it.

Why did I come? I knew I had made the wrong decision the moment I stood on the start line. I decided to sit down in my tent and drink some coffee and try to pull myself together; tears were rolling down my face now. How could I really expect to run well? What should I do with myself now? Should I drop out and admit defeat? It was a long, expensive trip to come for a 12 hour run and fail to complete any of my goals. I couldn't give up this easily, I must find out exactly how far I had run. The Australians had offered me help. I knew Mick Francis from many years ago when he was Scottish, but I was close to quitting and, although I didn't want to bother them, I really needed someone to talk to. I got myself up and walked to the lap recording person to ask how many kilometres I had run. She didn't understand. I left in a worse state. I needed to summon help. I saw an Australian shirt and it was only on asking for help that I heard that most of the Australian team had struggled and that Mick Francis had passed out, so help might be some time in coming. Well, I wasn't that bad, I thought, so I carried on walking, still upset and not knowing what to do with myself. It was only the next lap that I heard help was on its way, Mick's sister Hilary was making her way to my tent. I ran to the tent. I was in a state. I was hard to console. I was behaving totally stupidly compared with what I now heard of the rest of the field. Nearly everyone had suffered. Some thirty athletes had already dropped out, the Australian team had suffered with sickness and the course had taken its toll on the athletes. I was not alone. I had a glimmer of hope; even if I didn't run well and everyone ran badly there was a chance of making the top ten again with a lesser distance. Hilary had rung Bill, but the answering machine was on and Bill not home. Suddenly the mobile rang again, it was Bill; he had been in the garden. It was great to hear his voice; he was as supportive as ever, telling me how proud he was that I even attempted to come here on my own. Bill said if I wasn't enjoying it then not to suffer and injure myself, there were other more important events. I put the phone down smiling. He had done the trick. I was happy. Hilary had now found out my distances. My distance at 12 hours had not been anywhere near as bad as expected, 119 kilometres was actually a kilometre further than planned, but the last 2 hours had revealed 7 kilometres one hour and 4 kilometres the next hour. I had lost 10 kilometres being in my emotional state.

I was up and running again, on a high, my feet felt better, the little niggle in my knee magically disappeared. Had it been an injury or was it in my mind? So I had lost 10 kilometres, as my target had been 220 kilometres. "Keep running well and you should achieve 210 kilometres," I told myself, "All is not lost; I can still finish this race." I floated along, passing many international runners when the rain began. It got heavier and heavier. The course was waterlogged, ramps floating in the water, streams running through the tents of lap recorders, the ruts filled up with massive puddles. Did I get down about the rain? No. I noticed the field had thinned out. They were either taking a break or the rain was finishing them off, but there was no avoiding it, the rain had set in for the remainder of the race. The only disappointment was the news that fed back on my position. I had just taken the lead in the ladies open race before my "blip" and now was trailing by 8 kilometres. I could only hope that a strong finish would see me win.

Soon Hilary Walker was refilling my bottles again. Her advice was to put my waterproof jacket on. It was sixteen degrees Celsius, but a soaked body would soon cool down and knew that I would also slow down, so I took her advice and dressed appropriately. I took advantage of her being there and also got some coffee poured out for me. After she went I was more observant this time and noticed the piece of paper she left informing me that I had run 153 kilometres. My schedule had been for 162 kilometres, so I was 9 kilometres behind, but I had picked up a kilometre.

Mick's sister Hilary came across intermittently to check on me, but I was fine now. I had weathered the bad spells and knew I was running well and was going to finish in a respectable position. My feet were still very tender, but that was just normal now. At 20 hours Hilary Walker now confirmed I was in 8th place in the event. I was now three laps behind the Japanese leader in the open race. This was my race now. With the help of Laura Fleming of Teesside University I had now conquered my fear of the last 4 hours and could use my new strategy. Psychology was now going to help me win this race; those waffles and theories I had come to master had finally translated into concrete thoughts in my mind. I used to dread those last 4 hours and struggled through, unable to blot out the pain. Now I confidently looked forward to the last 4 hours, knowing I could be strong and instead of fearing it, I positively relished this section knowing I could finish victorious. It was now my strength that could shine through and I could dominate. In my head I always ran each 4 hours as an individual race and had to finish each 4 hour segment to make it to the next. At 20 hours I knew I would finish but I seemed to let go and this was the time where the race was won or lost. I was losing. I was in 2nd place. Could I now win? Now I could put this new strategy into practice. This was four blocks of 1 hour. I knew I could run strongly for 1 hour to get to the next, and so it was. Hour 20 passed; hour 21 passed and it was at that point I took the lead. For the next 2 hours I ran strongly and the clock ticked so fast. At 23 hours the distance was 205 kilometres; could I run 10 kilometres for one last hour? When 30 minutes remained there was a slim chance I could possibly make the magical selection distance of 215 kilometres, but the intense pace was taking its toll, my feet were really hurting me now and I was just running out of steam. It was just one challenge too far; the slight uphill section now felt like a mountain. I had done my best. I finally sat down when the 24 hours were up. Glad it was all over, I had probably achieved two of my three goals. The final distance came out at 214.5 kilometres, winner of the open race; 6th place in the World Challenge 24 Hours. Just listen to that again, 6th place in the world and I had still not reached the 215 kilometres required for selection. Only five women had covered 215 kilometres. Surely UK Athletics would reconsider for next year?

After the last bit was measured I hobbled back to my tent. I felt lonely again. There was no one here. All the supporters had their own athletes to tend to. I threw all the shoe boxes away, gathered my stuff in the suitcase and wandered off to find the showers. I knew I would get cold shortly and needed to find warmth. As I slowly began walking towards the stadium a local supporter came out to help me. He was very insistent that he must help and take my bags. I gave in. He was very friendly and typical of most Taiwan people, extremely kind people who go out of their way to help; he boosted my spirits enormously. Hilary Walker did come to find me, but I was sorted now and left her to continue her duties. Soon after it was the presentation and closing ceremony. I went on stage as winner of the open race and received a symbolic spinning glass trophy of a globe. My trophy was engraved "2006 IAU 24 Hours World Challenge, 1st place", sounded pretty good to me!

Then it was a back to the athlete's village to arrive by 4pm. It was 8am back home now and I rang Bill. What would he think? Last time I spoke to him I was about to withdraw, but he knew me better than I realised. "I knew you were too tough to drop out," was his response, but he was shocked at my distance. I had coped really well with the food and drink side, but had not coped well without the emotional support he gave me which was really essential for me to succeed.

Now it was back to the really serious stuff. Land's End to John O'Groats was gathering pace. There was much to do, constantly figuring out how to structure my race. How far to run per day? How much sleep to have? How many breaks in a day? What food to eat? How many crew members were essential? What duties should each crew do? How would the campervans follow me? How many sets of maps? How to follow my progress? What were the rules for ratification? This was all to take shape and consumed all my time with planning and alterations. Many of the questions would be answered with a trial. This would be good to see how practical my answers were. Three days should be sufficient to actually practise on the route to get used to the maps and know some of the course I was to run. Edinburgh was the biggest city to run through; so I wanted to run this as part of my trial.

But my plans were to be put on hold. The world record attempt was about to be postponed. I had not realised it, but I had picked up a serious injury in Taiwan. Two weeks later I was running the Redcar Half Marathon, but was getting pain from my lower calf, not initially realising it was my Achilles tendon. It wasn't until an ultrasound scan measured the extent of the injury and a Biodex machine at Teesside University demonstrated the weakness in my right Achilles that I realised how much trouble I was in. I had to take three months off running to rehabilitate and strengthen the Achilles. The date was put back from July to September, the last possible date before the cold and dark of the autumn months set in. To attempt a world record you must be in world record shape.

It was June by the time I was back racing and received an invitation to run in the Verdon Canyon Trail Challenge, Aiguines, France. This was a four day stage race with 7,000 metres of climbing in Europe's biggest canyon. Laurent Locke was the representative who kindly invited me. All I had to do was pay my expenses to get there. As it was such a lovely region, we used it as a holiday and spent a few days exploring and paddling up the canyon on the water before the race and getting used to running in the region. I was not back to full fitness, but running well. My performance in this event was day one, 10 kilometres, 57 minutes, 1st lady; day two, 25 kilometres, 4 hours 36 minutes, 2nd lady; day three, 45 kilometres, 9 hours 12 minutes, 2nd lady; day four, 35 kilometres, 6 hours 18 minutes, 2nd lady. I would class this as one of my toughest races ever. The heat was intense in the canyon, checkpoints a big distance apart and the terrain and steep climbs very slow going. As I had been invited to take part I put extra effort in to win this event and coming in 2nd place made me work all the harder. Winning races was sometimes easy if there were no challengers, but coming 2nd place was hard. It made me put in every ounce of effort to win, and if I could not win, it was because I was just not good enough. It certainly wasn't from not putting in enough effort. I had warned Laurent

I was not one hundred percent fit and he was aware of this and I put on a good show, but it was all good training for Land's End to John O'Groats. The hours spent running at full effort were ideal training. My ankles had been very weak on the rocky sections of the course and I lost much of my time on the descents. Twice we scaled from the top to the bottom of the gorge. Once we even climbed the sheer face of the cliff, suspended on ladders and clinging to ropes for safety. This was at the limits of my ability; the bit most people loved, I hated. There were only two British finishers in the race, myself and Luke Cunliffe. About sixteen British athletes had taken part. Many athletes ended up on drips or with heat stroke.

But home again and now it was time for the trial. I drove the entire course yet again, double checked all the maps, marking the parking places big enough for two campervans, checking every single mile, noting all road works (there was a big section in the South West that was obviously going to change with the construction of a new road). I was to carry out my trial in July, ironically the date I should have actually been attempting the world record. For the trial it was more about me and my strategy rather than involving all the crew, so there was to be just one campervan and Bill initially. Alan Young then volunteered to come with us, living not too far from where the planned trial was and we were to finish with a trip to the Orkney Isles which I had wanted to do for many years.

We met up near Lockerbie, at the house of the former world champion, Carolyn Hunter-Rowe. Alan was to leave his car there to collect on our return. Off to Moffat for the official start of the trial. I started at 7am, the same time as the event: four blocks of 4 hours of running with 1 hour breaks for food and rest and 5 hours overnight including only 4 hours sleep. The campervan was to leap-frog me, not directly follow me, as this was not allowed by the police. A cyclist could follow me and this was to be the routine. The cyclist carried supplies to keep me fuelled up and every 4 hours would take turns to swap over, Bill and Alan doing the duties on this trial. The routine worked well. I ran through Edinburgh and past Perth. Overnight was in Glenfarg. The trial proved very worthy for me to practice what I intended to do and to observe how Bill and Alan handled the crewing side of things. There was much to do: shopping, cooking, mix drinks, filling water, washing up, fuelling up, driving, repair bikes and much more. It helped me understand what I would feel like, how I responded to taking breaks. It answered many questions for me as the performer. This was not a general event that everyone could copy and do the same. It was my own individual plan, personal to me. It worked a treat and I was happy with my plans.

It was a wonderful trip following the planned route up to John O'Groats and we stopped overnight at Wick. From here we all used our bikes to hop across to Orkney mainland and then to the tiny island of Sanday to meet William Sichel and his wife Elizabeth. We were all made most welcome and kept busy the entire time touring the island. It is a unique way of life, away from industry and crime, but very remote with its own beauty. Although I loved the isolation this was just too far when you did need to travel and I could now understand why William always took so long travelling anywhere. I enjoyed racing most weekends and this would have been impossible on this little island and I am sure running around in circles on the island would not have got the best out of me. But each to their own; it was a great place to visit and see William's "Orkney Angora" business.

Back home and the plans had now reached critical stage. My entire race was mapped out: how far to run in each segment, the exact route to take, the crew all in place, a rota worked out for them, duties listed for each segment of 4 hours, publicity lined up, the schedule on my website so that supporters could follow and witness the attempt. I had a few sponsors lined up and the charity element for Asthma UK doing their bit. I was as ready as I would ever be and it was time to go. A great adventure into the unknown; it had taken me twelve years to summon the strength and determination from a little seed placed in a goal setting exercise at university to be brave enough to attempt this almighty challenge.

Chapter 10

The Biggest Challenge of My Life - Land's End to John O'Groats

The seed for this event had been planted many, many years ago. I had grown; strengthened both physically and mentally. I had planned the event meticulously, recruited a fantastic crew, had everything in place, had trained hard and specifically, had practiced with a trial and was fit and ready to take the plunge and attempt something far beyond anything before in my life. In real terms I was scared witless. I had gone highly public with this one, had some television coverage before-hand and the local papers were involved; my website was hitting thousands per week, all enthusiastic to see what happened. In reality I had no idea! When you have never done something and are going so far into the unknown there are many different things that can go wrong. I went public so that people could watch and witness the event. I published the route I was taking and where I expected to be every 4 hours. Guinness World Records do set down rules and regulations to follow: but it was easy to see these were not so stringent that you could not cheat. I went into great detail, far more than was required on my maps to prove where I was every few miles. I was rarely left alone with one crew member and especially not my husband Bill for fear of recriminations, so I could sleep at night and know that every single one of my crew would know exactly what I had done and could verify every painful step completed on foot.

Sandra Brown's record was still in place, the End to End record had only been broken twice in twenty-five years. I had known others try to run this, but I wasn't aware of anyone who had tried to break the world record in that time so it was a rarely run event. The planning and preparation for any such record attempt needed time and understanding. Sandra's record was 13 days, 10 hours and 1 minute. She was a far better race walker than me, but I was now a superior ultra distance runner. I could race walk and knew this would come in handy should I need it. I learnt from the Flora 1000 Mile Challenge how much easier walking was on the body compared to running, but this was distance against time and I did not have the luxury to walk this one. As always that clock would be ticking; would it be friend or foe? This was also not a direct race, there was just me in this race against the clock, to run from Land's End to John O'Groats faster than any female previously.

I had planned to run this in twelve days; a schedule was written to achieve this. If by some unbelievable chance absolutely everything went to plan this would be the result. But I was a realist and always knew that it would be incredible if everything did just slot into place and a magical twelve days was achieved. This plan had a built in "safety cushion". From my planned schedule to 13 days 10 hours and 1 minute meant I had a 34 hour cushion, 34 hours that I was allowed to slow down by to still take this record. At times this felt like a mountain of time, but again in reality this could go in a flash if something went dramatically wrong.

For this event I have made a diary of the exact journey, so you can follow with me with how many miles run, how much time each block of running took, what I ate, how I felt and exactly what happened. My schedule was a strict one. The first few days looked easy, I didn't know how continuously running so many miles every day would affect me. I tried to anticipate how I might be feeling, what my average pace would be. To control my pace I was not allowed to run any further than the schedule. I knew I would be fresh to start with and discipline and control was vital. I was capable of running 135 miles in 24 hours, but this was not a 24 hour race. I knew I would run further on the first couple of days and planned this into the equation. On the last day I thought I would be capable of running through the night and so planned extra miles for that occasion.

The Schedule

Day 1	A30 Rexon	84 miles	84 miles
Day 2	A38 West Monkton	70 miles	154 miles
Day 3	A466 Lower Redbrook	66 miles	220 miles
Day 4	A49 Leebotwood	68 miles	288 miles
Day 5	A573 Hermitage Green	66 miles	354 miles
Day 6	A6070 Kendal	68 miles	422 miles
Day 7	B7076 Ecclefechan	67 miles	489 miles
Day 8	A701 Penicuik	66 miles	555 miles
Day 9	A9 Dunkeld	66 miles	621 miles
Day 10	A9 Aviemore	66 miles	687 miles
Day 11	A9 Morangie	65 miles	752 miles
Day 12	John O'Groats	85 miles	837 miles

The planned schedule was to run in four blocks of 4 hours per day, interspersed with an hour's break for food, rest and showers. Overnight was a break of 5 hours with the hope of 4 hours sleep by the time I was washed, fed and undressed ready for bed and then had breakfast and dressed to go out again. There were five crew members on board most of the time; three crew members were in for the duration including my husband Bill Gayter; Ivor Roberts and Alan Young being the other two. On the first week husband and wife Andy Smith and Ramona Thevenet-Smith were to support, David Nicholson and Murdo McEwan to take over on their departure, a smooth turnover detailed in the plans. Two campervans were needed, one for me and Bill to sleep in and leap frog me the entire way. This was labelled as support van, to support me and collect the witness statements and adhere to the rules Guinness World Records had given. The second van, called crew van, was a larger campervan to accommodate the other four helpers, a large space for cooking, living and sleeping in. The crew van was responsible for cooking food for me and the crew, doing the shopping and other duties necessary to keep the event running smoothly. In reality the crew van leapfrogged each planned 4 hour block of running and was always prepared for me coming in for a break.

I was to be accompanied by a cyclist at all times; the bike had a basket attached to carry food and drinks required for the segment of running. Of the five helpers, one was allocated as a cook for the entire time and the other four each did one block of cycling, two blocks of driving and had one "rest block of 4 hours". This was calculated into a rota and the duties involved with each 4 hour block listed in a laminated sheet and stuck inside the campervans for all to read. My running schedule was also put in large font and stuck on the door for reference. Four sets of identical maps were used. One for each campervan: one for the cyclist on duty and one for myself. I was to do all the navigating myself, but the cyclist was there for support should I get tired or confused and should be double checking my every step to avoid going off-route and adding to the distance.

I wore a fluorescent yellow gilet, labelled with "Land's End to John O'Groats World Record Attempt," the charity involved and the sponsors. All money raised from this attempt was going towards Asthma UK. There were five sponsors involved. The only cash sponsor was EIM, the great Arki Busson who promised to pay the biggest expense of the campervans. Asics supplied shoes and kit, Mannatech supplied nutritional supplements, Expedition Foods supplied boil in the bag foods (quick and easy food to cook) and powdered sports drinks and Lucozade donated some bottled sports drinks and energy bars. Other expenses were mine.

Thursday 31st August

Alan picked up the campervan (crew van) close to where he lived in Dundee and drove to Guisborough, arriving late afternoon. It was enormous on the outside but the structure inside was not so good. The seating and cooking area was adequate and the bathroom massive with a tiny shower. This was not the most practical; more living space would have been better at the expense of the bathroom and I was not impressed by the tiny shower. I had hired a big four berth campervan, but everything inside had exactly that, four cups, four plates, four knives, four forks and so on. There were to be six of us but we would need more than six of everything and the pots and pans were not adequate either. I had anticipated this; so raided my cupboards to add to the equipment.

I had planned my food in advance, mainly high carbohydrate food and dried stuff such as pasta and rice that could be purchased in advance to save time with finding supermarkets and shopping. Bill and Alan transported the supplies from the garage where it had been stored into the crew van and I arranged it in the cupboards. Being a big campervan the cupboard space was plentiful.

Ivor was to arrive from Beverley later that evening and it was the first time Ivor and Alan were to meet. They were to have plenty of time to get to know each other on the long drive to Land's End.

Friday 1st September

First off was an early slot on BBC Radio Cleveland and the Evening Gazette took one last photograph as we left at 9am in the morning. Alan and Ivor were to drive via Stansted Airport to pick up Andy and Ramona. They lived in Surrey, but as they had generously given up a week of holidays to support me I needed to get them back quickly for work. So I had booked a flight back from Glasgow Prestwick Airport as it was easier for their return from Stansted afterwards. It also made picking them up less complicated finding an airport rather than a house while driving a large unfamiliar vehicle.

Bill drove me directly to Penzance where we were all booked in a campsite. We were originally to drive with the rest of the crew, but as it was such a long way there really was no point in adding to the journey. We had a good trip down and arrived at the campsite by 5pm. We were recommended a very nice eating place on the coast where we went for our final meal together. It felt a bit like the last supper; this was the last time I would eat alone with Bill for a couple of weeks.

The rest of the crew arrived shortly before 10pm. I had packed a mountain of sandwiches for them and a few snacks but they arrived hungry and Ramona cooked them a meal. We had a short gathering and we retired to bed.

Saturday 2nd September

We were up by 8am and after breakfast showed all the crew the food and drinks on board: a quick tour of both campervans so everyone knew what was stored and where and what food I would need. The weather was miserable, very windy and raining but mild. We then went to the lounge of the campsite for a briefing of the notes; so everyone was clear on how I expected the event to go. This took rather longer than expected but was good to ensure everyone had digested the information. It was also good for the crew to get to know each other. Although I knew everyone this week, the crew did not know each other. The only extra rule that the crew wanted imposed was on the toilet in the crew van. As on the Flora 1000 Mile Challenge this was a mobile event and emptying a dirty toilet was not always going to be practical and the crew wanted a "pee only" toilet. I adhered to this but my support van was the main van I would use and although I would use public toilets where practical, if I needed anything more than a pee then the support van (or namely Bill) would have to cope with the practicalities of emptying it.

It was soon time for lunch and last minute refuelling of the campervans and shopping trip for bread and milk for the next few days. We visited the local supermarket and also had lunch here. All food expenses were mine as the crew had dedicated the very precious commodity of time and commitment to helping me achieve my dream; this was a very small price to pay.

The afternoon was spent relaxing, signing cards to be given out en route and having one last massage from Bill. The last evening meal was jacket potatoes (freshly dug from my garden before leaving) with tuna and baked beans. Ramona was on cooking duties for the first week while the other four men Alan, Bill, Ivor and Andy were on cycling duties, in that order. The rota gave each crew man a cycling block, two blocks of driving duties and one rest period straight after the cycle ride. Bill and Andy were drivers of the support van and Alan and Ivor drivers of the crew van. I went to bed at 10pm.

Although I had massive confidence in all the build up to the event the last two weeks saw me dreading it and wondering what I had let myself in for. I knew this was going to be a long painful slog, but I began doubting that I really could do this; it was so much into the unknown. I was a very experienced ultra distance runner, Great Britain's best at 24 hours for the last ten years and I had confident ability at multi-stage races. In fact these were now my favourite races, but running almost non-stop for over twelve days at distances far beyond my previous achievements was very daunting. I felt now that I was just getting carried away with the event and was just following a course of action that I now didn't want to carry out. However, the event was organised, with seven different people supporting me, the campervans were booked and paid for; so there was no backing out now, I just had to get on with it.

In the previous month I had been busily breaking in over ten new pairs of shoes of various sizes from five up to seven, size seven were just too big to wear and I bought them on the off chance my feet should expand this much. Wearing in so many new shoes had given my left Achilles a little cause for concern and it was giving me grief in the last couple of weeks, but I had done no long distance stuff for the three weeks prior to this and had the biggest taper I had ever done to make sure there were no niggles.

DAY 1: Sunday 3rd September – 84 miles

The alarms sounded at 5:30am and were to remain at that time for the remainder of this event. Bill was up immediately and got into making

At Land's End with the official starter
Mayor Dennis Axford in misty conditions.

162

Ready Brek for breakfast. This was quicker and easier to make than porridge and was not as hot so I could eat it quicker. A shower and then off to Land's End. The crew stood in a line to greet me, all present and correct and ready for duties. They were a great bunch and gelled well without even having met each other. The weather was still miserable, wet, windy and misty and it was still dark. On arrival it was straight to the hotel to get the log book stamped and I immediately bumped into Dennis Axford, the Mayor of Penzance who had kindly agreed to officially start the event for me. What a lovely character! He seemed delighted to be here at this hour on a Sunday morning to see me on my way, assuring me it wasn't a chore but a pleasure; he had also brought his dog to have a walk along the coastal path after his duties were done. He convinced us that the weather would improve as we got further inland and it was often like this at Land's End. He was right.

The only other visitor at this hour of the morning was a photographer commissioned by the Evening Gazette. Photographic duties done, a small speech by Ivor, a shake of the hands from Dennis, watches and stop-watches co-ordinated, Alan did the count-down to the 7am start, with just me on the start line - yes, there is an official start and finish line at both ends of the country - and it was off into the mist and rain with Alan following on the bike. My epic venture was about to begin.

The wind was behind me as the run began; I was feeling my left Achilles but knew this would warm up at the sedate pace I was setting. My thoughts wandered for a bit, thinking of the almighty task ahead, 837 miles. How would I feel at half way? How would I feel at the finish? How many injuries would I have to battle? How badly would I be hobbling? I didn't expect this to go like clockwork, but when would the first incident strike? Would it be a massive blow or a slow grown repetitive injury? I somehow envisaged hobbling into John O'Groats at a pace of 2 or 3 miles per hour. Every night for weeks now I had gone to bed dreaming of this event, imagining how I would feel, the pain I would go through, the battered and blistered feet and tried to put this in perspective, knowing there would be pain, but somehow dealing with it, saying to myself "okay, this hurts, but it won't kill me, just stop me achieving my dream if I let it". I wasn't going to let anything stop me at any cost. This was a world record or bust. If I fell off the schedule beyond anything that I could pull back, then the record attempt was off. I was not here to waste people's time, I was not here to finish slower than fourteen days, the campervans were only booked out for that time and were due back on Sunday 17th September, so the crew knew exactly where they stood and would not be expected to carry on for days beyond the planned schedule just to say I had run from Land's End to John O'Groats. I would get no satisfaction from saying I had run or walked this like many others before me; this was a world record attempt, full stop. I didn't have any negative thoughts about this event, but it needed to be made clear to the crew where they stood should I fall off the schedule.

The first road was the A30, initially just a single carriageway, a quiet and gently undulating road. Alan was a bit behind me on the bicycle; Bill and Andy were in the support van leapfrogging every couple of miles. The crew van overtook going ahead to my first rendezvous at just over 23 miles with Ivor driving and Ramona passenger, beeping the horn and waving. This worked out well. On future days Andy would now be on his rest break but as Andy was still fresh for the start he joined up with Bill to help out and get the routine settled and watch how Bill carried out his duties for when he had to take over later. I had a bottle belt strapped to my waist, room for a three hundred and thirty millilitre bottle of drink, Bill had mixed the drinks and had a list of what to fill the basket with; Alan would give me the exact drink asked for on request. To start with I mainly had sports drinks alternated with water. All my drinks had Neovite added, a supplement to help recovery and prevent my body from break down and Ambrotose, a nutritional supplement from Mannatech.

My mind had drifted to the event as a whole, something I was only rarely to think about. I now had to concentrate on the task in hand: this was a 4 hour training run to be done as slowly as was practical and to finish with more in the tank. Each individual mile was marked on my maps and I could estimate where I was on the map to assess my pace. I wanted to finish close to the 4 hours which was approximately 10 minutes per mile. I tried to slow down and relax. It was gloomy and drizzling, nothing heavy but the temperature was mild; I was wearing tights and a long sleeved top beneath my yellow gilet. My gilet had two big pockets sewn into it, one for maps to use, the other for maps used and finished with. Map one covered the first 4 miles, no navigation to do, but I always kept an eye on them to tick off each mile. Just after 8 miles was the first roundabout. My map read: "At roundabout take third exit, right bend, left bend, at mini roundabout take first exit (left). At zebra crossing where cars can only go left (buses and taxis straight on) go straight ahead to shops. At Lloyds Bank round building with clock, go straight ahead (pedestrians only). At end of footpath bend right downhill on road, downhill to the Railway Station."

My maps were precise in detail, in places roads were named, as well as buildings, shops or significant observations around me marked. Navigation was very easy at this stage, as Penzance was not a big place, but descriptions such as these would be vital in the bigger cities that had to be negotiated. My memory was also still very fresh from having made the trips and drawing up these maps. There were two hundred and eighty individual A4 sides of maps, all numbered and covered in plastic sheets to protect them.

As I dropped down into Penzance we passed some people, the first we had met since leaving Land's End, I immediately checked that Alan was going to get a witness statement to check he was doing his job and saw him drop back. As part of the Guinness World Record rules witness statements had to be collected along the journey. A picture of me was on the statement book and witnesses had to sign to say where and when they had seen me along with their contact details so that this observation could be verified. I ran along the coast, as the weather was beginning to brighten up. The support van with Andy and Bill was at the coastal car park just before it joined the road at Longrock. Bill was collecting a statement and I was confused, as I had planned for the cyclist to collect the statements. However, the first obstacle had reared its head. Alan had been carrying these papers and in the damp conditions had already managed to get them wet. It was going to be more practical for the crew of the support van to collect the statements and keep them dry, so this was the first change to the plan. As long as the duty was carried out it didn't bother me who performed it, but I wanted to be kept informed.

At the next roundabout it was back onto the A30. There was a little more traffic now. Being a Sunday, I had not expected too much traffic and as it was almost the end of the school holidays I thought the traffic would not build up too much. Alan was still a bit behind; very little communication passed between us. I am never a big conversationalist on long runs anyway; I always like to drift away with my own thoughts. On the next section to Hayle, closely observing my maps and the distance covered had taken my mind off the overall big event and had got me focussed into "this 4 hour block." At Hayle I diverted through the little town, avoiding the bypass, and could remember getting soaked here on our cycling journey last year and drying out in a friendly tea shop eating toasted tea cakes. Then it was back to the A30 again where the noise of the traffic was beginning to build up and I reached the dual carriageway. I could see both campervans in the distance now.

At approximately 3 miles before hitting the first break of the day Bill rang ahead to confirm I was approximately half an hour from the meeting point so everything could be prepared. This was to be the routine before every break. This was vital just in case I was early or late depending on how that block of running had gone, easy when on fresh legs but sure to be useful as the event progressed. The routine was essential so that everything was in place and consistent. The first block of 4 hours was to be my furthest at 23.6 miles, I knew it would be hard to run slow at the start and was quite pleased when I arrived just 7 minutes early at 10:53am.

Warm kit ready, foot bath ready and pasta ready; even the weather was drying out now and I could change into a t-shirt. I dunked my feet in cold water on every break, initially as a preventative measure, as I knew from my 24 hour runs that my feet burning up could become a problem. I anticipated certain problems and did what was possible keep in good shape. The first meal of the day was always to be a pasta meal. I had packed all the packets of pasta with sauce for this, different flavours each day. Initially it was difficult for Ramona to estimate quantities with such a large group of people to feed; there was a hot cup of tea waiting along with bread ready buttered. Excellent! It all went like clockwork. The maps in my pockets were changed, used maps removed and next maps replaced them. Left pocket for new maps, right pocket for used maps. Andy did a quick interview with the video camera; Alan had started taking some of the many photographs that were again needed for verification with place names where possible in the shots.

The break seemed to last for a while and had to keep checking my watch. Crew had the duty to remind me 5 minutes before I was due out so that I could dress myself ready and put my shoes back on, trying to keep as close to the schedule as possible. As I had come in 7 minutes before the hour I tried to keep to exactly the hour to go out 7 minutes before the hour. The plan was that any accumulated extra minutes would result in extra sleep and not more miles.

I came in at 10:53am and left at 11:50am. Bill was on the bike now. Andy was driving the support van to keep overtaking me. Alan accompanied Andy; he was officially on his rest period now, but wanted to stay involved and he was also good company for Andy while the routine settled. Ivor now drove the crew van and Ramona was constantly on cooking duties. Andy got used to the leapfrogging well, using the same system as Bill. As for Bill on the bike, well we could hardly exchange a word as the traffic was so loud. I had known this from our cycle before and had hated this section even back then, but there was no alternative, this was the quickest and easiest route, the coast being far hillier and further. I just got my head down and had to get this section over with, but still control my running and not get carried away. The route was still along the busy A30, but at least there was a white line to run inside and so the traffic could easily overtake me without diverting out of lane. I jumped from a loud beep and shout as a couple who had been at the campsite overtook us on their way back home to Preston. The Achilles was feeling better than on the first run this morning. When I needed to exchange bottles with Bill I had to wait for a lay-by, as it was just impossible to hear each other and it was quite dangerous for Bill to come alongside, easier for him to stay behind. There were frequent lay-bys though and the clock seemed to tick reasonably quickly.

I likened my journey to a candle. At the start it was a tall, twelve feet high candle, over twice the height of me, each day was a foot long, each foot divided into three inch sections, each three inch section a 4 hour block. As I ran along I pictured the candle burning, all the three inch segments marked, burning and reducing three inches per block of running completed, each day a foot less high. By the time the candle burned out I should be at John O'Groats; half way at Penrith was marked.

The next stop was at Penhale near Indian Queens. We had again stopped here on our cycle ride; there was a McDonalds and a pub. I reached the stop very early, but the crew had rung ahead, so there was a rice meal for this break and everything worked like clockwork again. Pasta was to be on the menu for the first break of every day and rice meals for the second break, with different flavours again, but with tinned salmon or tuna added to improve the nutritional quality. This second session had been shorter than the first at close to 20 miles; it had taken 3 hours 20 minutes and I arrived at 3:10pm.

Leaving at 4:09pm it was now Ivor's turn to take over the cycling duties; Bill was on his rest break but accompanied Andy on his second drive of the day in the support van. Alan was now driving the crew van with Ramona as passenger. Back to the deafening A30 dual carriageway, and for the next 4 hours the only deviation from the A30 was to go through Bodmin. It was a relief to get away from the noise for a bit and I could actually talk to Ivor. The section just before Bodmin had been a source of worry to me, as when measuring the route I discovered there were major road works being carried out here building a new road and it was obvious the route was going to change. On the drive down we had checked the path of the road and amended the maps appropriately. Running this section there was a build up of stationary traffic and I didn't like breathing in the exhaust fumes. It wasn't that safe for Ivor staying on the inside of some the cars that liked to move into the kerb. It was down to single carriageway on this section. The route was quite undulating and there was a particularly stiff climb out of Bodmin by the castle. This was the first time that I stopped to walk, but as soon as the climb was over it was back to running. The light had faded as I reached the campervans just after Colliford Lake at 8pm. It was funny when I saw the campervans, as all I could see in the distance was a few yellow dots, the bright yellow gilets which were worn by all the crew and from a distance looked great and always made them easy to identify. They put me in mind of little working ants scurrying around preparing for the queen ant to make her appearance.

The third cooked meal of the day, or dinner, was to alternate between the Expedition Food meals and tinned steak and vegetable meals. Ivor was not a fan of the spicy chilli con carne and chicken tikka masala supplied by Expedition Foods and I didn't particularly want spicy food while running, so I opted for tinned stew for dinner. The rest of the crew enjoyed their evening meal and Expedition Foods were easy to prepare.

On leaving here at 9pm there were only 19 miles to cover in the last 4 hours. Bill was back in the support van doing his second driving duty, Alan was driving the crew van for the second time and Ivor was on his rest period. I had anticipated slowing down a bit by now: hence slightly fewer miles. I also knew that the route was gently rolling and expected this to drain a bit more energy. I had my head torch on and flashing lights attached to my bottle belt, front and back for traffic to see me. Andy also had the lights on his bike. I also put on a jacket as it was trying to drizzle again, but it didn't really amount to much. Andy had this horrible late shift, but he was a night shift person supporting my Flora 1000 Mile Challenge three years ago and had done such a good job that I had confidence in his ability to get me through this section of each day. He never let me down.

It was just head down and plod up the A30. I felt mildly fatigued on starting running, but it was easy to run and settle into a reasonable pace. The traffic was a little less now, but the road was featureless so it was difficult to follow my progress on the maps to see exactly how far I had run. The clock ticked really quickly and without knowing for sure exactly how far I had run there were the campervans up ahead in the distance. I walked the last 20 minutes or so, just to try to slow the heart rate down so I could sleep, as after 24 hour races I always find it difficult to sleep. The body works overtime during ultra distance events and takes a while to return to normal.

My plan during the day was to run each planned block of running; any time made up would simply mean extra sleep rather than run ahead of schedule, as this was to make sure I did not run too far in the early stages. I was pleased to arrive at the overnight stop at 18 minutes past midnight; this meant I would get around 5 hours rest, much longer than predicted for this first day. The routine was to return to the support van now. On all the stops so far my breaks had been in the crew van, having my meals with all the crew. Now it was time for sleeping, four helpers slept in the crew van and Bill and me in the support van. I sat on the bed, drank some tea while cooling my feet, got undressed, put compression socks on my lower legs and feet and lay down to sleep. But I didn't sleep, just tossed and turned all night until the alarm sounded. The clock dragged, ticked very slowly, I lay back in contemplation of the fact that I had accomplished my first day exactly on schedule; the candle was now eleven feet tall. It had been a good day. The crew had worked in harmony; all the duties had been carried out precisely. Everything had been ready for me the second I stepped into the crew van for my break. In reality I felt better than anticipated, hence being ahead of time for the 84 miles covered, but tomorrow was another day. I guessed I would feel the miles of today, but I had far less to cover, so was hopeful of completing everything as planned.

DAY 2: Monday 4th September – 70 miles (total 154 miles)

The alarm finally sounded at 5:30am, but I was still awake, just resting, waiting to go again. Bill made the Ready Brek and a cup of tea for me. By 5:45am breakfast was consumed and it was time for dressing and going to the toilet. I took off the compression socks; these were to stop my feet and ankles swelling overnight, another preventative measure. I weighed myself, again part of the routine, as if there was a sudden weight loss it would be an indication of dehydration. I had always been good at balancing my fluids but still didn't leave things to chance. I was a slim half a pound lighter. In the last few weeks with my big taper I had increased my weight marginally up to exactly 8 stones, 112 pounds (in metric this was nearly 52kg but the scales here were in imperial). Shoes were put back on. I had started in size five but now opted for half a size bigger. Although I didn't feel my feet had swollen at all, the long miles would have given them a slight battering and with the morning dawning sunny and bright I expected a warm day which could make the feet swell and bigger shoes would prevent squashed toes and blisters.

At 6am precisely I left the support van. I expected just Bill and Alan out of the campervans for a repeat of the previous day, but the entire crew was there to greet me and wish me on my way. I thought most of the crew would sleep in, with just Alan sneaking out to cycle with me. It was encouraging though and was wonderful to see the effort they were all putting in to support me. The A30 wasn't too bad to start off with, as it was quite early still. This was an hour earlier than yesterday's start to make use of the daylight hours. There was around 10 miles to run before I turned off the A30, then along the B3260 to Okehampton, reaching the centre around 8:30am. It felt great to get the A30 behind me and I had some nice quiet roads to settle down on. I was surprised that I was feeling really good and my legs didn't seem stiff at all. I continued along the quiet B3215, a pleasant change from the noise previously and could actually enjoy the countryside. Alan commented on reaching my first 100 miles close to the Countryman Pub. I stopped shortly after at 101 miles. It had become evident I was making up time again and I arrived early for my first break at 9:25am, just over 17 miles complete. The pasta was waiting and I was surprised to find that all but one of the crew tucked in heartily: pasta at 9:30am! Andy said it was on the instructions; so he was just carrying out his duty. Poor crew! Bill and Alan did a good job of polishing off any excess that Ramona cooked, still trying to get the portion sizes down to what was required, but better too much than too little.

Back out for 10:25am, onto the A3072 for a short section, turning off after Bow onto minor roads. The support van bumped into a couple of bee keepers who witnessed my run. It turned out that they had witnessed Barbara Moore completing her world record Land's End to John O'Groats many years ago in the Billy Butlin Challenge, an amazing co-incidence. The route was still very peaceful countryside by Coleford, crossing straight over the A377 to a minor road skirting north of Crediton. I met several cyclists on this section, all going on their way to John O'Groats and all planning on getting to John O'Groats more slowly than me! I was now drinking GlycoSlim, milkshake replacement meals from Mannatech. I alternated these with water, as they had far more energy and nutrition in them than sports drinks and I also wanted to keep up a good level of calcium as stress fractures were a serious risk during this event and would be the one injury that could curtail the journey. The massive climb out of Crediton loomed and Bill had drawn the short straw of cycling this section. I had marked this on my maps as "steep climb". I walked this section. Yet again I remembered cycling this section and crawling up hill with the weight of the trailer, but it went quicker than anticipated. Funny how when you know you have a big climb ahead and think it will take forever and really be draining that, because you know it is coming, it doesn't feel half as bad as expected. I got quite a surprise when the campervans appeared in the distance shortly after Stockleigh Pomeroy on

Passing Bow, on day 2 of LEJOG. © Alan Young.

the A3072. Ivor came out of the crew van to greet me, always with a smile and pleasant words. I had again completed this well ahead of time arriving at 1:51pm. The time and that clock were flying today.

Precisely an hour later I was out again on the steep downhill and onto the A396 to Tiverton. Ivor was with me now and, after the minor roads to Halberton, we turned onto the Grand Western Canal Towpath. The support van had to leave me here to rejoin at White Ball on the A38. It was a really pleasant afternoon, warm and sunny. As much as I really enjoyed this section being off road, peaceful and pleasant, the seats were inviting. I walked some sections of this feeling quite drowsy. I pictured myself lying on one of the benches, resting, catching up with sleep missed last night and soaking up the heat from the sun, but I had to snap out of it; there was no excuse for walking and enjoying this. I was on a mission, there was a job to be done and I needed to focus.

Ivor was good company. He didn't complain about having to get off the bike and walk. It was hard to cycle at a walking pace; so he walked with me, pushing the bike. It was the most tired I had felt so far, not really stiff in the legs, just sleepy tired and looking forward to my next break. This block of running had taken me the longest so far and it was the first time I had taken the allocated 4 hours. Can you imagine my disappointment when I emerged onto the A38 at White Ball to realise the campervans were not at the rendezvous point? Ivor quickly rang the crew who insisted they were at the allocated point at White Ball. Having put fine detail on the map, I could pin-point myself exactly, but I didn't know where they were. Were they parked on the route ahead or the route behind? Bill was first to respond to jump into the support van and find me, by which time I thought it best to continue to the next possible parking place at a pub a little further on. They had obviously stopped too early and not pin-pointed themselves exactly which was possible at this place. There were many places which were featureless where this was not possible, but as this one was easy to identify I felt I had a reason to be upset. As the support van was the first to arrive, I quickly got in and cooled my feet. I had dinner in the support van as opposed to the crew van where I was normally with all the crew. I was fuming. My crew had let me down. It was the first time I had really needed them to navigate correctly and they let me down. It was minor in the real scheme of things, but I had detailed the maps so precisely that this should not have happened. There were only a few places where the campervans were not to follow my exact steps and in future these needed to be scrutinised a lot better to ensure I would pass by them. The helpers sat in the crew van to have their dinner and left me alone. I knew they were all doing their best, but just as I had lost concentration so had they. My dinner was another tin of stew. Bill tried to calm me down and make sure I wasn't rude to the crew. I was angry and feeling let down. The duties detailed exactly who was responsible and I wanted words, but right now was not the time and Bill was right, I had to remain calm. It was obvious all the crew were upset by the incident and I needed to keep up morale, it was up to me. If I looked happy the crew would be happy, if I was upset it would upset the crew.

I had arrived at 7:07pm having taken 4 hours 17 minutes to complete the last 18 miles. I emerged from the support van with a smile on my face at 8:08pm. Problem over, it was on to the next section along the A38. It had only been a minor hiccup, but, now this problem had been identified, I was confident that more attention would be given to make sure this would not happen again. I was still running ahead of time from the earlier blocks of the day; so managed the first half an hour without my head torch.

I surprised myself by picking up the pace quite well. After having a walking spell with Ivor I wondered if this was the point where I was going to start slowing down and tiredness was going to take a hold, but the running felt quite easy to start with. I bypassed Wellington and was just approaching Taunton when I became aware of others around. Rob Wood had come out to join me, an ultra runner from Taunton who had said before hand he wanted to run a section with me, but all the contact had been left in the hands of Bill and whoever was in the support van with the mobile phone. I had completely forgotten about Rob, last meeting him in a 24 hour race at Tooting Bec the previous year. His time with me proved very valuable, as, although my maps through Taunton were very detailed along footpaths and canal paths, in the dark it was hard to identify the paths. Rob, however, knew the route like the back of his hand and I was grateful for his support and local knowledge that saved me valuable minutes reading maps and trying to navigate. I also enjoyed having different company. I wasn't too sure how I would be, but it gave me a break in some ways as well as different conversation and took my mind off the event for just a short while. Rob peeled off after running most of the section with me as I emerged back onto the main road north of Taunton, the A3259.

My running became intermittent again as I had started to walk and run and realised this time I was running out of energy. So I sent Andy ahead to ask Bill to prepare a potato snack (similar to pot noodles where you just add boiling water to a pot of mashed potato). I walked and ate this and it did the trick: I was soon back running to end the second day on the A38 after West Monkton finishing at 11:44pm. It was even earlier than the previous day. I had felt so tired earlier that I was sure I would sleep soundly. Alas, I didn't, I just tossed and turned again. But the candle had continued burning while I had run and, although I was still looking up to it, the days were reducing.

DAY 3: Tuesday 5ᵗʰ September – 69.8 miles (total 223.8 miles)

The usual alarm clock, the usual breakfast, the same weight ritual done, it was back on the road at exactly 6am. It had been so mild the last couple of days I decided to put shorts on for the first time today. It was to be another fine, sunny day. I could not stop the clock; the time just flew along the A38 through Bridgewater and Highbridge and the first 16 miles were over in just 3 hours and 2 minutes. Pasta was now at 9:02am and the crew were still following instructions and eating at this time in the morning. Ramona was now getting to grips with the portion sizes. I had provided five packets per meal but this had been far too much and a meagre three were needed. Bill and Alan usually managed seconds to finish off any leftovers; nothing went to waste. Ivor usually abstained at this time in the morning preferring just bread and jam; I think I would have done the same. I also had to get the scissors out to cut my first blister today, the first of many that I knew I would get, but these are never a problem, just a bug bear, and would never hinder this event.

It was day three and everything was sailing along. After a couple of bad spells the previous day the early morning session had been amazing. I usually walked for the first 10 minutes to wake the body up and have a warm up before gently breaking into a trot. The next section was great, another cycle path along the Strawberry Line, avoiding the roads and nice underfoot. Bill was with me as usual for the second session of the day and I got my first small niggle here, high up on the shin in the anterior tibialis muscle. I sat on a bench while Bill gave it a quick rub and was to have a better massage on this on my next break. The route emerged at Congressbury onto the A370 to Flax Bourton. This was my first error on the maps, the parking area marked half a mile away was actually one and a half miles away (later I made one mistake the other way around to even things up!). I had the next break at Flax Bourton where I turned off the A370 on a minor road to Failand. I completed this 18 mile section in 3 hours 36, minutes arriving at 1:48pm for the usual rice and salmon meal. Bill massaged my shin a bit more thoroughly and I was surprised how much it improved for my next block.

I was most impressed with my next section. When we cycled this we had remained on the A38 and gone through the middle of Bristol which had been a nightmare: big busy roads to cross and miles of heavy traffic, roundabouts and traffic lights to negotiate. My route was to avoid Bristol completely but it did involve some proper footpaths. I had gone back and measured this with a surveyor's wheel on the bike. The next block was with Ivor. He was great company in the afternoons and I settled into a chatty mode with him. Each part of the day seemed so different. The morning was always quiet with Alan, then Bill and I had the odd bit of banter. Ivor joined me in the afternoon for a really good chat and then Andy again in the evening where I settled down to being a bit quieter again.

We set off at 2:50pm. I was now into size six shoes. We trundled along the footpaths to Easton in Gordano. Ivor had quite a tough section now, very undulating on minor roads and footpaths, one very muddy footpath up and over stiles with the bike, but the exhilarating experience of crossing the bridge next to the M5. The rough section resulted in the bike getting its first puncture. A quick ring ahead to Andy in the support van for the next possible meeting point to swap bikes. There were two bikes in anticipation of this occasion, as it was easier to swap bikes; so the person on duty in the support van had time to fix it and I didn't have to be without a cyclist. Poor Andy had never fixed a puncture in his life; so learnt on the hoof and there was the original bike ready for Ivor a few miles down the road. I found this amazing, what lengths the crew would go to. Had I been a member of crew I am sure I would have left it for someone else to deal with. It was great running up the Severn Way alongside the estuary; we could see the campervans ahead for miles as well as the bridges.

The last break of the day was just short of the original Severn Bridge. This was the first time I noticed the duck tape holding together the back light and panel that had been broken on the crew van. I found it very annoying that I had not been told and had to see it for myself. Nobody wanted to tell me anything because they didn't want to worry me. This just frustrated me, something like this wouldn't affect my running, but I needed to know what was happening and didn't like being kept in the dark.

This section had been a break from the norm, with the footpaths, bridges, coastal section and then grass tracks and stiles. Evening meal was on arrival at the A403 junction with the Severn Way, a fraction before the Severn Bridge. It was steak and tinned vegetables for all of us tonight; I had second helpings for a change. The last 17.5 miles had been completed in 3 hours and 1 minute; the change had done me good and I was well ahead on time today. This was the first time I was to have a shower. I had forewarned the crew from the last break to ensure the water was hot and the water tank full. The shower was tiny compared to the size of the bathroom area. I am not a big person but it was hard not to hit the doors of the curved enclosure. I had anticipated the water tank not being large; so showered quickly. Even so, the water turned cold shortly before I finished! I had not wanted a long shower anyway, as time was miles and I tried to do this all within my hour's break, but I wished I had done a bit more homework inspecting the inside of the campervan I had hired.

It was Andy's turn for the last section of the day, leaving at 7:55pm and running over the Severn Bridge to Chepstow, quite a landmark and well out of the South West and into Wales. The light was fading as we crossed the bridge and I was feeling rather full from having eaten too much with my second helpings, but the weather was surprisingly mild and not as windy as expected. The shower had refreshed me immensely: it was wonderful to feel clean. On reaching the support van the other side there was Ann and Norman Wilson waiting. Norman was coach to many ultra athletes and on the selection committee. He stayed for a couple of hours leapfrogging with the support van offering encouragement, as well as

trying to scare the living daylights out of us with his spooky howling!
It was great to see such people, to know they had made an effort to see me,
as it was a long lonely run in the real sense. A bit like the Flora 1000 Mile
Challenge, bang in the centre of London but cocooned on a bus. Here
I was out in the great wide world, but completing a long lonely quest to
achieve a dream. I think he was quite surprised at just how well I was
running and I must admit I was quite amazed at myself. Today had gone
really well until now and nothing really bad had come up on the trip so far.

I remembered cycling the next section along the A466 from Chepstow the
previous year and it was one of our favourite sections through to Tintern
Abbey. We had stopped here for a massive cream tea and were hardly able
to get back on our bikes again. Running through in darkness was also
wonderful; the Abbey was all lit up and a spectacle to see. I then had a
choice of routes. There was the off-road path on Offa's Dyke or I could
follow the undulating road. My feet were beginning to get hot again and
this was going to be my last opportunity to run off-road for some time, so
I decided to take the Offa's Dyke route. I am not entirely sure it was the
best decision, as darkness had set in and the grassy path was covered in dew
and soaked my feet. It certainly felt good to be off the tarmac but it also
slowed me down significantly and I had to walk as the surface was quite
uneven in places. I was also not able to see that well under the head torch.
Bill was in the support van and becoming concerned at the time it was
taking me to reach the bridge where I hit the road again. He had tried to
phone Andy, but the signals weren't connecting. I had also opted to run a
little further tonight, as far as Lower Redbrook, to reach a better parking
place for the campervans. This would shorten the next morning's first
block of running. Bill was relieved to see us when we emerged to cross the
River Wye. Bill went immediately ahead to Lower Redbrook for the
overnight stop on one side of the river and Andy cycled the gravel track
with me on the opposite side of the river along the Wye Valley Walk. After
the last section of walking I started running well again and crossed over the
bridge just short of where the campervans were parked. We reached here
at 40 minutes past midnight. The last 18 miles had taken 4 hours 45
minutes. Surprisingly I still struggled to sleep again! But as usual I thought
about that candle burning brightly. It remained above head height, still a
long way to burn, but it was lowering nicely. At night it returned to a glow,
almost on hold until the running began again.

DAY 4: Wednesday 6th September – 64.2 miles (total 288 miles)

Off for another 6am start in the sunshine. Along the A466 and I arrived
in Monmouth within half an hour of setting off. David Davies, MP for

Monmouth jumped out of a car and joined me. There had been several telephone calls trying to establish the time I would run through Monmouth, co-ordinated by Asthma UK so that David could join me. He took me through the centre and out onto the A466. For anyone that knows this route there is a big hill that climbs out of Monmouth. David ran this section with me before turning off to make a circular route to run home. He had a couple of young children; so was up early anyway. The crew were trying to take photographs and video us, as was an official photographer. David was very chatty and said he would follow my progress with great interest. I was honoured to have someone of high prominence join me at this unsocial hour at the exact time I was running through. For me, chatting to someone different provided a short break from focussing on the run.

The route ahead was still quite undulating and the first break was near a place called Wormelow Tump, a tiny village with a shop, but what a welcome! The people from the shop all came out to cheer me on and as I reached the campervans there was another group opposite shouting and cheering. Apparently the crew had filled up with water at the industrial unit there. I was still running extremely well and came in very early at 8:50am, but I had run 3 miles less this morning due to the extra run last night. The crew were now getting used to eating pasta at this time in the morning. I wondered if they would keep it up when they got home!

The quick start to the day was useful, as during the second run of the day I was to hit a problem. Exactly an hour after arriving for my break I set off again at 9:50am. As usual at this time it was Bill who was on the bike with me and we soon joined the A49 to hit Hereford. It was mid-morning now and road works had left a long tail back of vehicles heading into the centre. I could smell the exhaust fumes as I overtook the traffic. I was fighting for fresh air, but the route exiting Hereford was just as bad as traffic was also queued up here as well. Unsurprisingly my asthma started to affect my breathing and I was forced to sit down and take my medication, as the wheezing got worse and I began to feel a bit light headed. A passing cyclist had seen me sitting down with the support van ahead of me and informed the crew I wasn't running and looked as though I was in trouble. Andy was on duty in the support van and rang back to check I was okay but I wasn't far from him by this stage.

There was little point in sitting around for long, as the only way to improve was to get out of the congestion and fumes that were causing the asthma. I walked on slowly and finally escaped the pollution but I was unable to run; my lungs could not manage any extra exertion. There was another big climb shortly afterwards to Queen Wood Country Park. I even had to walk the downhill section here and all the way to the end of the block planned. The route then diverted off the A49 onto the minor Hereford Road. Not surprisingly this section took far longer than the planned 4 hours, but as I had time in hand from the morning's run, I could afford to take my hour's break. On taking the break the crew had asked for permission to park and were amazed to hear that the garage chosen for parking had already heard about me running through the area on the radio; so were more than happy to oblige with parking. That section of just over 18 miles had taken 4 hours 20 minutes, ending at an Industrial Estate just before Leominster.

The next section with Ivor was still a painfully slow one. Whether it was because of the knock-on effect of the asthma or of being on my feet a bit longer, I am not sure. I still struggled to run, my feet were also burning up more and the clock starting ticking very slowly again. I progressed though; the candle was still burning. On through Leominster: onto the B4361. We did have a short rain shower just before Ludlow, where Andy came back in the support van to check if we needed our jackets; it was only a short shower; so we refrained. The gilet was reasonably waterproof anyway; so it was only my arms that got a little damp.

This had been my favourite place when we cycled the route the previous year, a wonderful little town with superb food stops. Unfortunately I did not arrive here at the right time for eating. The route was now out by the race course on a minor road. I was struggling more and more and could not get into my proper zone for running; it was just too much effort and I was out of puff immediately.

It was during the afternoon sections that I began to eat more. My morning weight had been stable: in total I was one pound lighter than before I started. Ramona would make up sandwiches cut into quarters for me and I would slowly nibble these as the day wore on. I would usually eat more during the afternoon session with Ivor. I tried intermittently to run, but the next 18 miles took even longer than the previous 18 miles, arriving 5 hours 7 minutes later at 7:18pm.

There was a big surprise waiting for me at a tiny little village called Onibury. It seemed as though the whole village had come out to welcome me, along with Donna Rourke, from the nutritional product sponsors Mannatech. I was signing cards for all the onlookers and Donna came in the crew van for a quick chat while I ate my food and cooled my feet.

There was much more ice in the cool box now, as I had felt the water was not getting cool enough with the one pack of ice cubes that was being put in per stop. The crew had now purchased ice from the supermarket and this certainly froze my feet. It also froze me, as the temperature had dropped significantly and I went into shivering mode and had to be bundled up in a pile of blankets and given more hot drinks. The crew used to overheat when I arrived, needing all the doors shut to prevent me cooling down. I would put extra clothes on immediately, while some would leave the crew van as it was too warm for them.

The shivering fit over; it was time to dress up in plenty of kit and a woolly hat to continue into the darkness. I had begun dreading these sessions now. I hated running in the dark, tripping and stumbling over the debris in the road that I could not see properly. It was that time of the year when conkers were falling off trees and the councils doing the last bit of hedge cutting for the summer which created much debris. I was only delayed by 10 minutes by the shivering episode and set off 70 minutes later at 8:28pm, almost immediately back onto the A49.

This was a very busy road, but as it was getting later there was less and less traffic. Again I could remember cycling this section and hating the noise and traffic, but this was probably the only advantage of taking longer to get here. My feet were now much cooler, the air much fresher and I began running well again after the last two very slow sections where I was barely able to run. I was soon undressing again; the hat came off first, then the jacket. The highlight that night was the amazing response from supporters. There were several pockets of people waiting in the street to cheer me on with flags and shouts of encouragement; what a lift! It left me with a smile on my face.

The darkness continued and eventually I started running out of energy again. Andy rang ahead to get Bill to make another hot potato snack up and I reached him just as it was made. This was crew members working in harmony: exactly what you want when you need it. It was also an appropriate time, as it wasn't that far from the overnight stop and I didn't have to go too far before the campervans appeared just after Leebotwood. I had run well in the last session of the day and made considerable time up to stop at 11:34pm. The last section, a bit shorter at 14 miles, had taken 3 hours 6 minutes. I crawled into bed again after the post running routine. Every night I laid my head on the pillow I would say to myself, another day done; another day nearer achieving my dream. I was still going, still running and the dream was still alive. Tonight, amazingly, was the first night I slept properly and didn't wake up until the alarm sounded.

DAY 5: Thursday 7ᵗʰ September – 66 miles (total 354 miles)

Exactly 6am again and I was out of the support van, Alan waiting with his bike as usual and the crew all there to cheer me off again on another day of this adventure. This was now my fifth day of running and I was surprised I was continuing running so well. I never dared to think of the task ahead and would just focus on each 4 hour block. I think the crew were getting used to my mentality now. I never wanted to know how far I was running each day or where I would finish. I just needed to know what was in the next planned block of running. Although the support van and the cyclist had maps, I always carried my own maps and did all the navigation myself, constantly looking at my maps and counting down the miles until the next stopping point. Then it started all over again, just another 4 hours. This morning's run went well again, hitting the outskirts of Shrewsbury around 7:30am. I had spent ages finding the best route though here and again had some intricate detail on my maps, with the best route avoiding some of the congestion and following a footpath by the river, out by the station and now out on the A528, continuing my northwards journey.

The first run in the morning had always been planned to be a bit shorter, the second and third runs a bit longer and the last run a bit shorter to walk before going to bed. The reason for the first run being shorter was to allow for walking first thing on getting started when I was stiffer to avoid injuries, but in practice when I got running this was always a good section where I could run well before my feet started burning up. In hindsight I would now probably increase this section, but the schedule had been done in advance and I didn't want to change a plan that was working so well. The next stop was at Harmer Hill, 15.8 miles run in 3 hours 7 minutes, including lots of time wasted trying to cross busy roads in Shrewsbury at rush hour.

The weather was much cooler today and I kept my tights on. Bill left with me at 10:08am on the next section of the B5476 though Wem and Whitchurch. There was a succession of mini roundabouts here and the maps were again finely tuned to direct me correctly; so I safely navigated my way out to the A49 again. The breathing problems of yesterday behind me, I was back running again. In real terms my legs were not that bad. I felt mildly fatigued and getting up and down the steps into and out of the campervans I looked a sight, but in general, once running I was pretty good at maintaining pace, occasionally walking the odd steeper gradient. My feet, however, were another story. The size six shoes had been required a while ago, and although I didn't feel I needed a bigger size, my feet were more regularly starting to burn and became more and more tender as the block of running continued. They would really hurt for the first 10 to 20 minutes on starting a block, while I grimaced and suffered the pain to start running; then once I'd been running for a while the pain from the blisters would subside.

The third section of the day was not so good, running along the busy A49 with a few wagons getting quite close. At one point, where a lorry was overtaking me slowly, a car turned into its path and the lorry screeched to a halt. The car stopped too and had to reverse out of his way. I hated this section and was relieved when a footpath came up to feel safe again; there were quite a lot of conkers on the path that made running quite difficult. My feet were beginning to groan again and getting very hot. Every time they really heated up I seemed to get a couple of new blisters and my feet were looking a little battered now, with several blisters and some getting a bit ugly. In addition, my little toes were rather crushed as my feet had expanded. Size six shoes were the biggest that I had requested Asics to supply: I am not sure they really believed me when I asked for different size shoes, but they did oblige with four pairs of different sized shoes. I had a short reprieve from the A49 on the quiet country lanes that avoided Tarporley, slightly more undulating but worth the effort and the route was also slightly shorter going anti-clockwise around the little town. It was a relief to stop at Cuddington as my feet were in desperate need of freezing water. That section of 19 miles was completed in 4 hours 14 minutes, arriving at 6:50pm.

I had made very good time today and there was still some daylight left as I left for my last block of running at 7:54pm. I was not looking forward to the next section; it was just a big conglomeration of places from Warrington through to Preston and I was looking forward to getting out of here and on to Kendal where Lakeland beckoned and half way would be achieved. The route started off not too bad, but it soon deteriorated. I was trying to run on pavements where possible, but the darkness and conkers and rubbish were making me stumble and I was becoming very frustrated. To top it all Andy got another puncture on the bike. The hedges had recently been trimmed and cycling over the trimmings was to cause a lot more punctures. Luckily Bill wasn't far away with the replacement bike. The built up areas were quite quiet at this time of the night and roads were not too bad to negotiate and cross, but had to keep a close eye on the maps. Andy was always reassuring me that he was following the maps and keeping me right. I always followed the maps myself, but this was helpful for me just in case I made an error. As the night progressed, the inside of my left quadriceps muscle (front thigh muscle) was gently pulling at me, probably caused by twisting and turning over the millions of conkers trodden on. I decided to run on the road now, as this was beginning to hurt and the roads were much smoother than the pavements and there was less hedgerow debris. At one point I decided to stop and get Bill to give my leg a quick massage, as it really was beginning to tighten up. It didn't seem to do much good though and I was aware I was not running smoothly.

As I ran through Warrington a fire engine overtook me with firemen waving at me. They were probably thinking what was this idiot up to at this time of the night, running all over the roads. Further down the road I discovered that I couldn't have been more wrong! They were standing outside their fire station offering me sports drinks and the use of their facilities should I need them, such as toilets, showers, an overnight stay or a rest. Several big handsome hunky men on offer and I had to graciously decline for the sake of my husband and the confined space of my support van just a few miles down the road! They encouraged me on my way and promised to follow my progress.

I needed to get to bed. The quicker I finished; the more sleep I'd get. On reaching the outskirts of Warrington, just crossing the roundabout with the M62 we heard sirens coming at us. It was our friendly firemen on their way to a call, lights flashing, and all I could see were hands waving at me and big smiles. I was smiling too at this stage, as now it was only a mile to my bed and I was feeling tired with the quadriceps muscle (quad) giving me more grief. I was now walking to give it a break. There was a small diversion from the A49 onto the A573 now to stop near Hermitage Green. I was relieved to finish and was given a proper massage on the quad from Bill before going to bed. If I was going to get an injury this was the best time to get it, when I could officially stop and have a bit of rest. It was my earliest night so far, reaching the support van at 11:17pm, but it was still probably mid-night by the time I had my massage, cooled my feet and drank my Horlicks, but I slept well. I lay my head on the pillow again, reflecting. Well, I had had a few problems now: an asthma attack, my feet were getting sorer, my quad pulled, but I was still going. Tomorrow I wouldn't be far off half way and I had still not fallen off my schedule at all. The fact that I should have finished the day at 1am said it all. I had been cruising, but all was about to change.

DAY 6: Friday 8ᵗʰ September – 60.5 miles (total 414.5 miles)

It was an even colder start this morning. I had my woolly hat on for the usual 6am sharp start and my feet were very tender to begin again.

The quad was also grumbling at me still. I finally succeeded in running again after half an hour of walking and was just approaching Golborne when I was aware of a runner alongside me. I assumed he was a runner out for his morning training, so, as I turned to say "Hello", I got a shock: it was Martin Dietrich, a local runner who lives near Great Ayton, just a few miles down the road from my home in Guisborough. He was working in the area that day and had made a special effort to come out early to see how I was getting on and run a short section with me. It was little efforts like this from people that really made me feel special. He had been following my progress on the website and was able to follow the route well enough to find me. At times you just feel you are out there against this big time barrier, running distances beyond what people think is possible and no-one knows you are out there. But a little effort from someone and you know people are thinking of you. Thank you Martin; it was a very nice surprise.

After a good chat Martin had to retrace his steps. He was running in the Robin Hood Marathon at the weekend, his first road marathon for many years. I checked the results after I got home and was delighted to see he got a massive personal best. As the morning continued I was feeling the quad more and more. It really felt as though it was twisting in knots after a couple of hours and it was getting very painful; so I was becoming somewhat concerned. After going over a railway bridge approaching Wigan and the A49 it really started seizing up and going into spasm and I had to walk. Bill was not far away and I decided to get some more treatment on it. He massaged it again while we were parked in some church grounds. The vicar came out and duly signed the witness statements. It had been a joke with the crew that they were going to get a vicar and a policeman to sign the statements! Alan took his picture next to the support van and he wished me well. I hoped he was going to pray for me, as at this stage I needed all the help I could get!

I continued walking. This was hurting. I decided I would now walk to the end of the block, to give the muscle a break, a rest from the immense workload it had been forced to complete. I had to stop again and tried a compression bandage to see if this would take some pressure off the injury. I was making very slow progress now and felt very uncomfortable. I completed a very steady walk while the clock ticked too fast and eventually arrived at the planned rendezvous point at 10:36am; over half an hour late. The first block of the day had always been my best, always the one I picked up most time on. Those 14.6 miles had taken me 4 hours 36 minutes; that averaged 17.2 minutes per mile compared to the 12 to 14 minute miles I had been averaging. I immediately decided this was a major problem; it wasn't going to go away quickly and I knew I would have to walk for the rest of the day. I changed my strategy to taking shorter breaks to try my hardest to keep as close as possible to the schedule. My schedule was to finish in twelve days but I always guessed I would slip off this demanding schedule. However, I never knew when this would be. I had a 34 hours to play with. In my mind it was six blocks of running that I was allowed to lose.

I set off a mere 32 minutes later at 11:08am instead of having an hour's break. Bill was with me now and the route a little undulating, it was on the downhill that the quad would really spasm and I was reduced to bad hobbling on these sections to dampen the pain. After a few miles we hit the edge of Preston where the support van was about to leave, as the route was along a cycle path. Just before the cycle path I had to go under a motorway bridge carrying the M65. The steep descent made my quad completely seize up and I ground to a halt. I had to stop in agony. Bill tried to massage it. It didn't help. I hobbled around the corner to where the support van was. This was a very worrying moment. I was nearly half way from Land's End to John O'Groats and barely able to walk. My mind was saying I could take a complete day off and still have 10 hours to play with, but the thought of pulling out never even entered my head.

In the support van Bill suggested I remove the bandage, put on a pain relief patch and take some ibuprofen. I had not even thought about pain killers; pain was just something I knew I had to put up with. The pain relief patch felt much more comfortable than the compression bandage and I did take a couple of ibuprofen tablets, the first pain relief I had taken since the start. I also put on compression shorts to support the quad as it was a beautiful warm sunny day now. Bill also suggested maybe taking a rest for the remainder of the 4 hour block or even possibly the rest of the day to give the muscle a chance to heal, as there was still plenty of time in the bank. This suggestion was immediately rebuffed. As long as I could continue and cover a reasonable distance in 4 hours I felt I needed to continue, as I never knew what other unpleasant things might be lurking around the corner waiting to pounce. Each mile further was a mile nearer the finish line. My 4 hour race continued, the candle continued to burn.

I was able to walk on again. I was relieved to still be on my way. The next section was dead flat along a cycle path that was an old railway line; this was the perfect surface to walk on. My mental maths was busy now, adjusting the times in my head if I had to walk from here to the finish. Could I still break the world record? In reality I had started this block at 11:08am; that was only 8 minutes behind the schedule. I had been running faster than the schedule; so even if I slowed down a few minutes behind the schedule with 30 minute breaks to minimise time lost, I could even finish in twelve days, but I really doubted this would be the case.

I emerged from the cycle path into the busy centre of Preston; to my surprise the support van had managed to park accurately on the route in the middle of Preston on a quiet road on double yellow lines. The traffic warden had come up and even allowed Andy and Alan to stay there after they explained the reason and gave him a card (I had postcard-sized pictures of me on flyers explaining the Land's End to John O'Groats world record attempt). My support crew were not needed, but it was nice to see them and the effort they were making to ensure I was progressing. Leaving Preston and reaching the A6 was a nice feeling. This big section of built up areas was now behind me and I was now heading into quieter places. I always felt the first half was the worst for built up areas and everything would be much better after Penrith. I made the planned stop just after Bilsborrow at 4pm.

By the time I left at 4:32pm I was now half an hour behind schedule and knew I would probably have to fall behind a little today. The bike was now ditched by Ivor, as I knew I could only walk and it was pointless walking with a bike. Ivor was a great chatterbox and I enjoyed walking along chatting with him. It took my mind off the quad, which only gave twinges when going downhill and stepping off kerbs. I had first met Ivor at a 24 hour race many years ago and was always bumping into him at races. He had offered his services back in January at a race called the Tandem. He had heard about my plans from another friend and as he had taken early retirement from teaching he had the time to give me. I bet he was wondering what he had let himself in for, sleeping in a campervan at close quarters with three others! The crew were all getting on magnificently, with a sense of real camaraderie among them. They were a joy to be with and it was always a jolly atmosphere when I arrived for food. I diverted through Garstang to save a few metres and was soon walking on the A6 again. We passed the new campus of Lancaster University. Ivor pointed out the new buildings; he was a mine of information. Time soon passed and we stopped right in the middle of Lancaster in a supermarket car park. This was the first time the schedule was altered, stopping a few miles earlier than planned. I was feeling tired now, sleepy tired, and could easily have just put my head down and been out of it, away from the pain, the sore feet, the continuous fight against the clock. It was 8:40pm when I arrived and I left again at 9:19pm.

I had covered 13.5 miles in the last section and planned another 13 miles for the final session of the day. By the end of the day I would be around

8 miles behind the planned schedule; not too bad considering the problems I'd encountered. Andy decided he would walk with me too, as it's very hard to cycle at a walking pace and all of my crew were fit people. Bill was probably the least fit, but that was due to his arthritis; he had been on the waiting list for a new hip for nearly six months now and was anticipating the operation not long after our return. The last section followed the A6 to Carnforth, then the A6070 to Kendal.

This section wasn't too bad and went reasonably quickly. I was more comfortable walking now and knew that, even if I had to walk all the way to the finish, I was still capable of breaking the world record. I was now at the end of six days of my journey. I had planned for just twelve days, but my head was slowly getting around to the fact that this would go beyond that; so could not consider myself at half way yet. I had covered some 414.5 miles by the time I stopped just after Clawthorpe Hall Hotel on the way to Kendal; this was 5 miles short of the half way point of the total distance of 837 miles. I could now afford to lose a 4 hour block per day if I so wished, but I always wanted to remain as far ahead as was possible. The sooner I finished, the sooner the pain would stop.

It was 36 minutes past midnight when I reached the support van. I climbed into bed and thought of another day done, but I dreaded the thought of my poor sore feet in the morning. They were really beginning to deteriorate now that I was out there for longer and the breaks were no longer feeling like breaks, just eat my food, dunk my feet and get back out. I lay down again, content in my own mind that this world record attempt was still on. I had come this far, I was not going to break down now. I would have to do this all again if I failed. I put that thought straight out of my mind. I would not fail. I was here to break the world record and that was going to happen. I remained positive: the walking wasn't so bad, the miles were still accumulating and I was a mere 8 miles adrift after six days. The candle was reduced to a fraction above head height now, coming into reach so that I could it see easily. Very soon I would look down as it continued to burn.

DAY: 7 Saturday 9th September – 59.1 miles (total 473.6 miles)

I was 2 minutes late in starting this morning and after a short road section I joined the flat grassy canal path for a bit. It was nice and tranquil and there had been very few trail paths since the Offa's Dyke Path, but like that path my feet got wet with the dew. The weather was still fine. I had been extremely lucky so far, I thought, as I continued on through Kendal. The crew had become rather ingenious now at adapting to the restrictions of living on the move in a confined campervan and the parking spot at the leisure centre was the perfect place for them to clean up and have showers. It was amazing how much water cooking and washing up for four meals a day was taking up. There was little left for showering and heating up the water. Their gilets displayed with the world record attempt and charity element and postcard-sized flyers helped gain access to many places to supply water or take showers where facilities were scarce. They also probably helped with the witness statements, showing that they were officially a part of this team.

Kendal done and it was back to the A6. I had been beeped and called out to by someone in a black car. Apparently the person had been following me on the website and, as I was passing close to where he lived, he had come out just to see me and cheer me on. He spoke to Bill for some time and leap-frogged with the support van a few times. The next stop was the Plough Inn after Garnett Bridge. A distance of 14.8 miles walked in 4 hours 20 minutes arriving at 10:22am. I had completely forgotten that Dave Nicholson was to join the crew now; he stood out in his super clean gilet. I had not realised how grubby ours had become from pounding the streets and they were actually quite faded from the sun. Andy and Ramona were going to leave us tonight; their full week of support complete. Dave was the only member of the crew that I had not met; there had been plenty of emails and a chat on the phone. He was a neighbour of Alan Young and had offered his services and very kindly made his own way to the convoy courtesy of his wife. He had also brought along his daughter. He was to be with us to the end now. Andy was busy showing him the ropes and where everything was kept. He even told him to take over an additional duty that I had not requested of him, to gently remove my socks and shoes every time I stopped! It was much easier than doing it myself, as I got stiffer and stiffer at bending down and it was nice to have a little bit of attention. I was never the kind of person that wanted sympathy. It was my desire to do this and to put my body through the pain; so I could see no reason for sympathy; I was doing this to myself for my dream to come true; I just needed some assistance.

The next section was also to be full of surprises. It was to be a long plod ascending on the A6 to eventually reach Shap, having left at 11:01am. Bill was on the bike again. Both Bill and Alan still cycled rather than walk; Bill would not have been capable of walking with his hips anyway. It was a long drag and I kept my head down counting off the miles until I could stop again. Ahead I could see Andy had stopped in a lay-by. He had the video camera out again and I noticed that a car had pulled up and a couple got out. Shame, I thought, they were going to get in the way of the shots. As I came closer I realised who they were. It was a great surprise to see Michelle and Shaun O'Grady with little Bethany; they were on honeymoon in the lakes and made a special effort for the short sighting they got of me. There was not much time for chatting as I had to keep moving. They knew I was coming through, and had made their way to Shap. When I didn't turn up at the scheduled time they had taken a drive down the road and found me. I gave them a brief hug and thanked them and left with a smile on my face.

It was shortly after this I had some more visitors. Ian Thompson and Carys pulled up alongside in the car; he had also made the journey west to see me. Although he had planned to push alongside me in his racing chair for a bit with Carys on the attached bike, it wasn't the best of roads to do this. We had a quick chat and I got a jelly baby from Carys before they continued on their way. His wife Tanni Grey-Thompson was away competing on international duties. He had also kindly brought a spare video camera if we needed one. The one we had was generously borrowed from friends Trevor and Lynda Russell.

On through Shap and we met a few more Land's End to John O'Groats cyclists. This was the first group that we had met who were going to finish on the same day as me, although they were taking a different route from us after Moffat. They had Todd's campervan as support. My feet were getting hot in the sunshine and as we went through Shap an inviting bench beckoned me for a quick rest. Bill popped into the shop for an ice-cream. The crew caught us and recorded the evidence on video camera!

The next section also proved very eventful. With both campervans ahead we could see a great plume of smoke, as though something had just caught fire. On getting closer it looked like a campervan. Bill did have a joke about Ramona's cooking and it turned out to be a caravan. Just as we approached, so did the fire engine that promptly extinguished the flames.

The next event was when Bill nearly fell off the bike. He often drifted off into his own little world while cycling, but this time he fell asleep, wandering onto the grass verge which woke him up, just stopping short of falling in the ditch. He was promptly ordered to get some sleep on his rest break coming up and also informed the crew he must be left to sleep. All the crew could either sleep in longer in the morning or go to bed earlier than us, depending on the rota. Bill was the only one who was driving on

A donation tin and the postcard flyer at the Shap Chippy.
© Alan Young.

the first and last block and could not get any extra sleep; his 4 hour rest period would have to be used for this. The crew van was always parked up around half an hour after leaving the final feeding place of the day and by 10pm the crew could all go to sleep if they so wished. It was always Andy

189

who had to creep in late at night and try not to disturb the crew if they had gone to bed. Keeping the crew fresh and happy and enjoying the event as much as possible was quite important. It was always Bill who got the short straw: the first and last stops and having to mix all my drinks, still mainly alternating GlycoSlim milkshake and water. I had very occasionally had some coke. I also had a protein drink twice a day to prevent too much muscle loss, as happened during the Flora 1000 Mile Challenge, but in general my diet was far better on this event. Cooking facilities and food were limited, but as it had been planned ahead it was appropriate for the energy required. The next stop was another pub at Hackthorpe at 4pm. I had my second shower here and still managed to get out again by 4:32pm.

The third section of the day was to take me through Penrith, another big barrier for me, as this was well over half way now at 451 miles and was also the nearest point on the route to home, a short jump across the A66. My feet were really, really tormenting me again now and walking was very painful. I stopped half way through my block of running and put my feet in freezing water again. This did the trick and I was almost race walking by the time I arrived at the next destination after High Heskett at 8:52pm.

There had been some changes built into the rota today. This section had been done with Andy as opposed to Ivor. Ivor was now to drive to Glasgow Prestwick Airport to release Andy and Ramona from their duties. Ramona cooked the last meal and farewells were said. It was really sad to see them go and I didn't really want to change the atmosphere we had going. I felt they were also upset leaving, but unfortunately they had to go back to work. They had both taken annual leave to join me and be part of this team. It had been an incredibly big-hearted offer from them and I would feel different once they had gone. Both had done a sterling job.

Ramona, our "little chef", (she was the shortest of us all), had cooked every single meal in the crew van, all carefully prepared precisely on time and plentiful to feed us all. The crew van had been kept thoroughly spic and span throughout, the bathroom was spotless and washed up continuously, far more than was expected of her. Ramona was training for an ultra distance event herself; so I didn't want her cycling and she also needed time to do her training between cooking duties. After breakfast there were three cooked meals a day to prepare. She had to tolerate sleeping in a crew van full of men! Andy my "night owl"; had had the unpleasant task of the last shift at night, always in the dark and often into the early hours of the morning. He had been faultless in every way and I could not have had a better crew alongside me at these awful times. He had "the knack"; he understood me well.

Although they had arrived together for the week, there were probably few times when Andy and Ramona had actually been "together", as for 8 hours a day Andy was driving the support van while Ramona was in the crew van and another 4 hours were spent cycling with me. So Andy's rest block of 4 hours was the only time they were together and Ramona was always washing up and getting ready for the next meal, prepared in an instant when a phone call would come in to say "running early", or as the case was now "running late".

The last section of the day was down to Alan for this night only and what a night it was to be. I had been late in leaving at 9:42pm with the depressing departure of our happy couple. Ivor, Dave, Andy and Ramona were sleeping in the crew van; so all departed to sleep at the airport, dropping them off for an early morning flight and then hopefully returning in time for the first cooked meal break, but a contingency plan was in place just in case they never made it back in time. That left Alan on the bike and Bill driving the support van as usual. The last section had seen me take an extra few minutes half way through the block as my feet were just boiling over and the pain immense. The extra ice foot bath had numbed them for a bit; so I was able to walk strongly again. The quad had progressed slightly and, although I was still completely unable to run, it was far less painful to walk on.

Now going into the night again and having left at the latest time so far on my journey, the sleep deprivation and time on my feet were catching up with me. This section was horrendous and I hated every single minute of it; the only break was getting a policeman to witness the run, another minor goal achieved. My feet were rebelling, screaming at me to stop. They couldn't take much more. They were killing me. Swollen to two sizes bigger than normal, blistered, burning, throbbing agony, causing me excruciating pain with every step. It was like treading on glass with each foot strike, with every step I was now staggering, moving sideways more than I was forwards. I was ignoring these signals, suffering the pain, soldiering on in ignorance. It was my mission, one mighty mission to become a world record holder. My head may have been telling me to stop, but my heart was insisting I should carry on. I was doing this of my own free will. Hell and agony all rolled into one. Self inflicted torture. An ordeal, call it what you like, but it was what I wanted to do, my own desire to make my dream come true.

It was midnight and I was approaching Carlisle; not good timing and sleep deprivation was hitting me. I was unable to maintain my co-ordination. It was as if I was drunk, but not a touch of alcohol had passed my lips.

Maintaining forward momentum was difficult, but time was distance and distance was important and the clock kept on ticking. I wanted the time to pass to get nearer the finish, but it was also the enemy, the miles needing to be run before the clock ended the day. I was testing my body to its limits and pushing beyond all boundaries while in such a state. I was on my epic journey and had been running, walking, staggering and suffering for nearly seven days now, accumulating blisters and muscle injuries, my feet throbbing with the constant pounding and hammering as the tarmac beat them and sleeping on a minimum of just 4 hours per night.

I was lit up like a Christmas tree: flashing cycle lights tied on my back and waist, torch strapped on my head. I was dressed in a bright yellow gilet with fluorescent strips. I was the focus of the local binge drinkers as I staggered all over the road; unable to walk in the direction my head was telling my legs to go. The local drinkers were the same. Crash! Another big hit with a party reveller! I stubbornly continued forward pushing these intoxicated party goers out my way. Alan was following on the cycle but he was not faring any better, hijacked by a group of merry jokers, "What are you doing? A sponsored walk? John O'Groats is a long way", they laughed, not realising that really was my goal. A few shocked minutes later they realised I was for real and kindly found a few coins to donate to Asthma UK.

The torture continued. This was the last stint of the day, but it was getting harder and harder. Could I really make it just one more hour until the Little Chef on the A74 which was to be my overnight stop? Did I say overnight stop? It was gone midnight, it would be past 2am by the time I made it to my support van and bed and the alarm was set for 5:30am every day. I really wanted to stop now. Why could I not just keep moving forward? I had got to concentrate: just 3 miles now. I remembered the route, but it was dark now. It would be difficult to find the cut through from the industrial estate to the A74 dual carriageway, not that this bit saved time or distance, but it did save noise and the risk of being run down. I looked at the map; the next mile was taking forever. Surely I must nearly be there? The tears were rolling down my face now. I knew I couldn't stop. I had just got to make it. I had already lost a few hours off my schedule. This was relentless. Time doesn't stop. It was a continuous fight against the clock. It was an emotional roller coaster: as much as I wanted to stop, I didn't want to stop. It was a battle, head against heart, head was saying stop, heart saying continue, heart won over yet again, I would not be beaten.

It was pitch black in the industrial estate, with no street lights, well away from the night life of Carlisle now, but I was still unable to put my feet

192

where my brain was directing them to go. The finish for the day was so close, but it felt so far. I wasn't sure if it was the pain of my feet or the emotion that made the tears keep rolling, or frustration even, as my body was just not doing what it was supposed to do. I was staggering badly. Luckily it was quiet here and I was not in danger of being hit by traffic as I don't think I could have stayed on a footpath even if there was one. I think even Alan was staying well clear of me. I would probably have bashed into him if he came alongside. I was not sure if he could even see the state I was in. Not a word was said. But I probably preferred it that way. I hate sympathy. This was my choice, no-one was making me do this, I was making me do this, as I said, self inflicted torture.

Finally I found the cut through to the A74, just a mile or so still to run along the hard shoulder of the A74. The hard shoulder was a good width and the road pretty quiet: good timing to make up for the bad timing of Carlisle. Ouch! I kicked something black. My feet were sore enough already but my head torch just didn't light up all the debris that was now getting in my way, bits of tyres and all the rubbish people lazily chuck out of vehicle windows. It's not only disgraceful, it hurt. The misery and distress just continued. I kept checking my watch. The time kept ticking, but the miles were not. Surely it couldn't be more than a mile now? Surely no more than 15 minutes? Just where was the sign indicating that the services were just a mile away? I knew there was a sign for the services. Maybe I'd missed it with my head down, kicking and stumbling over yet more rubbish? Finally: a sign. I was almost there. Just half a mile now. At last I heaved a big sigh of relief and the tears stopped. I was going to make it. Another day finished. Sleep at last and a break for the feet.

Once I could read the services sign, the lights could be seen and I just focussed on that with such great satisfaction. My goal was still in my sight, another day closer. What a welcome sight the services were, but I couldn't see the support van. Where was my support van? Over there, phew, that's a relief! Great, one last effort to climb the steps Bill had put out for me and finally a sit down on the edge of my bed. It was 1:35am. Shoes off and my feet were instantly into iced water while I drank a nice hot cup of tea. What sheer luxury; pain over and sleep beckoning. I felt content now. Over half way, 473.6 miles to be precise (that meant 363.4 miles still to go), but it had been one hard day. I was now around 4 hours behind the planned schedule of twelve days. I had completed my worst daily mileage yet, only 59.1 miles today.

By the time I drank my tea, washed and undressed ready for bed it was gone 2am, no 4 hours sleep that night. I laid my head on the pillow, relaxed, with such a great feeling of self satisfaction that I was a day closer to my goal, but I didn't dare think the horrendous thoughts that I had to go through this all again the next day. This was only a temporary reprieve and that agony of putting my shoes on first thing in the morning would be real again in just a few hours time. I went out like a light now, not like the first few days where I lay awake unable to sleep after the day's exertion. I felt I just dropped off when the alarm sounded; surely it wasn't 5:30 already? But yes, Bill was immediately out of bed and making tea and Ready Brek. The ordeal was to start all over again. The clock just never stopped. The previous night it ticked so slowly going through Carlisle, but, while sleeping, it went like a flash.

DAY 8: Sunday 10th September – 53.4 miles (total 527 miles)

After just over 3 hours sleep it was back to the A74 again. It was 6:03am and I still felt very tired and my feet were the most sensitive yet. That was the first morning that I got up and did not feel refreshed after a few hours sleep. I did not feel revived at all and wondered just how much more abuse the body could take. I was not about to give up though, this thought never even entered my head. The thoughts were more about, "How can I deal with this extreme tiredness and pain in my feet?" It was not pure fatigue, just sleep deprivation and feet that really didn't belong to me. The scales surprised me that morning, though. Over the first six days I had lost the total sum of one pound. Today, however, I was three pounds lighter than the previous day. I wondered if this was extra fluid loss or maybe the support van was on a tilt and giving a wrong reading. It was noted and I made a point of making sure I drank plenty and "peed" regularly and also tried to eat a bit more, as this could be pure weight loss.

The pain in my feet was beyond belief that morning; I took ibuprofen for the feet today. I wasn't walking fast enough for the quad to even give me pain and I had completely forgotten about that injury now. The previous night was spinning through my head. Did I really experience that? How had sleep deprivation caught up with me so suddenly? I knew there was a general "sleepy tired" feeling on stopping for each break and that my feet were progressively deteriorating, but I was frightened at the thought of another such night. I had to avoid being in such a state. If I had been on a major road and staggering all over the place it could have been plain dangerous and I was not here to put life and limb at risk.

The section on the A74 was only very short, but the clock had slowed down again and it took forever to reach the slip road for Gretna Green.

194

We had been married here over fourteen years ago. It was very quiet at this time on a Sunday morning, but the quiet roads were a pleasant relief. It wasn't long before I saw another face I recognised on the B7076: it was Carolyn Hunter-Rowe cycling towards me. It was great to see Carolyn, but, feeling at my most delicate, it was even better to talk to her and take my mind off the task in hand and try to turn off the thoughts of pain. I struggled sometimes to get my words out and was speaking far slower than usual, something I had occasionally experienced at the end of 24 hour races when extremely tired. Carolyn cycled with me, as Alan hit another puncture. Ecclefechan was the destination for the end of the first block; this was exactly where we should have been last night and was only a couple of miles from Carolyn's house. Those 14.8 miles had taken me 4 hours 20 minutes and I was quite surprised it wasn't slower. Carolyn had done her job well and another block of miles accomplished. I could now look down on a shortening candle, still glowing very brightly.

The crew van had arrived back after travelling to Prestwick the previous night; they had left the airport at 6am after only getting there after midnight to sleep. Ivor had cooked the pasta this morning and it was a lot quieter with only four crew members on board. Carolyn had made a walnut and banana loaf, my favourite; I had a slice and asked for a couple of slices to take on my next block rather than the usual sandwiches. I left at 11:10am and Carolyn continued for a little further to Lockerbie before doing a real training session on the bike. It was nice to catch up as earlier in the year I should have met up several times with Carolyn, but, due to my injury, we had missed each other. I had also been selected to run in the World Challenge 100 Kilometres in Korea a few weeks after this event where Carolyn would have been team manager, but unfortunately had had to withdraw as I would not have been in a fit state to represent my country so soon afterwards.

With Carolyn gone my feet were the worst yet. I tried to put on some shoes that had the toe boxes cut out; these felt comfortable, but I knew I would not be able to walk long distances in these. Bill suggested taking some ibuprofen again: what a good idea! I just kept forgetting painkillers might just help. I stopped again to put my feet in freezing water and now tried wearing sandals. These felt good on my feet and were certainly a lot cooler but I felt the cushioning was poor and that there was no heel lift for my Achilles tendon which might cause problems. My Achilles that had bothered me a little on the first couple of days had completely gone now; the body was a most amazing machine. I stopped yet again and this time put on my only pair of size seven shoes, brought for such an emergency but never ever worn as they were just too big. These were Nike Presto and they did the trick. My feet were comfortable at last but the effects of the previous day were about to hit me.

I had wrestled all morning with tiredness and now I was unable to walk in a straight line again. I was very aware of what I was doing and Bill was having a rough time with me: I had been stopping and starting all the time, dipping my feet, changing shoes and it was the first time Dave had been on support van duties on his own. I dreaded to think what he thought of me. How on earth was I going to keep on time if this was all I did? It was mid-afternoon and the emotion and tears of frustration were getting to me. I had to carry on; I didn't want to stop and needed to pull myself back together again. But how to do this? How to rid myself of this lack of concentration? That was all it was. I was motivated and capable. I only required the concentration to keep moving and preferably moving forward the way I wanted and not stumbling aimlessly around. Eventually I just had to pull the support van back, as I was unable to continue. I could not concentrate and felt unable to walk properly. The accumulation of lack of sleep since having to walk was taking its toll. The sub 4 hours sleep last night was just too little. It was another lesson learnt the hard way and was put back to bed by Bill for exactly an hour. I had stopped so frequently during this block, that this was an even slower pace than my nightmare block through Carlisle the previous night.

It was while sleeping that friends Ella and Geoff arrived on their way back to Guisborough after a week of climbing Munros. They appeared 10 minutes after I went to bed and had a long wait for me to emerge again. I lay down in the support van. It was just a short reprieve from the long journey. But far from feeling I went to sleep I seemed to lie there with my eyes closed aware of vehicles passing as we were parked close to the road. The hour felt like an age, unlike last night. When Bill came in the support van I was instantly awake and eager to get on my way. I felt more human again now and had my rice meal and a cup of tea before continuing. I also took more ibuprofen anticipating the pain in my feet.

Vicky had been doing my website up until now and Ella was going to take over for the second week. She took a few photographs but couldn't stay with me for long, as it was quite a trek back to Guisborough and she had already wasted an hour while I was in bed. I felt much more alert now and the hour's sleep was well worth it to feel sober again. I had done 12.3 miles in my last block, the least so far and had taken a 90 minute break. The next block was also to be cut short, as I was not quite sure how I would be and thought it would be better to get my head around a shorter section. I left at 4:45pm and covered a mere 11.7 miles, now joining the A701 and passing through Moffat. I was pleased to hit this section, as it was where I had started my trial and although I knew there was a long climb out of the town I knew what to expect. A big group of motor cyclist enthusiasts were in Moffat. They roared past us beeping and waving in support; they had generously donated to our fund for Asthma UK. My anticipation of the massive climb had shrunk the reality into a gentle stroll and reached the top of the ascent with ease.

I was feeling chirpy still and the haze of confusion had not returned. I could concentrate. The next section was with Dave; this was the only change I was to have to my support. Andy had gone and Dave was the replacement. He was doing an excellent job and although the company was different everything else remained unchanged. Dave had also taken annual leave from his employment to support me, again a wonderful gesture from someone who didn't even know me, also from his selfless family for allowing Dave to join me on this wonderful adventure. I certainly don't think it was fun for the majority of the time, but all wanted to take part of their own free will and all would be rewarded as being part of the world record run.

My break had been from 8:10pm until 8:56pm and it was the coldest night so far. This was quite a high section of the A701; I had to put on extra kit: jumpers, hat and gloves. The night was still and very few cars passed us on this remote road. One did stop, however, to offer a lift, thinking we had been caught out in the night! It was very kind, but obviously not needed. Dave continuously talked to me, trying to keep my spirits up. I mumbled occasionally, but probably switched off for a majority of the time. He read me well though, counting down the miles for me, diligently following the maps and understanding why I counted down the miles for just that small block of time I was in. Again, he was faultless in his execution of his duties.

I managed 14 miles to the stop at Crook Inn, arriving at 1:07am. It was great to be back to 4 hours sleep again. This had been my worst day for mileage: I had completed a meagre 53.4 miles, but at least I had never missed out a block of running and I was well within the record schedule. Although this was some 30 miles off the original schedule, this only amounted to two blocks of running for me. I still had another four blocks to play with and in theory could do three blocks of running per day and still break the world record. I had now begun to count blocks of running left until the finish, as it was easier than miles somehow and even now

I rarely thought about the event as a whole, only that tiny 4 hour block of time I was in, trapped in a time warp of 4 hours that I had to repeat over and over again. It was similar to the ground hog day experienced on the Flora 1000 Mile Challenge. The candle was shrinking rapidly, burning away continuously, but the flame glowed well; it was not to be extinguished yet.

DAY 9: Monday 11th September – 56 miles (total 583 miles)

This was day nine of my run. I was very confident now that the world record would be mine. It was just a case of keeping going. I still knew there were around five days of running ahead and I just had to keep focussing on each block of running, but there was no way at this stage I would fail. My feet were crippling me, my quad was straining, I was sleep deprived and rapidly losing weight now, but my confidence was high. On the scales today my weight had plummeted a further three pounds, now seven pounds in total. I knew it wasn't dehydration and guessed it was possibly the anti-inflammatory ibuprofen I had taken that was reducing the swelling accumulated in my legs and this was the reason for the rapid weight loss. For the last two days I had been trying to increase my calorie intake: with each block of running I ate a large bag of chocolate minstrels. Usually I love chocolate but on long runs I can't often eat it, but during the walking phase the chocolate had been going down well. Running and eating chocolate didn't work, but walking and eating chocolate did. I had bought a box of these anticipating going through a "chocolate phase" but would not have guessed I would eat none for a week and then around four packets a day!

The day went steadily. I set off at 6:05am and continued up the A701, joining the A72 for a short section by Blyth Bridge. Next was Mountain Cross for the first break of the day at 10:40am. The slightly later mornings were due to the time it took to put my size seven shoes on. I had pressure blisters that were now very ugly on the sides of my heels. There was nothing I could do about them but to continue and ignore them. I never tape my feet; any blisters are instantly popped and I get on with progressing on the journey. If I taped my feet the continuous wetness from cooling my feet every break would see the skin shrivel and any tape would fall off. I was able to cope quite well with walking down hill now and the quad was improving all the time. It was amazing that the body could heal itself while I was putting it through such a gruelling task.

The route had been fantastic so far today: wonderful scenery, a quiet single carriageway road along the A701 and the next segment was even better,

198

apart from a small shower of rain. Starting again some 32 minutes later Leadburn was reached; then I took a nice canal path missing the centre of Penicuik to arrive on the outskirts of Edinburgh. The second break of the day was close to the roundabout joining the A703. I could see Murdo waving ahead, my last crew member to arrive and boost us up to five crew members again. I had not realised how much the crew hated cooking; so it was a relief to have Murdo on board, although he probably hated cooking too and had to cook for six! Murdo had only recently finished a very successful run of the Tour du Mont Blanc and was in recovery mode so didn't mind not having to train at the moment. He lived nearby in Edinburgh; so this was a convenient place to join us, with his wife Jo kindly escorting Murdo to our little mobile set up. I had competed in ultra distance races with Murdo, but like Dave really didn't know him in terms of personality. All I knew from the communication we had prior to this was that he was again a very diligent person who took his role in this adventure very seriously and I knew he had been on contact with Ramona regularly to establish his duties.

A journalist from a Scottish running magazine 'My Race' was also here to greet me. He did an interview while walking out on my next section and took a few photographs. The mobile phone was ringing non-stop at that moment, as Willie Rennie MP was supposed to be running with me on the Forth Road Bridge, but as I was behind schedule and not due to hit the bridge until darkness it looked as if it was all off. I wasn't too bothered; this was all about getting a world record and I could not run according to other people's plans and photographs, although it was disappointing as this had been planned for some time. Ivor was with me again for the afternoon chat of the day. I was dreading the next section again. We arrived at 3:15pm and left at 3:50pm to tackle Edinburgh. I won't detail the route except to say that as it was a busy built up place it was another battle with my feet. Murdo had kindly brought some homemade flapjack cut into tiny pieces. Just perfect! I love flapjack and had a few pieces wrapped up for each running segment instead of sandwiches. I liked having something different and it encouraged me to eat more. I was concerned by my weight loss and trying to eat more, but it was a losing battle.

I had planned to meet up with my crew at a leisure centre just before the Forth Road Bridge and both campervans were to go direct to the meeting point as it was pointless trying to follow me through Edinburgh, but my feet were refusing to play ball, screaming at me to stop again. It was frustrating. I wanted to ignore them and get on my way but they kept fighting me, crying out for a break and some ice. I could not block out the pain. I relented. The feet were getting hotter and hotter and I had already found out that the time spent taking a quick dunk in freezing water was always worthwhile as I got back to a good walking pace again. My pace had slowed with the grief the feet were giving me; so Ivor called in the cavalry. We sat on a wall at a cross roads to give the feet some relief and poor Bill managed a much needed shower in the leisure centre. It was his rest period and he should have been catching up on sleep. But his wife was in distress and it was into the support van, masquerading as an ambulance, to race to my rescue. It was a race against the clock. The quicker he could get to me, the quicker the feet would be cooled, the quicker the relief from the pain and the sooner a better pace would be achieved. I was on the B701 just off the A90 by the time they found me. Bill parked conveniently on a side street where he found us.

It seemed to me that my feet were very weather dependent: the warmer the weather, the hotter the feet and the sorer they got. This was why I didn't seem to struggle so much on the first and last block of the day when the weather was cooler and the tarmac not so hot. I was now pleased that the trip had been put off from July until now, as the roads would have been hotter still. I love running in the heat and hate the cold which is why I had planned the event for July, also for the longer day light hours. However, putting this off until later in the year was now a blessing in disguise. I was also pleasantly surprised as Adrian Stott and his daughter from Run and Become shop in Edinburgh also arrived. Alan had told me that Adrian was trying to get to see me and asked if there was anything I needed. 'Socks' was the reply. Adrian was preparing for the Sri Chinmoy 24 hour race to be held at Tooting Bec, London in October and I had known him for many years as a race organiser and international 24 hour runner.

Every time I stopped for a break I put on clean socks. I had a bag with forty eight pairs of socks, twelve days at a rate of four clean pairs per day. Adrian brought me some socks from the shop. I had realised I would probably be running another full day, another four blocks of running; so would either have to get socks washed or put dirty ones back on (not really an option, as the blisters were leaking quite badly now and staining all the socks I was wearing). He came at a most appropriate time and I was immediately able to put the new socks into action. Adrian also walked with me for the rest of that block and I was able to pick up the pace again. He is another very friendly runner and he was telling me stories of when he supported the great Don Ritchie on his world record breaking John O'Groats to Land's End run many years ago. Don ran in marathon blocks at a fast pace and had long breaks. During this section the route was along a cycle path leading to the Forth Road Bridge. This was a longer distance than following the main A90, but pedestrians and cyclists were forbidden from taking this more direct road.

I reached the leisure centre at Queensferry at 8:20pm with Ivor and Adrian. The car park was full of children all excited about my arrival and wanting cards signed. Murdo did a fantastic job with cooking dinner and getting used to the facilities. The dinners had been planned in advance but a few extra things had been used and Murdo made the best of what was left. Dinner was a kind of stew and pasta that went down very well with us all.

The last section of the day should have been the first section of the day, as I was now three blocks behind schedule. The Forth Road Bridge was uneventful for me. I had done this before. Leaving an hour later, I continued my tortuous walk. Dave was with me now busily chatting away. No Willie Rennie MP. It was dark now and the only surprise was the other side of the bridge where I could see Bill waiting with someone. I wondered if this was a photographer. No, it was Bert Hannah, a lovely character who had been following my progress. The Land's End to John O'Groats Association had informed him of my run and he had been really eager to walk a section with me. Unfortunately he had not realised how far behind the schedule I was and had turned up and waited since 10am in the morning. It was now around 10pm! He had been home and had managed to get contact via the website and mobile phone and made his wife drive out in her night-dress just to walk with me. He had walked this in sixty seven days for Cancer Research UK and was so enthusiastic. It was an honour to walk with Bert and he did a really good pace with me. It was great to talk to a fellow Lands End to John O'Groats achiever and hear his stories; just a shame he had such a long wait and it was dark by the time I arrived. The Lands End to John O'Groats Association had been in contact via Jack Adams when this event had first gone public in my local Evening Gazette and had sent tremendous messages of support that I was getting on route via mobile phone. In addition, I had heard that Teesside University was also giving £500 of sponsorship.

Bert joined me suitably clad in fluorescent yellow and torched up too. We shared many stories walking through Inverkeithing, to Crossgates and the B981. We were stopped temporarily by a police car as we walked up the middle of the road three abreast at Cowdenbeath, a very quiet road at this time of the night, but the police simply wished us well and we continued on our way. Bert left at Kelty on the B917 where his wife picked him up to drive home. I had slowed down significantly now, even though I thought I had set a good pace the time was ticking by as it was nearly 1am. The planned stop was over 2 miles away and the thought that this would result in less than 4 hours sleep again was more than I could face. I was getting tired, slowing up, fighting to keep going. I couldn't stop peeing either. I had taken over three lots of ibuprofen today for the first time and guessed this was fluid from the swelling still being excreted. I decided to call it a day at Kelty. Bill just parked up the support van and sent David on his way to the crew van. I stopped at 1am exactly, having only managed 12 miles for that block. I laid my head down, content that this was the right decision, content that the record was in my grasp, but still never counting my blessings until the ordeal was over. I had walked 56 miles today, 583 miles completed, 254 miles still to go. It was still an awful long way to contemplate; best not to think about it as a whole, just the 4 hour blocks, but the end was getting closer. I was aware the crew were getting excited too. I was no longer wondering if I would I finish, but now tried to guess my finishing time. I really didn't have a clue other than that I knew it would be faster than 13 days and 10 hours. Even now there was time for this to go pear shaped; there were problems I might hit, time to lose, and that clock which never ever stopped, but the candle continued to burn down.

DAY 10: Tuesday 12ᵗʰ September – 65.5 miles (total 648.5 miles)

I awoke to drizzle for the first time. It was quite dark and gloomy outside and a local photographer had been ringing to find us since the alarm sounded at 5:30am. He pulled up just as I stepped gingerly from the support van. There couldn't be a worse time to photograph me, unable to barely walk! Bill now hated watching me put my shoes on in the morning, squeezing the feet that were now pretty shredded into my shoes. The sores on the side of my feet disliked being pushed by the edges of the shoes and I had to hold my breath and wince, eyes tightly shut as the pain shot through my body. One shoe on, one more to do; it was taking me longer and longer in the mornings now, but it had to be done, there was no way round it. Shoes on; next on the list was getting moving, this was even worse. Both my feet felt as though they had been battered to a pulp, continuously thumped, the way you would beat a carpet or crushed in a vice to squeeze the life out of them. I wasn't sure how much more they could take, how much more pain a pair of feet could produce. I really wanted this to end, but for the pain to stop I needed to get to the finish.

Several times Bill had commented that it was no disgrace to withdraw having run so far. But that was the point, having run so far it would not be any better if I gave up and tried on another occasion. You can't train the body for this level of battering. All you can do is train to be as fit as possible and then it's a case of mind over matter, pigheadedness, stubbornness, determination, fighting the pain, ignoring the pain, living with pain. Pain, pain and more pain; the pain was not going to stop until I stopped. Only three more days of pain, that was all it was. I could cope with that. I never ever would want to do this again. I just hoped all the pain was worth it and that the euphoria of being a world record holder would feel like heaven. I wanted to know what it felt like to be a world record holder, to have run this route faster than any female previously. It kept me going; there really was no stopping me now.

I lowered myself out of the support van, with Bill's assistance, and balanced on my heels. I was unable to walk properly in the morning. I just pigeon stepped along, taking tiny little steps and strides and bit by bit the pain would subside, not wearing off, just becoming a bit less painful. The photographer looked on and decided that as the light was still poor he would drive a couple of miles down the road and wait for it to brighten up. He had planned to take pictures of me coming across the Forth Road Bridge, but as it had been dark he had decided to get some shots of me this morning. I looked at the state I was in trying to walk down the road. I had to laugh through the pain. Just what did I really look like? I could barely walk and yet I had 254 miles still to go; he must have thought it was impossible. If I looked at myself I would have laughed and thought, 'never in a million years'! But I had fought a very different pain many years ago, and, just as it did then, the clock would tick, the days would pass and life would improve.

There was also a call saying that Alan was on his way back on the bike to meet us. Dave had told him I was 2 miles further back. I emerged onto the B996, it had gradually been getting darker every morning as the nights had drawn in; today was particularly dark with the gloomy weather. Murdo had said that the forecast was for rain and that Tuesday would be the worst. I had been very lucky with the weather up until now as I had never had a trip to Scotland where it hadn't rained. It even rained heavily on my trial for the first 8 hours.

Alan had not been looking at the maps again and stayed on the B996 bypassing Keltybridge. Just as I was approaching the photographer for the last time I tried to run again, to try to look as though I really was a world class runner who could complete a few more days. The quad was painful but I was not experiencing the twisting spasms that I had had earlier in the event. It had been improving bit by bit and most days I had given it a little trial to see if it would take any running. I had been really frustrated at not making it to the meeting place last night. I had now been walking since day six; that was almost four full days of walking. I had been taking ibuprofen for the last couple of days and, knowing that in the process of repair to an injury swelling normally stops after three days, I was ready to give this a go. If I couldn't run I had nothing to lose, as I knew I could still walk this and achieve my goal. The running continued to my amazement and that of the crew. They all cheered as I ran by, a sight they had not expected. The only one of the crew missing was Alan and it was now that we realised he was heading back to the Forth Road Bridge! Bill went back to find him and bring him back.

Running meant that instead of stopping the crew short of the planned distance I was sending them on ahead, further and further along these minor roads and through tiny villages. The planned stop near Glenfarg was extended to Bridge of Earn, which I reached at 9:50am. I was ecstatic, likewise the crew. I had finally completed a block in less than 4 hours again; I had run 17 miles in 3 hours 50 minutes. I could allow myself a whole hour's break again. That was fantastic! I felt like I had eventually had a break at last, the whole crew seemed on a high again and all seemed in shock. I wasn't sure I would continue running though, as I could feel the quad the whole time I was running and could not run downhill at all; I could only run on the flat and uphill. The weather also began to improve, as after a couple of very wet hours it dried up.

Alan had rejoined me after his extra cycle ride that morning. Luckily he used the cycle still. Alan was a fit person. In a previous chapter I mentioned my debut in the 24 hour race at Tooting Bec in London. Alan was a previous winner of this race and had run in excess of 140 miles. A back injury had halted his running career and he now supported many ultra distance athletes worldwide on various exploits. After taking early retirement from work he had gained great enjoyment from supporting others. This was a long trek for Alan; the run may only have taken a fraction over twelve days but by the time Alan finally returned home it would be eighteen days away.

After my whole hour break I left at 10:50am. The next section was through Perth was a nice section along the river on a cycle path. This was very pleasant and I was surprised that I was still able to run before emerging onto the dreaded A9. This was horrendous. I hated it. I found it worse than the A30 in the South West. There were only small segments with white lines to protect us and sometimes even these disappeared. I felt the traffic was very close to me here and was just really glad I was running again, as this would mean getting over this dangerous section quicker with less time spent on the road. The next stop was just after Dunkeld, some 19 miles, easily achieved in 4 hours 2 minutes. Bill was so chuffed I was running again. I had even eaten the flap-jack that Murdo had brought along; he saved it for me so that I could be drip fed this every day for the rest of the event.

Ivor had to get on the bike again now. He had ditched it since I had been walking, but now I was running he had to cycle. I left at 3:53pm; the route continued along the A9 until Pitlochry, then the B8079 to Killiecrankie and the next near disaster. A police car overtook us and I saw it pull in further up the road; I just knew it was for us and spelt trouble. The two policemen made me laugh, as they got out of the vehicle and one walked to the back and held up his hands with arm signals and ordered us to stop as if we were a car. Was I really going that fast? They asked what this was about and said that it was dangerous to run or cycle on this road and that they pull all cyclists off the road. They also wanted to know if I had informed the police about the run as they could have helped plan the route. Fat chance that they would have let me do the shortest route! I showed them my maps as I sat in the back of the car (my choice as I wanted to sit rather than stand on my sensitive feet). I had around another 6 miles on the A9; so they got an ordnance survey map out to try to get me off the road. Eventually they decided there was no alternative and would only let me continue the next 6 miles if I ran and Ivor cycled on the uneven grass verge. I wasn't about to argue, as if they carted me off it would be the end of the world record attempt as I would have broken the rules of 'End to End on Foot'. I was quite convinced they could not take me off the road, as there were no signs to stop pedestrians or cyclists and this was just a normal A road. There had been signs on the A90 prior to the Forth Road bridge forbidding cyclists and pedestrians to use the road but an alternative cycle path had been provided. For the next few hundred metres I ran on the grass verge, worrying that it would pull my quad again and my feet did not like the uneven surface. Once they were out of sight, however, it was back on the road, but luckily just a short way later a cycle path appeared on the opposite side of the road, part of General Wade's Military Road. Unfortunately following this on the opposite side of the road, sometimes a short section away from the route, David was with the support van and missed us overtaking him. We could see the support van but could not see David. Eventually I sent Ivor back to try to find him to tell him where we were. He had missed us and probably would have sat there for a very long time.

Back on the A9 again and David was driving back down the opposite side of the road again. I was puzzled. Where had he been? No problem; he was back with us soon. Thankfully we reached the B8079 without seeing the police again, but it was getting dark and the clouds were gathering. We were in for one almighty thunderstorm and downpour for the last hour and just managed to get our jackets from the support van in time. Amazingly after several stops for different reasons I still made it to Killiecrankie ahead of time, arriving at 7:30pm, but the weather was still poor.

It was continuing to rain when I emerged fully clad with Dave at 8:38pm. Wearing the head torch for the last section of the day was sending me dizzy. I could not run with the rain drops flickering in the light and eventually took it off and ran by the light of the bike headlamp. After Bruar, there was about a mile on the A9 before hitting the cycle path at Calvine. I had ridden this cycle path and knew that it was a single track road that was driveable for some distance with just two or three houses; so Bill drove behind us and I ran in the beam of his headlights. Absolutely brilliant! This was parallel to the A9, but there was a big distance between the A9 and the path. It also seemed to be all uphill; at its highest point it was around 1,500 feet. The crew van was parked up on the cycle path where it hit a road at Dalnacardoch Lodge. Local knowledge had come in handy here, as there were few land marks to indicate how far we had run and to plan which lay-by to stop in. Dave directed the crew van and knew almost the exact distance. What a day! I had run all day. I had run nearly 10 miles further than yesterday, had taken an hour's break between each block and was finished at 10 minutes past midnight. If I could continue this it would make life so much more bearable, less time on my feet and more time to relax. I lay my head down, smiling. The pain was less, the running over quicker and morale was higher. This was really happening. I was running again. The candle was barely knee high, the end was closing in.

DAY 11: Wednesday 13th September – 65 miles (total 713.5 miles)

It was still drizzling when I left in the morning. My shoes were soaked from the night before and I had no others to change into, as I was in the only size seven shoes I possessed. At 6:07am I set off to continue along the cycle path. There was quite a strong tail wind too, but it seemed to buffet me around and I did not like it. The climb of last night gave way to a gentle downhill and I was able to run this now. The quad was improving all the time; quite amazing considering I was still running over 60 miles a day. The cycle path that Bill had driven along last night had now gone and I was on a narrow, gravel cycle path with Bill just parallel on the A9. There were less than 200 miles to run now, but it still seemed such a long way and still required three days of running. The rain gradually eased, the cycle path disappeared and it was back to the A9 again at Wade Bridge. There was a big white line to run inside here and it was not for long as the campervans were ahead again. They were parked short of the distance anticipated which was quite frustrating as I was trying to maintain the maximum mileage I could in the 4 hours. This stop was at lay-by ninety-seven before Crubenmore Lodge, (all the lay-bys were numbered). Although running well, I was just expecting another problem around the corner and never dared risk not running the maximum possible, as I might regret it later if something else happened and I looked back and realised I had not done everything possible to keep ahead.

I stopped at 9:38am, the weather dried up for the next block of running and the wind started to ease. Leaving at 10:45am the route soon left the A9 and went back to a cycle path to Ralia picnic area. Here the B9150 road took us to Newtonmore and Kingussie. Dave knew the person running the sports shop here and managed to get some better lights for the cycle donated and the Co-op donated some ice for my feet. Dave was a dab hand at this; earlier he had managed to persuade a restaurant to give me some ice from an ice making machine. He was very ingenious. I ran along the A486 for a little way and then the quiet B9152 to stop just after Kincraig near a campsite.

A clean crew greeted me. They had been taking showers at leisure centres and campsites on the way. Although the crew van had a shower, it was very small, had an extremely small tank of hot water and was not practical for the crew to use. I was the only one who used it; I probably had a shower every three days as it took time and effort to shower. I learned after the first shower to just wet myself, turn the shower off, lather up and then rinse off, otherwise it ended up cold.

During the last section I was getting tired again and had stopped to walk intermittently finding it hard to concentrate. For the first time I took a quick nap in my seat at the table in the crew van. It didn't do the job and I should have known better and gone to rest in the support van. It also meant all the crew left the campervan to leave me in peace. Luckily the sun was out now.

The break lasted from 14:31pm until 15:38pm. The sun had come out again and but I could not get running again; there was a bad camber on the road and my feet were almost unbearably uncomfortable. I stopped again just half an hour into the block to freeze my feet. Job done, it was back to

SHARON GAYTER

running through Aviemore and I had another excellent run after that back on the A9. Initially, after having had such a bad start to the block of running I pulled the crew van back a couple of miles, but then, after getting going again, Ivor had to phone back to revert to plan A and stop at the original plan after a ski centre, another 14.8 miles completed in 3 hours 47 minutes.

For the last section the sun had gone and I decided to freeze my feet again before getting out as well as when I came in. I had a superb last section running the 15.5 miles in just 3 hours 17 minutes to arrive at the picnic area near Daviot Wood at 11:42pm. Just two days to go now, I was so looking forward to going to bed and not having to get up and put shoes on these poor, poor feet. I had over 5 hours sleep that night, pure luxury.

DAY 12: Thursday 14ᵗʰ September – 64.1 miles (total 777.6 miles)

After finishing so well the previous night I was disappointed to crumble in the morning, when the route along the A9 was a big downhill to Inverness. I just could not hack the pain of running on my feet and tiptoed all the way to Inverness. Having left at 6:05am I started running again as the gradient eased and crossed Kessock Bridge. Fantastic! There was the first sign for John O'Groats; my journey was coming to an end! Alan behind me on the bike was on the mobile phone and ahead of me Bill was there with the video camera catching the moment, but it said still 109 miles to go! The A9 now was the worst yet, with no line between the kerb and the road and traffic thundering behind. I was getting beeped at and I abhorred it; shortly afterwards I saw a cycle path on the opposite side and told Bill I was taking it. The path didn't last long and ended up on a minor road. The maps showed this as approximately half a mile further than the A9 to Tore, but I felt it was worth taking, as this was really dangerous and also at that time of day, around 8:30am, it was probably the worst time to run this. Alan rang Bill to tell him where we were and to rejoin the A9 at Tore. Bill was parked there as instructed, just in time as the early spitting was now turning to rain. I pulled the campervans back a couple of miles, as the very slow start and extra half a mile were adding to the time on my feet and stopped just after Cromarty Bridge at 10:14am; 16.9 more miles accomplished.

It was raining heavily now as Bill got kitted out in full body cover waterproof clothing. The crew filmed the seals happily settled opposite. I hated putting on sopping wet shoes but there was less than a hundred miles of running left now. The route continued up the A9, but the traffic was easing now. The further north we travelled, the less traffic there was; it was out of rush-hour as well. It was just a long plod up the road, with me jumping off the road at one point as I heard the screech of a vehicle behind us. I turned round to see Bill already on the verge and a white van swerving on a completely empty road. What was he up to? Obviously engrossed in something else, he must have suddenly looked up to see us in front of him. He waved apologetically and continued. My heart rate took some time to return to normal!

The rain was getting heavier with lots of spray from vehicles coming by. I was getting tired and wet. I had never really completely recovered from my sleep deprivation at Carlisle and often struggled on the last run at night to keep a straight line. I was making a great physical effort to keep going now, but didn't want to take extra time out, as I needed to finish this the next day and before midnight, because it was Bill's birthday and for the first time ever I had not purchased a single present. This was his present, a wife as a world record holder. For Bill's fortieth birthday I had bought him forty presents, all wrapped in newspaper. He loved his presents being wrapped; so this was a cheap and easy way to wrap them. Bill always had "a birthday week" where he unwrapped several presents every day. I won't tell you what I get for my birthday by comparison! The best solution now was to have my rice meal in the support van, get out of my wet clothes and get my head down for 45 minutes. I had run well in this block and made up around 40 minutes taking just 3 hours 20 minutes to run 16 miles. I did this as planned and, although I arrived at 2:40pm, I was late out at 4:03pm. I never really slept but did feel a little better, probably a psychological improvement in that I felt I had taken a sleep, even though I had felt the campervan rock with every vehicle that passed.

I had used up my last clean pair of Asics tights; I had taken six pairs. Bill pulled a dirty dry pair from the washing bag. I had brought sufficient kit that no washing needed to be done; it wasn't that practical really, being on the move continuously. The rain continued on the next section though and I diverted from the A9 to go through Tain. Although the rain was progressively getting heavier, I ran well again, covering 16.7 miles in 3 hours 30 minutes. May be the rain soaked feet kept cooler and therefore didn't give me so much pain.

I must have been getting slower at getting out now, as the last break lasted from 7:40pm until 8:55pm. For the last section of the day Scotland did its best: there was absolutely torrential rain for the entire last block of running. It had rained all day and the roads were over ankle deep in places. The rain completely drenched my woolly hat. I had to change my wet tops after a couple of hours and put more layers on and yet another woolly hat. Dave had suffered the coldest night on his first night with me after Moffat and now endured the wettest night; even he had to pinch Bill's hat to keep warm! He was always such a happy character, though, and never moaned. I often wondered what the cars overtaking us thought: what was this idiot doing out on a night like this in the pitch black? I did wonder myself!

Having had enough of the incessant conditions, with my head down trying to avoid the stair rods of rain in my face, I nearly ran straight by the campervans! As the rain was so heavy I just waved to Bill every time I overtook him to make sure he had seen us; on the last occasion he was parked in a lay-by just before Lothbeg, which had a section between the road and the support van and I could not see the crew van parked either. Bill had changed his head torch from white to red to tell me it was stopping time and had to run out to me to pull me into the lay-by as I ran by. What a relief to finish and get out of the rain and dry my shrivelled feet out! Just one more day of running left now and I still felt no excitement. There was just less than 60 miles to run, but this entailed another four blocks of 4 hours of running. Still 16 hours of running to go. I could not relax. I knew I was going to finish. I knew I was going to smash the world record. I knew there would only be one more morning of running on these excruciating feet but there was no emotion, no excitement and no butterflies. I was sure I would feel differently the next day. I arrived here at 35 minutes past midnight and wished Bill a happy birthday, but would have to wait a while before I could give him his present. One last time I lay my head down; only one more morning of walking like a cripple, one more day to suffer four blocks of 4 hours running. My time had come, the flame flickered low; the clock was still ticking. It was soon to end and I would be able to sleep to my heart's content.

DAY 13: Friday 15th September – 59.4 miles (total 837 miles)

The last day, the last time I had to get up in the morning and wince as the dripping wet shoes were forced on. Even the weather was looking up after the rotten finish to the night. The entire crew were out for me; all got a hug as I ventured out for the last day. It still felt like a very long day; there were still four blocks of running to do. Initially I had planned to run through the last night, but I knew with the sleep deprivation already experienced there was no chance of this. The world record would still be broken; so it would be pointless. The route ahead was to be very hilly. I had marked this on the maps just in case I was tight for time, as I knew it could take a little longer than average. The first big climb was after Helmsdale and I walked up the long steep hill. I only had to do four blocks of 15 miles for this last day; the first block went quite quickly despite the massive climbs. I didn't realise at the time, but looking at the log book now it records leaving at 6:17am. I froze my feet again before setting off this time; so I took a bit longer getting ready. The first break was at a snow-gate before the next and biggest of the dips and climbs at Berriedale. I reached it at 9:36am. At 3 hours and 19 minutes it had been a tough section. The break was pretty good. Bill got a birthday card from the crew and a bag of sweets, as he had eaten the large supply he had started with (with a bit of help from the crew).

Worse was to come on the route. I started out on the steep descent with escape lanes for out of control vehicles; it was back to tiptoeing painfully all the way to the bottom followed by a long, long steep climb out again. The climb circled away well into the wide expanse ahead. It was Bill's turn on the bike yet again, but he managed to cycle it. After that the hills lessened, I made it through to Latheron where I took the A99 that would take me through to John O'Groats. The road signs were counting down the miles to John O'Groats, but all I could think of was another 4 hours to run. Even at this stage I could not think of the finish. The sun came out and my feet were burning up again by the time I reached the next stop near Occumster at 2:25pm. Yet another celebration for Bill, another card and chocolate cup cakes supplied by Murdo, with a few appropriate newspaper clippings inside, some about tinned food we had been living off and conkers.

ITV had been in contact now; they did some filming before the event. The original plan of talking live on air at 6pm had changed and it was now better to have an interview at 4pm that they could edit for later. This actually worked out quite well, as when I set off again my feet were screaming again and I could not run. They were a throbbing, battered mess and I wondered how long they would take to repair. I stopped again after half an hour and froze my feet again; just as I was finishing this the mobile phone rang for the interview. I sat in the back of the support van while I had the interview, much easier than walking along the road where passing traffic would severely hamper my hearing. Interview done and feet frozen, I was able to run again, on and on for another 4 hours, through Wick and stopping before Reiss, just 14.2 miles to the finish.

The message was coming through that Mike Amos from the Northern Echo was on his way up from Darlington to witness the finish. His train was to arrive at Wick at 10:08pm, but the crew were unable to pick him up due to the risk of missing me finish; so a taxi was organised for him. I set off for my last block of running with Bill; he wanted the glory of being with me at the finish and I wanted him with me too. One last hug from the crew and the finish awaited. My last break was from 7:01pm until 8:05pm.

It was quite cold now as I set off and the mist was starting to roll in. It was eerie in the pitch black when the mobile phone started ringing again as we approached Keiss, about 10 miles from the finish; first Ella for the website, then ultra friend Chris Finill. Just one more block to run, just 14.2 miles and this would be over. I had thought I would fly along, high on the adrenalin knowing I was going to finish and break the world record. But no, I was struggling to run yet again as the route went uphill by the Hill of Harley and then Warth Hill. I stopped for a bag of minstrels to keep the energy up for the last few miles just as a taxi came whizzing by and stopped in front of me. It was Mike, but there was not a lot of time for talking, as this had to be over before midnight. I left Bill to update Mike and continued on my way, 3 miles to go and around 10:45pm now. I could not believe that even at this stage of the run I had no pangs of excitement; I was just so looking forward to getting off my feet and taking my shoes off and sleeping.

Downhill now, the mist was lifting and finally in the distance the street lights of John O'Groats could be seen. It felt a long way winding around the roads to the source of the lights. On through the village and there was barely a soul that I could see. Did nobody know what was happening? After all, I was about to break a world record. On by the signs to the hotel, the finish was probably only 400 metres now, but where was everyone? Finally Bill pointed out the campervans and as I came jogging around the corner there was a long white line above the finish line. It was a toilet roll tied to my campervan. I ran up to the line and not until within 50 metres of the finish did I see just seven people, four of whom were my crew members; Murdo, Ivor, Dave and Alan. The others were Mike Amos and his photographer and John Green, councillor and official finisher. I took just one step over the line and broke the toilet roll, hands in air. I had finished, my dream had come true; I was a WORLD RECORD HOLDER! I had taken over 17 hours off the world record, finishing in 12 days, 16 hours, 22 minutes and 3 seconds.

It was freezing; I dared not take my hat off as I knew I would start shivering. I finally wished Bill a very happy birthday and hoped he liked his present that he could only hug and not open. He was a very proud man and probably just as relieved as I was to finish. He had hated seeing me suffering and had tried to gently persuade me several times to take an extra break or miss a 4 hour segment out, as I was still ahead of the schedule, but I always refused.

After a few photographs on the line it was a big hug from everyone and a fantastic achievement for all of us to experience, all nine of us that was (including me and Bill this time). John Green had kindly brought a very large pottery plate from the Tain Pottery, which I had run by the previous day as a gift, a very nice memento to mark the occasion. Just like Dennis Axford at the start he had kindly given his time to witness the occasion with no fuss at all.

Where was the champagne? I had brought two bottles in anticipation of breaking this world record. Glasses were soon clinking as I finally sat down on a chair in front of my support van and Dave did his last delicate removal of the shoes. I was starting to get cold now, as a blanket was put on me for a group photograph. A few last photographs at a sign saying "Journeys End" and it was off into the bar to sign the official book wearing my sandals now and the blanket around my shoulders. Oops! The bar shut at 11:30pm. I had finished at precisely 11:22:03pm and it was not going to close a minute later for the world record holder to sign. Tough luck! That was a few extra steps I didn't need to walk! Mike was ringing the Northern Echo to confirm Saturday's front page news and Bill was ringing Ella who had stayed up to update the website for you all to read.

There was no point in hanging around much longer. Everyone was tired, the goal had been achieved, it was cold and misty and there was nothing

End of LEJOG, David, Murdo, Bill, Ivor, Alan. (Picture courtesy of Newsquest (Yorkshire & North East) Ltd©).

much to see. I climbed in the back of the support van to be driven for the first time since leaving Land's End just under thirteen days ago. Mike came with me to do the interview he had made such a long journey for, as Bill drove us back to Wick and the campsite we had finally been booked into, also the first since Penzance. I was absolutely shocked that I still felt no emotion. I had expected to burst into tears and jump for joy, but all I experienced was just sheer relief at finally being able to get off my poor throbbing, swollen, blistered feet and sit down in the warm. I almost felt human again after being on a determined mission for nearly two weeks. I was still wrapped up in a big blanket with just my feet sticking out to cool down. It was great talking to Mike; he had known me for many years since my first major successes just before breaking onto the international scene in 1994. The first major headline had been 'Wicked Witch on the Run'. I think I have certainly lived up to that name now!

Mike left us at the campsite around 1am. He had been offered the floor of the crew van or the reclining front seat. We had blankets and pillows for him, but he left us to our well deserved sleep and wandered around Wick until his train at 6:20am, obviously practising being on his feet in a sleep deprived state. I bet he slept on the train on the way home though! I laid my head down; the flame of desire had been extinguished, what remained was just smouldering at ground level, a bit like my feet still cooling down. It felt good.

Saturday 16th September - no miles!

I tossed and turned all night, my feet throbbing, and I was wide awake just after 5:30am fretting that I should be out running and Bill had forgotten to set the alarm. No, I had finished and did not have to put my feet through any more running. I told myself to turn over and go back to sleep. Awake again, it was day light. Quick panic! Why hadn't the alarm gone off? Why hadn't Bill woken me? I remembered yet again. Oh! I have finished. I wished Bill would wake up as I was longing for a cup of tea. Bill finally awoke and had a nice hug from his world record breaking wife. I really could not face any Ready Brek on that morning. I was fed up with the stuff and only forced it down for energy. I don't think I ever really felt hungry on the entire trip; food was just energy to keep me going that I had to eat. I had lived mainly off pasta and rice the entire trip, with the odd tin of salmon or steak added.

So what was for breakfast? I was looking forward to a bowl of cereal for a change, but all I got was a cup of tea and a bag of Maltesers; the crew had eaten all the cereals! I crawled out in my sandals to get a shower. Well done

Bill! He had parked right outside the shower block, less steps to walk. As much as I looked forward to a nice, long, hot shower I could not stand on my throbbing feet and wondered just how on earth I had managed to put shoes on these battered feet and run. For the first time I could see how much my body had shrunk and I knew I had suffered a significant weight loss. It turned out to be over ten pounds and I now weighed in at seven stones and three pounds. I had put on a few pounds in the last three weeks leading up to the event and was just hitting the eight stones mark at the start.

The crew were all shopping in town, their duties fulfilled. A card for me signed by all and flowers from Murdo and it was time for the long journey home. Ivor was finishing his collection of postcards that he had been making from the start. He couldn't get any from John O'Groats though, they only sold ones of Wick. Sorry, but I had no intention of going back. We drove in convoy back to Inverness and had a celebration meal there in a place Dave recommended. The telephone never stopped ringing the whole way, with calls from various friends, supporters and media. Even while eating my meal Alan had planned another interview when he knew I would be next to him to answer the mobile phone. Steak and chips made a change, but I couldn't manage a pudding. Bill did, of course! We continued back to Perth, where we left Alan and Dave. Alan had the task of returning the hired crew van to the hire centre, not a pleasant task due to the damage sustained: broken back bumper, broken back light, broken back panel, two side windows blown out and a stained carpet. The problem was mine though and it cost another £930 extra! Arki Busson from EIM was the only cash sponsor I had, and, believe it or not, he coughed up the extra to pay the excess sustained, so all ended well. Not a cheap trip, but a worthwhile one now that the dream had come true. I just wished I could bask in the glory, but I was merely a passenger relieved not to be on my feet.

Ivor and Murdo now joined us in the support van. I sat in the back with my feet up, chatting to Murdo; he was to leave us at Edinburgh. Murdo had done a sterling job, with all the mish-mash of food left over he concocted some lovely kind of pasta stews that were enjoyed by us all. One final stop on the A1 somewhere after Berwick for a coffee and chocolate bun courtesy of Ivor and it was the final drive home. I was dropping off and just dozed for the rest of the journey. We arrived home at around 10pm. Ivor had to continue his journey to Beverley.

The house was decorated with balloons and congratulations outside. The balloons were each decorated with "World Record Holder" and the time achieved. Inside, all the walls were covered with congratulations banners, clippings from local newspapers had been carefully cut out and stuck on the patio doors, there were flowers, chocolates and even a chocolate "WORLD RECORD HOLDER" that I was very reluctant to eat, despite my love of chocolate. It was a great homecoming and two very well looked after dogs greeted us. Thanks go to Martin, Denise, Sarah and Matthew for doing such a good job here, as my little dogs are very sensitive and have never been in kennels. Walnut is too scared of other dogs and would spend the whole time crying. They had been well cuddled and cared for.

I finally climbed the stairs to sleep in my own bed again. I laid my head down reflecting. What a journey! What an adventure! What an experience! Did this all really happen? I felt so content. I had dreamt of this for twelve years. Planned, cycled and driven every single step that I would have to take on this course. It had been one very long journey. For twelve years that clock had ticked waiting for this day to arrive and for twelve days the clock had ticked while I ran. Was it friend or foe? It had been a great friend. It had given me an enormous challenge. I had battled with it throughout and I had won. It had driven me to want this goal, to fight against the clock, a fight I wanted to be in; a fight I had won supremely. I slept well that night.

Chapter 11

More Extreme

I had now run the race of my life, run from one end of the country to the other, and guess what the first question was? What's next? What can be harder, longer and more extreme than this? But my next challenge was already waiting. I didn't want to run a greater distance, so it had to be more extreme: higher, hotter, and more remote. My next goal was to take part in a desert race, The Libyan Challenge 190 kilometres next February.

Two weeks after completing Land's End to John O'Groats I was still no more excited than when I finished. The only thing I liked was getting my van livery changed. It brought a tear to my eye watching a big white line covering up the word "attempt" and replacing it with the word "holder" and realising it really was me who achieved this, just like my chocolate "World Record Holder". I still could not bring myself to eat it (but the Thornton's chocolates soon went!). I had put on two pounds in weight since the challenge. The blisters went, but the soles of my feet did continue to peel for several weeks after. My legs felt fine, my feet were not tender but were still "sensitive" and I was sure they would not have liked a long run, but I had been for a couple of short runs of half an hour exactly two weeks after I finished and for an hour a couple of days later. My heart rate was still a little elevated; normally around thirty-eight to forty beats per minute, it was up to seventy-five beats per minute two days after finishing and now was around fifty beats per minute in the morning.

My next race back was just over four weeks later, the Grasp 3 kilometre track trial organised by my club, New Marske Harriers, at the local track at Guisborough. From my longest ever race to my shortest ever! I had never run a 3 kilometre race on the track. I did a few more races and some off-road marathons but eventually my left Achilles tendon decided it was going to give me some grief and I took a few weeks out towards the end of the year to strengthen and rehabilitate it. The other news at this time was that Bill finally had his second "Birmingham" hip resurfacing operation and was to be pain free at last.

My crowning glory did finally break me down into tears of emotion. To finish off 2006 I reached the finals of three sports awards. The first up was the Local Heroes with the Northern Echo. I was nominated by Mike Amos. This was a big marquee affair at Hardwick Hall with nearly one thousand guests invited. I had an invitation for myself plus three others. Bill of course was one; the other two were my great friends Roy and Marie Bainbridge. There were eight award categories; mine was the first up with "The Most Remarkable Achievement". A resume of the three finalists selected was given with photographs and I was very honoured to win this award, the presentation being made by Steve Cram. I could relax then and enjoy the rest of the awards as the butterflies settled in my stomach. It was a marvellous night out. I thoroughly enjoyed every minute; dinner was also excellent. By the end of the evening I had forgotten that the winner of each category was then put back in the hat to select an overall "Local Hero for 2006".

The Northern Echo editor, Peter Barron, ran though all the eight category winners. He then began to announce the overall winner. I was listening intently; having had a bet with Bill on whom we thought would be the winner. I never win big awards as I am an ultra runner and learnt this many years ago; "Britain's best kept secret", I used to call myself. But as the introduction continued Peter was dropping hints: "she" and "remarkable" and I was left speechless as I was announced. I didn't quite know what to do with myself. I had not anticipated this; I had been content with my individual award. I gave Bill a big hug and kiss and had to walk onto the stage to collect my engraved glass trophy from the England team manager at the time, Steve McLaren. I felt so small, as all around me stood and clapped with a standing ovation. It was overwhelming and I had to fight really hard not to collapse into a blubbering wreck. I was glad Peter didn't expect me to say anything because I really don't think I would have been capable. Yes, I was a world record holder, had given the readers a great story with my long journey of asthma, pain, traffic, blisters, big feet, determination and fight to achieve my dream and all had rewarded me with this title. It was amazing. I never slept a wink all night, as I just could not contain my excitement, reliving the moment I was announced the winner. I cried with much joy that night. I wanted the clock to slow down; my epic journey had been honoured. It had been worth the effort. The next day I was front page news yet again.

The BBC awards were not so good and I never so much as got a mention, but this was what I was used to. For the final one, the Evening Gazette Sports Awards, I was again quite hopeful, as I had now been recognised. I was one of three finalists. The other two were Chris Newton, a cyclist who won a gold medal in the team pursuit at the Commonwealth Games and now lived near Manchester and Stewart Downing, from Middlesbrough football team. Rather strange I thought, local awards for someone living in Manchester and a professional footballer for grassroots sport. Chris Newton was the winner. I was also number one in the Commonwealth but, without my event being in the Commonwealth Games, I could not get this recognition. Yes, I had built my expectations up this time and came away a little disappointed. Bill was chuffed, however, as I got my photograph taken with Stewart Downing, being a big "Boro" supporter.

Preparation for Libya was fantastic. I had much help from Teesside University, Darren Cooper in helping with the strengthening of my Achilles and Matthew Wright in strengthening my body and both were present for the heat work done in the world class facilities in the "environmental chamber" at Teesside University. My longest session was 6 hours long at thirty-seven degrees Celsius, with various tests going on. Fluids were measured, so that I knew how much water should be carried between checkpoints and they measured the energy burned, to find out whether I was burning fat or carbohydrate and at what stage my body switched energy systems depending on what I ate and how far I had run. This was to be a self sufficient challenge and eight thousand calories of

Training in the environmental chamber at Teesside University.

food needed to be carried. My usual custard and potatoes was not on the list for this one: too heavy to carry.

I love the heat and couldn't wait to experience a run across the desert. I trained with a pack of half the weight first and then increased it up to the full weight anticipated, around eight kilograms. There was a big list of compulsory kit for this one: sleeping bag, anti-venom pump, compass, first aid, anti-sceptic, pen knife, torch, salt tablets, spare batteries, global position system and food. My fitness improved enormously in the last six weeks and I adapted well to carrying the pack.

The journey was a long one, first to Paris and then up at 3:30am to get to the airport for the 6am chartered flight. A flight to Sebbah Airport and then a long bumpy coach journey to base camp near Ghat. The heat on arrival and the journey were astounding. I had seen the Pyramids and Sphinx in Egypt, but this was a whole new vista. Stunning rock formations, rich coloured sand, skylines of high mountains. It was phenomenal! The coaches followed the last sand track and ground to a halt in darkness. I had been allocated a mud hut with fellow English athlete Lizzy. The accommodation was better than I had anticipated; with straw roof and a big moulded mud lump that felt like concrete for a bed. There was just enough space to fit the suitcase around it. The toilets were primitive, a hole in the ground. The showers were from an underground thermal spring that occasionally reached luke-warm and went down the same hole as the toilet. Opposite were plastic tables and chairs in an open-sided, straw-roofed hut. The meals were mainly chicken and couscous, but perfectly adequate.

The next day was kit check and collection of numbers and a flare. Medical forms were also given in, a simple process. The camp site was like a little green oasis surrounded by rich coloured sand dunes, just as I had imagined with a few camels to one side. The food I carried was mainly the GlycoSlim powder from Mannatech, decanted into plastic zip lock bags for five hundred millilitres of water, some Nutri-grain bars, a few fig-rolls and nuts to complete the calorie count. That night was the race meeting and going through the route description and what we would expect to see. It was superb and I couldn't wait to see the landscape for real. The road book listed eighty-six global position system points with sketch diagrams.

The start the next day was around 10am and from the cool conditions overnight you could feel the temperature rising by the minute. I had opted for a long sleeved t-shirt to avoid burning. The pace at the start was fast, on a kind of gravel track and I started to get used to my new hand held global position system. The route was tough. It felt like climbing Ben Nevis, with steep hair pins up boulders and rock, but the vista on reaching the top was amazing. I had carried nearly three litres of water and using the global position system as a guide it was easy to gauge how much to drink and how far to the next checkpoint to reach more water. The global position system detailed the pace accomplished and the kilometres covered. The early checkpoints were over 20 kilometres apart, becoming closer towards the end.

After the big climb was a gentle downhill with a bit more sand and then more sand and gravel tracks, but the panorama was amazing. I had never imagined a desert to be like this. It was stunningly beautiful, with rock formations beyond anything I had ever seen. The view kept me guessing as to what was around the next corner: it was absolutely unbelievable! The field of runners soon whittled down and I was left with Paolo Barghini, a wonderful Italian who kept me entertained most of the night. I was quite scared of the night section; pitch black in the middle of no-where with only a global position system for guidance. What if it went wrong? What if I had put one of the grid references in wrong? What if I went well off-route, how would anyone find me? What if I collapsed and there was no-one with me? Who else might I bump into in this desert with Nomads? Paolo's presence was reassuring and I enjoyed his company. He had been a member of the Italian 100 kilometres team. Late on into the night Paolo's feet were becoming sore, as his gaiters had let him down. As we were leaving a checkpoint two other women were approaching. I had been the leading lady and soon shot off, eventually leaving Paolo as we could see the torch lights catching up with us. Paolo was insistent that I should continue without him as he was struggling at that moment and I was stronger and he knew I wanted to proceed.

It was initially quiet without Paolo and I missed his presence, but I had become more confident with the navigation and braved the route alone. Soon I was to climb onto one of the plateaus; I had skirted around a few and went up this one. Once on top I could not believe my eyes, as a whole new world opened up before me. It was like nothing I had ever seen before. It was as if the entire surface had been covered in shiny black polished stones that had been carefully placed next to each other, absolutely stunning! I felt as though I was on another planet, it didn't feel real. I had to stand and look and adjust. The narrow path could be seen for miles in the distance. I had never experienced anything like it. It was difficult to put into words but breathtakingly beautiful. On and on and soon the sharp descent began. I was much higher now and was pleased to hit this steep zigzag path in daylight; we had been warned it was dangerous at night.

A checkpoint was at the base and then an almost white soft sand track. I began feeling tired on this section. My feet were beginning to throb from the many rocks I'd stumbled across and I was feeling very drowsy in the afternoon sun. I had been going for over 30 hours now. I was fading, in need of a quick rest. The sun was baking down, no shade in sight. "Ah, a rock, that will do nicely", I thought. Just as I approached a snake slithered across my path. I didn't sit down and it instantly brought me back to reality. I was in a desert. Now I knew why I'd brought that anti-venom pump. "Not much longer now", I thought, "only two more checkpoints to go". At the next checkpoint was the only sustenance given other than water, a can of very welcome coke. It was fantastic, just what I needed to wake me up. I got going nicely and the darkness fell for the last few hours.

I made hard work of the last sand dunes, trying to find the finish. I was on point eighty-five; point eighty-six on the global position system was the finish. Up and down I went, but I just could not see the finish. I felt like I was going around in circles, making no progress at all. The dunes were massive. I had to run up them on all fours, sit on the top and get my breath back and slide down on my bum. I was getting more and more frustrated as the clock kept ticking and the global position system seemed to be all over the place; the arrow directing me would not stay constant. One last really big sand dune loomed. I got to the top. I sat on the top, around half a kilometre from the finish line but I could not see it. I then became aware of something about a hundred metres to my left. I kept looking into the darkness at it, then realised it was a person in Arabic dress standing like a statue with one arm straight in the air holding a light stick. Was he here to show me the way to the finish? He was silent. I stood my ground and asked, "Finish?" I got no response and didn't dare go near him. I thought he might be here to kidnap me and was very unnerved. I took two steps forward to go down the dune and he sprung into life in Arabic. I sat looking at him again and asked for, "Finish? Libyan Challenge?" Only to meet with silence again. I walked about a few metres towards him and asked again. He turned and pointed in the distance and could see a second person with a light stick. A little more confident now, he turned and walked towards the second person and I followed up and down a few more dunes. Then more words were spoken and I could now see the finish in the distance. Relief swept over me as he took my hand, dragged me up the remaining sand dunes, and guided me through a barbed wire fence, over some water pipes to the place where the air horn was sounded as I finished.

It had been the most amazing adventure I had ever been on. I'd been frightened in some places, in awe in others. A desert was nothing like what I expected, instead of monotonous sand, constantly changing scenery, with

Libyan Challenge outside the mud hut in the campsite.

lots of rocks, hills, plateaus, colour, and rock formations like none I had ever seen in my life. The result was fifth overall, first lady, 36 hours 46 minutes and a new course record by around 7 hours. Good friend Anke, from Germany that I met in the Moravian Ultra Marathon was one of the joint winners from the previous year and had improved her time this year. It was a good first trip to the desert, a magnificent experience I could hardly believe I had seen.

Next up was another international race, the World Challenge 24 Hours, at Drummondville, Quebec, Canada. This July trip was fraught with problems from start to finish, from travelling extremely late to the event, flying from London the Thursday before a Saturday race, to a sack-full of restrictions on training before the event. In addition supporters were not allowed to travel with the athletes or even stay with the athletes and we were not allowed to travel early or come home later after the event at our own expense. Spencer Barden from UK Athletics was explicit on this, we had to travel "as a team", supposedly treated like all other teams under UK Athletics rules that I had heard before. It was pointless my bringing Bill; I was supposed to pay for him to travel independently, book him separate accommodation and even then he would have to "seek permission" to approach the feed tables to be permitted to support me. UK Athletics had no understanding of the requirements of this event and how to get the best performance out of the athletes. These rules and restrictions conspired against the athletes. For the first time in ages there were both male and female teams selected, the standards having been relaxed some-what after the extreme selection criteria previously made. The men's team comprised John Pares, Chris Finill and Jim Rogers and the female team Pauline Walker, Sandra Brown and myself.

The event was my worst ever experience in life. I complained of chest pain that no one did anything about, eventually collapsing on the course after around 10 hours. I was stretchered to the medical tent, looked at by a first aider (not a doctor!), left for a couple of hours accompanied by Val (a friend of Pauline Walker's), before team management decided I should be taken back to the hotel by taxi. Still feeling very light headed with mild chest pain I passed out again and there was no choice but to take me to hospital, where at last I could find the source of the chest pain. The ambulance arrived with lights flashing and I was immediately wired to an electrocardiogram and was told there was an abnormal tracing. Blood tests at hospital confirmed I had simply run out of salt and was getting cramp in my heart. Either heart failure or kidney failure could have resulted imminently. I had hyponatraemia and my legs were very swollen. I spent the night in hospital on drips. The following morning after more blood tests to confirm my blood salts were normal I was released by the doctors and was taken to the hotel and left on my own until the evening when the team arrived. I was left with nothing, despite passing the race venue I was not allowed to pick up my case on the way; I was given the choice of "hotel or venue". Not feeling great and with the weather still very hot the hotel was the best place for me. We had checked out of the hotel, as the night of the race the hotel is not needed because we should be running; so we had to take all our belongings with us to the event to save the cost of the hotel (which incidentally athletes had to contribute to as the allocated accommodation was not ideal for the little amount of sleep we would have after our long journey). It was a long, lonely wait. My mobile phone was at the race; so I could not even call Bill to talk to him. I felt very low, stunned at what had happened, annoyed at myself for not insisting on seeking medical assistance, frustrated at the management for not taking responsibility for more prompt and appropriate action. The team returned in the evening after the awards ceremony, with below par performances due to the circumstances they had been put into. I had eaten nothing since breakfast the previous day and felt famished. By the time we went for an evening meal I was beyond eating and could barely consume a morsel. On returning home, despite having eaten little, I was still several pounds heavier, not direct weight gain, but fluid retention. Within a week I was considerably lighter!

There were a few complaints about that event and the result was no funding for next year's event. There was no attempt to fix the issues and support the athletes, everything was just brushed under the carpet and the athletes were forgotten. My reflection on this event was one of pure contempt. I have never put my life at risk from running. I run hard, run stubbornly, run in extreme conditions and over extreme terrain and distances. I have sustained minor injuries but have never, ever risked my life. I know that possibly I could have stopped and insisted on medical help, but this was a world championship event. I had trained long and hard and had arrived in probably one of my fittest states ever, having had no problems in the build up to the event. I had informed my helper of what I was experiencing and had expected appropriate action; my mind was fixed on the race and winning a medal. How would this experience have been different had Bill been with me? The answer would have been the minute I complained of chest pains he would have ensured I was seen by a doctor immediately. When I collapsed I would not have been left in a medical tent with just a first aider, he would have insisted on getting proper medical advice. I felt very let down. The clock nearly stopped ticking that day. Had I been left longer in the medical tent or made it back to the hotel without passing out it just might have stopped altogether!

I was very nervous on my first few outings after such an experience and paid a couple more visits to the doctor for advice on how to progress. I felt very despondent and unsure of myself for some time. I was nervous to push hard in training. My first long run back was the Finnforest Boston 12 hour track race at the end of August. I ran steadily with a goal of just completing the event healthily with a plan of running 10 kilometres in each hour. The result was exactly that, 120 kilometres and first person. This evidence that my body was functioning normally again was just the boost I needed.

I followed this with a run around Tooting Bec, London again. This was the usual 24 hour race; I ran 212 kilometres, apparently a stadium record. This kept me ranked number one in Great Britain. The last event of the year was another challenge into the unknown. Having run the 837 miles from Land's End to John O'Groats my distance at six days could have been vastly better; so I decided to have a crack at the 'Six Day World Record' in Monaco. For the first time I had support from Darlington Building Society to pay for all my expenses. The course was not conducive to a fast run for me; it was very crowded, with many charity walkers, push chairs, dogs, and children and it also involved cobbles, sharp corners and u-turns.

I tweaked my ankle very early on, resulting in some bad swelling. With two days not complete there was no point in continuing, though a few more lessons had been learned.

The next year, 2008, was the year of the hot races. I planned to run the Badwater Ultramarathon, the "world's hottest" race, 135 miles across Death Valley. I wanted to run some races in the heat to prepare and it was easy to make the decision to navigate the Libyan Challenge again. It was just as spectacular as the first time, the route had a few changes, including an amazing purple landscape and more amazing rocky outcrops, the only problem being that my gaiters were not so good (I bought some rather than make my own) and my shoes let the sand in, trashing my feet as a result. I had to stop frequently to empty the sand and relieve the pressure, but I was still the first lady again and lowered the course record by a small margin.

Three weeks later was the Marathon des Sables, where I was supported by EIM again. Arki Busson (EIM) had heard of this race and was keen to support me to run this. It had long been on my list of "races to do", but with my feet barely recovered from Libya it wasn't my finest hour. The

*Marathon des Sables, tent mates, Sharon, Gavin,
Paul, Colin, Steve and Andreas.*

desert did not have the beauty of Libya. But living in a tent with five men for a week developed many new friendships! The Sandblasters team consisted of Steve Partridge, Paul Mott, Gavin Pilcher and Colin Lyall. The last member of the tent was Andreas Doerfler. After a bad experience previously in this race, he came back to correct this and had a superb run. I could not have faulted one of them; they were a great bunch of supportive athletes, although there were mixed fortunes with the results.

I had also changed running clubs now, from having spent many happy years at New Marske Harriers, a great supportive club that I still have great respect for and would recommend to many runners, I joined North York Moors Athletics Club who were developing and progressing all the time. Their runners competed in many more of the races I competed in most weekends. In addition, when I left New Marske Harriers there were few runners in the club of better standard than me at the shorter races. By comparison, when I joined North York Moors Athletics Club I never even made the top three for team places in several races and had to fight hard to get a placing. This challenge was what I needed and I liked to be part of a team event where possible. North York Moors Athletics Club also boasted some ultra distance runners, not necessarily 100 kilometre and 24 hour runners, but runners who regularly competed in races up to and over 100 miles.

After sustaining a stress fracture to my left hip while running the Surgeres 48 Hour Race in France in May, I missed my big race for the year, the Badwater Ultramarathon. All the preparation races in hot conditions had been for nothing. The stress fracture was put down to the poor diet during the week-long events in the deserts where food was restricted. In the Marathon des Sables you have to be self sufficient for a week and I lived off dehydrated foods. The heavy pack, long hours and poor diet had a cumulative effect, with the stress fracture the consequence. I finally resumed light running by the end of August and after three easy weeks, three hard weeks and a two week taper I went to Tooting Bec, London to attempt to maintain my rank as Great Britain's number one for the twelfth consecutive year. I always knew I was pushing my luck with fitness and the contingency plan was to assess the distance covered in 12 hours to see whether I was fit enough to achieve my goal. There had been one good performance so far that year by Pauline Walker at 210 kilometres; so knew I had to beat this.

I ran well for 11 hours and then started to stiffen up in the hip region and my pace began to drop. At 12 hours it became evident that, if I continued to slow up, then 210 kilometres was beyond me and I was not prepared to fight hard with a body that was not strong enough to deliver the goods. So I turned to plan B which was to stop at 12 hours while still in reasonable shape and give myself another chance later in the year to try again. Vicky Skelton went on to pip Pauline by a single kilometre finishing with 211 kilometres; both ladies ran very good personal bests to achieve these distances.

Within days of returning home I knew I could not give up without a fight and scoured the internet for one more attempt at a 24 hour race that year. With winter closing in, knowing that the cold months are not my best time, as I suffer with asthma in cold and windy conditions, I wasn't sure that I would even find a suitable race until I came across the Bislett 24 hour indoor race. Now that fascinated me! I had never run indoors. It took out the weather conditions: no wind and rain, no wet feet. It sounded perfect! A quick look at the website and I saw the first obstacle. The race entry had closed back in September with a full entry and a waiting list for those waiting for a place from anyone that might drop out. I emailed the organiser anyway, in the hope that, as a foreign athlete with a good distance to back me up, I might gain entry. I was in luck and got an amazing email back. Not only did the organiser Bjoern already know who I was, he sent a picture of me running at Tooting Bec past my sign written van along with an immediate entry into the race!

The training began; extra gym work for the hips, racing twice most weekends with a short blast in the regular 5 kilometre time trials at Albert Park, in addition to above 80 miles during the week, hill repetitions and weights. I had another seven weeks to get fit. My 5 kilometre times improved initially but took a nose dive on the last two weeks due to the cold conditions as the asthma took control.

The weekend finally arrived and I was in good shape, no niggles at all, all planned training complete and a new bonus thrown in to challenge me. I had found out that the British indoor 24 hour track record stood at 207 kilometres as set by Eleanor Robinson while running in a 48 hour race. Other information had also come to light on selection criteria for the following year. So I was going into this race with five goals to spur me on:

- **Goal 1** – 200 kilometres: selection distance for the Commonwealth Championships 24 Hours the following September, Keswick.
- **Goal 2** – 207 kilometres: British indoor record.
- **Goal 3** – 212 kilometres: Great Britain number one for the twelfth year.
- **Goal 4** – 213 kilometres: UK Athletics "A" selection standard for the World Challenge 24 Hours, Bergamo, Italy, 2009.
- **Goal 5** – 218 kilometres: to beat my personal best of 217.5 kilometres.

This was a unique 24 hour race and a journey that you might like to experience. What is it really like to run for 24 hours? Could I really come back strong after having been side-lined for three months with injury? How much did I really want to hold onto my Great Britain ranking? Was I kidding myself or was I still the best Great Britain had at running for 24 hours? It had been highlighted that the best British performances came at Tooting Bec. This was my last-ditch attempt to claim back my place. Could I achieve it against all the odds? I was now forty-five years old.

Having flown to Oslo on Thursday, it was Friday when Bill and I visited the famous Bislett stadium. It snowed all day. The track we were to run on was amazing. It runs under the main seating area and was just two track lanes wide. At points there were exit doors to the main 400 metre outdoor track that was about ten steps above where we were to run, but they were all locked and the track obviously not in use. As for our running track, there were several athletes training here already, doing some sprint work. It was a 545 metre track. In the clockwise direction there was one downhill section and two shorter uphill sections, and the track was not uniform. There was one straight of around 100 metres which also had a parallel four lane straight track to the side. The rest all appeared to be on a slight arc that varied in the angle of the curve, but was far less severe than a 400 metre track. There were also several sets of open double doors to run through. One section was heated and classed as a "warm zone" of approximately forty percent of the track, the remainder of sixty percent was the "cold zone".

Luck would have it that the first person I approached was the organiser, Bjoern. I had not recognised him from Tooting Bec, as I only ever saw the back of athletes and never saw their faces. He had supplied me with lots of information and photographs of the track beforehand to help me understand this race. He was also very aware of my goals for this race and how important it was to me. Because he was an ultra runner himself, I just knew this was going to be a well organised race and the previous results spoke for themselves as there had been some very good performances here. My last request was for a table and chair to set ourselves up in order for Bill to support me during the race. These were supplied immediately and we chose our spot in the "warm zone". There were one hundred and twenty athletes competing, thirty-six of these were in the 12 hour race that started at the same time so space was at a premium. Everything in place, it was now back to the hotel for one last massage and time to relax and eat.

Saturday arrived and it had finally stopped snowing, but it was bitterly cold and was even cold by Norwegian standards. Reports were of minus two degrees Celsius for the day and minus nine degrees Celsius for the night. It was hard to know exactly how cold I might feel with the continuous cycle of "hot, cold, hot, cold" but Bjoern had warned me this race would be cold and that it was more important to dress for this, especially as the race progressed and the pace dropped. He was not wrong.

We arrived around 9:30am for the midday start and sat at my table drinking coffee. The temperature was reading seventeen degrees Celsius in the warm zone. I met several friendly faces: Kim, with whom I had raced in Libya and who was a member of his national team and Per Lind, the Norwegian team manager, whom I had met several times in different countries. I was number eighty-two and had a personalised number with my name and national flag printed on it; very nice. The not so nice bit was having two very large champion-chips to strap to each ankle. These were different from all other chips I had seen and I just knew they might cause a problem resting on the tendons on the front of my ankles later into the race, but the good news was you could concentrate on the race and not worry about a lap recorder missing you.

At 11:30am we were called to the starting area for a small opening ceremony. This was very pleasant. Each athlete was grouped by nationality and their name read out and national anthem played. I was the only British athlete; so felt very proud that the British National Anthem was played just for me.

The race finally got underway at midday. I was feeling relaxed. My schedule had been written to achieve 214 kilometres, but on a good day I could stretch the odd couple of kilometres if a personal best was within my reach. The starting pace was the key, a vital component, and had planned this precisely: no faster than 3 minutes 5 seconds and no slower than 3 minutes and 10 seconds per lap. I started close to the front, knowing this was a big field, and hoped that I was one of the best in the field. I was aware of Sharon Broadwell. She had run 211 kilometres at this stadium last year and was ranked one below me in the world rankings the previous year (I was eleventh and she was twelfth), she could prove to be a powerful adversary.

Off we went and after starting in the warm zone we ran into the cold zone and down the slope and bang! Shock! This was really, REALLY cold! I was wearing long tights, a long sleeved shirt and a short sleeved shirt; it was absolutely freezing and I could feel the cold take my breath away as well as the cold on my arms. My immediate reaction was that I needed another long sleeved shirt on. This was far colder than I anticipated, even indoors.

I was told it should not get below five degrees Celsius, but an athlete who slept in the stadium the previous night told me it went down to minus five degrees Celsius in the cold zone and would be even colder tonight. Bill was sitting waiting for me to circle, so I asked him, "Get me the long sleeved blue shirt for next lap please; it's too cold." The warm zone was good to get back to, but did not last long. On my second lap round I took off my t-shirt while running and tucked it in my tights ready for putting on my extra layer. Bill smoothly handed me the shirt and I continued on my way. Three top layers on now; would this keep me warm enough?

I went back to concentrating on the clock and getting my pace right; it was 3 minutes 20 seconds for the first two laps and I had noticed that Sharon Broadwell had overtaken me while putting on my extra shirt. One more lap and my time was too slow. This was very rare for me, as the first couple of laps were usually too fast and am usually slowing myself down. Was this a bad omen indicating that I was not as good as I thought or was the cold having an immediate effect? I increased the pace slightly and got onto the tail of the other Sharon. She was with a big group of around fifteen athletes and I bit the bullet and overtook the lot to get into free space. A 3 minute lap was the result. "Settle down and relax now", I was telling myself and soon the laps were like clockwork, spot on 3 minutes and 5 seconds. The laps ticked by but it was difficult to completely relax. It hadn't taken me that long to catch up the back markers and a continuous overtaking phase began, but there was no chance of running on the inside of lane one, I was more often on the outside of lane two, then weaving between runners. It was not great and I had to concentrate and be careful to anticipate runners who suddenly moved out in front of me to overtake an even slower runner in front of them.

I soon just got used to this, not completely happy and relaxed, but this was the race and was what I had to do. At least it would thin out as the clock ticked and time progressed and the 12 hour runners stopped. The hot and cold zone was a novel experience and was surprisingly easy to adapt to and did not cause any real problems. The track was also one of my most weird running experiences ever. It is hard to describe and put into words, but part of it felt like running through someone's living room, if felt carpeted with a warm feeling and low ceilings, lined with tables full of athletes' personal items, then through a set of doors and a kind of "tunnel experience" almost Dr Who-like. The walls were immediately either side of the two lanes, white and with low ceilings you could almost touch bending around an arc, then another set of doors and out into the shocking cold, downhill and a massive communal food and drink area from the organisation. This was probably one of the best displays of food and drink I had ever witnessed in a race: really long tables lined up, cups of drinks ready, hot and cold, all kinds of suitable foods on display, hot food available at certain times, masses of room for the runners to easily access the tables without tripping each other up and getting in any one's way. It was excellent.

After this was the first short uphill on a bend, then through another set of doors and then the long straight which almost felt like an underground car park with big concrete pillars holding up the stands above. Then the curve began again that led to the next short uphill, enclosed by more white walls and on through one more set of doors, back into the warm zone. Noise, music, cheering, a large screen with runners' distances flashing on it, and then Bill and my table draped with the Union Jack. Round and round and round. I somehow didn't feel I was in a race. I was aware that although my pace overall for time was stable, I was often putting on small spurts of speed to overtake a group of runners or squeeze between runners two or three abreast. There were only a few occasions where I did hit a complete brick wall of runners and requested a passage through, which was always courteously given.

The clock continued to tick away and with the first 4 hours complete, 41.9 kilometres was the distance which made me first lady with Sharon Broadwell fourth lady, some 4 kilometres adrift and obviously not in top form. My schedule was for 41.4 kilometres, so to find that I was one lap ahead of schedule, just 545 metres too fast after 4 hours of running was very pleasing. I was in sixth place overall in the race.

The next 4 hours ticked away easily with absolutely no problems and the result was then 82.8 kilometres compared to the schedule of 81.7 kilometres. So I was now two laps up on my schedule and had moved up to joint second overall. The champion-chips did cause some puzzlement initially, because when running through the warm zone the lights on our ankles flashed red, obviously recording data and when leaving the zone stopped flashing again. There were also quiet little beeps as you entered and exited the recording zones, but better than the loud "chirp chirp" that is heard from the more common champion-chips. I saw many runners trying to look at their ankles to see if their lights were flashing.

It was now approaching midnight and the temperature was dropping. I stopped and put on another long sleeved shirt to keep the cold out. The results at half way were now 122.0 kilometres compared to my schedule of 120.9 kilometres. I had heard that I was equal first after 11 hours, but I was caught up in my own challenge to achieve my goals and winning the race outright and fighting so early on was not part of my plan.

232

As I was now above my schedule my fight was not to lose the extra kilometre gained and finish with a better distance than the 214 kilometres schedule and the glimmer of hope that all five goals might be achieved. I was in second position overall, a lap behind the leader with the second lady over 20 kilometres behind me, so no worries there.

The 12 hour runners now stopped and all kept out of the way of the 24 hour runners while they waited for their last part of a lap to be measured. The field seemed to be so much thinner now and I could finally get through to the inside lane for the majority of the time. It was also evident that quite a few of the 24 hour runners had called it a day, Sharon Broadwell had exited a few hours ago obviously having a bad day, it is a long race and hard to get everything right on the day.

All of a sudden half way around the track we were being turned around. I had forgotten that there was only to be one change of direction and that was after the 12 hour runners had finished, it was not far from 1am now. Initially it feels very strange changing direction and feels like a completely new course. Instead of one down and two ups it was now two downs and one up, but I was still enjoying the change of pace that these small slopes brought about and it certainly helped to use different muscles. A live band had also set up in the warm zone and played for over 2 hours. There had been almost constant music. Beforehand we could put forward our favourite music to be played and it was interesting to hear the various tracks the runners liked. I was also being continually photographed and wondered how much was being relayed back to the supporting public watching the race via the website. The feedback we were getting during the race was fantastic. Although I could see the screen, I preferred Bill to read it and give me the information, so I could concentrate on the race itself. Every hour he was feeding me my distance and position and how close other runners were to me.

My pace usually slows in the second half and it's usually a case of, "keep moving and the distance will increase". I find it hard to eat and run now; so after 12 hours of non-stop running (apart from toilet visits and extra clothes) I now stopped to walk and eat my various foods. These were mainly small sandwiches, custard, bananas and mashed potato. Then I got back running again. The cold was still creeping in though, and, as I already had four top shirts on and felt like Michelin Man, I added my hat and gloves.

I was pleasantly surprised to find that by 16 hours my distance was now 157.5 kilometres compared to my schedule of 153.6 kilometres. If I could keep this going then a new personal best was on the cards, but I had become very aware since about 13 hours that the champion-chips were weighing heavy on the tendons on the front of my ankles, the left one felt particularly bruised. I had seen many runners bending over and adjusting the Velcro straps on these and decided that now was the time to stop and put on some padding underneath in the form of a pain relief patch to prevent further bruising. This would waste time, but would be worth the time in the long run. Although the right one was not too bad, I thought it best to cut my losses and patch up both ankles while stopped rather than just do the left one now and find out a few hours later that the right one needed doing, requiring me to disrupt my pace and schedule yet again. I had to stop and take both socks and shoes off in order to do this and must have taken over 10 minutes out. I knew I would lose some of the distance gained but I should still be ahead of schedule.

I had run for 20 hours now and the distance came back as 188.5 kilometres. The schedule was 186.3 kilometres; so I was still 2 kilometres up and now was the time to dig in and fight to reach my goals. They were to come thick and fast and I wanted to achieve as much as possible. Of all the goals listed, the most important one to me was to maintain my number one status for the twelfth year. After all, this had taken twelve years to achieve!

I was surprised at how clean and tidy the track still was. There were plastic boxes placed at regular intervals around the track and everyone heeded the rules to place rubbish in the boxes. Other cleanliness issues that were also pleasing to observe were that everyone was using the trackside toilets, a rule not always complied with by the men on outside courses when there is a grass verge and this even extended to the poor runners who were sick. They also used the rubbish bins. Pity the people cleaning them out!

It was still dark outside. Although you could see the track through the couple of exit doors there was little sensation of daylight and darkness. It turned dark shortly after 3pm and light around 9am, but I had not seen a bright day yet and it was always very overcast. Inside, the track had continuous strip lights above the entire track for the full 24 hours; so the light never felt like it changed.

I was fighting hard to keep going now. Initially after 12 hours the tops of my hamstrings and my buttocks had felt fatigued. It was now the turn of the quads to scream at me with every stride that landed. I was also very aware that I must have a big blister on the inside forefoot of my right foot, as it was very tender, but these are all just normal aches and pains of ultra runs that you have to ignore and just get on with the job. It was a long hard race. Now at 21 hours of running and a distance of 195.6 kilometres I was still to achieve a single goal, but they were approaching and I was continually doing the maths in my head, as I really wanted all five goals.

Goal one of 200 kilometres, the "A" standard selection distance for the Commonwealth Championships 24 Hours to be held in Keswick the following year was finally achieved at 21 hours 37 minutes, but this was the least of my goals. By 22 hours the distance was 202.7 kilometres and goal two of 207 kilometres and a new British indoor 24 hour track record was achieved some way after this. By 23 hours the distance was 210.3 kilometres and a new goal had been brought to my attention: the Bislett stadium track record was held by none other than the worlds' best ever 24 hour runner, Edit Berces, world record holder of 24 hours at that time and previous world champion. Her record here was 214.3 kilometres and it was obvious that the organisers would be thrilled to bits to have a new record set here that should confirm their status as an excellent venue for good performances. I duly obliged but was dead set on my own goals of a new personal best which was very "touch and go".

Goal three, the one I strived for to maintain my status at the top of the British rankings for the twelfth year, of 212 kilometres, was finally achieved and soon after goal four of UK Athletics "A" standard for the international 24 hours the following year was behind me along with the stadium record. Just one more goal left to achieve now. The excitement was mounting, the noise was deafening and the crowds were growing, the cameras flashing and my pain increasing. I couldn't get so close and not achieve my last goal. I needed the distance on every lap after 23 hours and 30 minutes of running, so that I could do the maths to achieve my last goal. Bill was standing at the screens relaying the distance every lap. With 25 minutes to go I needed five laps. Easy, that's one lap every 5 minutes. On and on, I dared not even stop to have food now, as this was just too close for comfort. My strategy was a minimum of at least one item of food per hour, but this was the last hour and there was no time for food. It was happening; this was going to be my best ever run! With less than 10 minutes remaining on the clock my final goal was surpassed with that magical 218 kilometres being flashed on the screen. I could relax now and wave and acknowledge the crowds of supporters spurring me on; it was fantastic. I had not realised just how many people were now here. It was one of those wonderfully warm feelings where I felt like just bursting into tears and jumping for joy, but I think the legs would have collapsed in agony had I tried. I just plodded on, very content that the money that Darlington Building Society had invested in me coming to this race was to bear fruit and success was to be finally achieved after the months of recovery during the summer.

It was now time to switch on to the finish and avoid collapse. With such a hard last hour I was running on empty; food and heat were the priority. So the request was, "Mashed potato and a down jacket the minute I stop running, please Bill". As I ran through for my final lap I caught up with the first man, German athlete Ralf Weis. He had spoken to me a couple of times during the race as he had a battle to keep ahead, since he had run the Spartathlon at the end of September and was not fully recovered and 10 kilometres below his best distance. The countdown began and we finished together, Ralf first person, me second. Unfortunately we had just hit the freezing cold zone! Organiser Bjoern was immediately there with the camera; what a good shot, the two winners finishing at the same spot. Photographs taken, it was on with the jacket and down with the food.

We were not that far from the starting area; so within a few minutes our part laps were recorded and we were free to go. A big hug from Bill and I staggered back to the table. I had a quick lay down on one of the many camp beds that the organiser had provided. There was a complete room full of beds for the athletes to use from the night before the race and all through the race. After 10 minutes or so I was feeling a bit better and the mashed potato was doing its job and I needed to take off my numerous

World best indoor distance for 2008, Bislett, Oslo.

236

damp tops. Bill held the Union Jack up to shield me while I stripped the top wet layers off in exchange for dry ones and just put my track bottoms on top of my tights as these were not too damp. Next it was removal of the shoes and just one blister, but it was a big one. That burst, it was time to relax with some hot tea and wait for the presentation.

I was first up on the podium and was presented with the biggest, heaviest trophy I had ever seen (it has now been weighed at twenty pounds or nine kilograms). I had to put it down as the second and third ladies got on the podium as I just didn't have the strength at this stage to hold it for the entire presentation. Per Lind, the Norwegian team manager presented me with my prize. He is a really nice person that I have met several times and was very encouraging; along with a few other prizes I also got a Norwegian hat as I kept moaning it was cold. I was very grateful as I only took one hat and that was now damp and smelly.

Then we had the effort to walk back the 2 kilometres to the hotel, with Bill carrying the kit bags and me the trophy. That didn't last long as Bill had to keep swopping and carrying the trophy as well. The temperature outside was absolutely raw, but at least it wasn't snowing. Back at the same hotel above the shops in the centre, we took the lift up the four flights of stairs to the reception. This was an experience in itself, one of those doors that you pull open, step inside the lift and then there is no door between you and the different floors, nothing automatic here. Room 528 also gave us a little smile, as right next to the door, written on the wall was the word "legend" with an arrow pointing to the door, most appropriate as I had been called this several times already this year!

We had some food and a little rest and Bill fed the seagulls on the window sill with left over sandwiches. They were enormous and he had to shut the windows quickly to stop them flying in the room. After even more food and a shower we finally went to bed at 9pm, but totally unable to sleep, I tossed and turned as usual, got up, made tea, rested again, made some couscous at around 3am and more tea and was drinking tea yet again when Bill finally came back to life around 8:30am. My resting heart rate was now seventy-six beats per minute compared to its normal around thirty-eight beats per minute; so no wonder I wasn't sleeping! Then it was off for the flight home.

On reflection I was just relieved that this came off. I knew I was in a much fitter state than for Tooting Bec, but there was still that niggling worry that three months of no running might still affect my performance later into the race. I ran a steady controlled race, had no excessive time out, just a couple of stops for extra kit and to put patches on my ankles. I ran continuously for the first 12 hours and then only walked to eat. The cold area probably helped in some ways, as there was no way that I could have walked in the cold conditions as I would have got too cold. My nutrition had been spot on, no major energy dips or feeling sick at any stage and the results just speak for themselves. In reality I had my schedule written for 214 kilometres, as this was what I anticipated I was fit enough to run. I always hoped for a personal best, but I really didn't think I would be fit enough this year. The fact that I had gained a personal best in this race now gave me the confidence to know that I could still go further. The conditions in this race were really cold and having four layers of clothes on can't have helped. Also, all the overtaking in the first 12 hours must have added considerably to the distance.

As for the event itself, Bjoern had done an absolutely fantastic job of organising it: the venue, the equipment supplied, such as beds, table and chairs, the food and drinks table, the technical equipment for measuring and displaying the results, the fantastic trophy and prize giving, the amazing support and encouragement, the music playing, the perfectly clean track, and the fact that rubbish bins were continuously emptied along with clean track side toilets (not very common!). Now back home with the 24 hour statistics at hand it was obvious how good this performance really had been, so here are some statistics showing what I had achieved:

- Ranked as Great Britain's top female 24 hour runner for 2008 (twelfth year).
- IAU world 24 hour ranking 2008, including indoor, outdoor, road and track events - number 11.
- World best indoor 24 hour track performance for 2008.
- Bislett stadium 24 hour track record.
- British indoor 24 hour track record.
- World best indoor 24 hour track record, veteran woman 45.
- World best indoor 12 hour track record, veteran woman 45.

With my renewed fitness I had been planning the next big one for some time. It was another six day world record attempt, but this time on home soil with a perfect course. The only problem: I had to organise it. Darlington Building Society generously sponsored this event again. Croft Circuit near Darlington was to be the venue. The big recession was now biting though and Bill had been made redundant just before Christmas with no sign of any jobs on the horizon. I, too, lost a contract leading up to Christmas; so for the first time in our lives we both had to sign on for Job Seekers Allowance. But at least it gave me time for the organisation of this race.

The other good news to start the year was my first sponsor for shoes; new to this country from America were Spira shoes. These shoes use spring technology for the cushioning and energy return. They were revolutionary new shoes that I was eager to try. Many people say they can feel the springs in the shoes. I personally couldn't but I really couldn't fault the first few outings in their lightweight racer, the Stinger, combining the lightness of a racer with great flexibility and my legs after races felt like the results from a heavier training shoe, no stiffness at all. I took nearly all the North York Moors Athletics Club veteran female 40-49 records within months of wearing these shoes. The more supportive structured training shoes, such as Striker, would have to wait until they had been tried and tested in some long events before I could be confident of their use.

The Croft Circuit Six Day race being held in February was not the best time of the year, but it had been the only time I had space in the busy calendar to fit this in. I had a great referee in the form of Ian Champion, who travelled all the way from London for this one, referee of many Tooting Bec races, London Marathons and London to Brighton's, not forgetting his efforts in the Flora 1000 Mile Challenge. My other experienced six day race volunteer official was Roger Lawton, whose wife badly broke her leg the night before the event; so he was unable to make it. Course measurer and lap recorder was the good old faithful Alan Young from Dundee.

The event started after a week of snow in the North East. Alan and Ian arrived the night before the start and slept in a caravan provided for the officials at Croft Circuit. There was a sprinkling of snow by the time Bill and I left the venue on Sunday evening, after setting out the course and organising the food and sleeping area. At 10am on the Monday morning Tanni Grey-Thompson set us on our way, a very small field of runners to adhere to the rules for setting a world record. I made some great friends here and the support given by people I hardly knew was amazing. After Roger had no choice but to drop out, officials from Loftus and Whitby Athletics Club stepped in with little notice; that was Brenda and Tony Hare. Andrew Russell ran his first ever marathon, Linda Guy was amazing for the hours of running completed, as was Shirley Gibson, going for her first ever 100 miles in a week. Their husbands, Alan Guy and Will Gibson were stalwarts, doing what they could to keep the track clear of snow, stones, and other obstacles and doing what they could to support. Runners such as Lydia and Martin Dietrich joined in the event as much as possible, appearing at all times to support me the best they could. Peter Rowley, Chief Executive of Darlington Building Society came every evening too and brought along a friend to run with me. Peter had given me some good

Start of Croft Circuit Six Days, Martin, Lydia, Sharon, reporter, Shirley, Andrew and Tanni with the starting horn. © Alan Young.

battles over the year, nearly as many races as me considering the high powered job he held at the time. This was just a few of the many supporters that came, watched, helped and even cooked welcome meals for the officials.

For my part it didn't happen. Everything was pretty much on schedule through the first two days. Before going to bed on the second night my left shin was becoming painful and by running at first light I became aware of what it was heading towards. The injury was directly on the bone, not a soft tissue injury and I recognised the signs immediately. I was heading towards another stress fracture. I withdrew at that stage knowing there would be no point in continuing until the bone fractured, as the world record was off and I was not here to run six days. Like Land's End to John O'Groats it was world record or bust. It was frustrating, as the public support and media interest had been amazing and I knew that if I could break the record this would be the place to do it, but it would have to wait for another day.

After pulling out of the world record attempt Bill presented me with a gift. The other thing I now had time for was going back to a long-lost childhood love of doing jig-saw puzzles. For many nights as a child I had engrossed myself in five thousand piece puzzles that passed the time away, waiting for the clock to tick. Now, while Bill watched his films I would put together jig-saw puzzles. We were in the same room, could still have a take-away and eat chocolate and popcorn, and we were both happy with our individual relaxation jobs. I had now got into shaped jig-saw puzzles, such as the shape and picture of a lion or dolphin, usually around one thousand pieces that I could finish in a day. While researching for more puzzles I had joked with Bill about finding the world's biggest jig-saw puzzle; that came in at twenty-four thousand pieces and was a beautiful, brightly coloured image called "Life". It was made up of an incredible planet system, hot air balloons in amazing colours, some sailing boats with bright sails; an array of animals running across the land, some exotic underwater sea-life and a destroyed underwater village. "Life" was an amazing piece of artwork, full of variety, activity, colour, beauty and drama.

Unknown to me, Bill had got one as a joke, supposedly to make me rest after my six days of exertion. He now presented it to me to help me with my recovery. It did put a smile on my face, as he had teased me with it for weeks. What I hadn't expected was for the media to pick up on it. It attracted very generous attention and I was continually being asked if I would actually attempt the puzzle. I thought it was a joke present and one to sit on the shelf and wait for retirement, if I hadn't forgot about it by then. But the media attention and the fact that I was not going to be able to run for the next few weeks due to the injury changed my thoughts. It was a really interesting picture, extremely colourful, appropriately named and in some ways I couldn't resist the challenge to complete it. I had no idea how long it would take, probably many months.

The size of the puzzle was the next obstacle. It was enormous measuring in at 4.28 metres by 1.57 metres (14 feet by 5 feet 2 inches). We purchased some wood and then put together a table that took the entire length of our conservatory. There was hardly any room to manoeuvre. I had to go out of the back door and in through the conservatory doors to access the puzzle. The patio doors into the conservatory were out of use. I spent over a day sorting all the pieces into different buckets and containers including the straight edges and set to work. The sails of the boats were first to go into place, followed by the hot air balloons and the stars and planets, next up was the sea and boats followed by the animals. All this was pretty easy and constructed quite quickly. The underwater village was by far the hardest and after progressing really well for the first two weeks it took me a week to complete this small section of just a few thousand pieces.

The media kept ringing to check on my progress, a picture had been taken by the local Evening Gazette on the first day of this new challenge with all the edges pieces in place demonstrating its size and heaps of pieces scattered all over the table. I spent about 5 or 6 hours a day on the puzzle initially and thoroughly enjoyed my leisure time. I then began to realise it could be done far quicker than I had initially thought and as it took up so much room it was best to get it done and finished and put the house back to normal. The interest in the puzzle also spurred me on. I was doing aqua-jogging in the local swimming pool as part of my rehabilitation (running in the water wearing a floatation device around my waist) and many recognised me as, "That runner doing the big jig-saw puzzle". I got stuck in and finished the puzzle in 4 weeks and 13 hours; promptly getting a photograph taken by the Evening Gazette again the day I finished. I was stunned when Barbara Argument, the feature writer came back after some investigation to tell me that it looked like it was a new world record. I was gob-smacked! I didn't even know such records existed.

After submitting the evidence (the local media helped enormously here), I did some research myself. I had not realised that the four packs that the puzzle came in were in fact four separate sections of the puzzle. I had mixed them all together unaware of this! Even if I had known I would have been a purist and mixed the pieces together anyway, as this would otherwise have made four puzzles of six thousand pieces and defeated the whole idea of being the world's largest jig-saw puzzle. Mike Amos also did his bit in the Northern Echo, a whole page featuring jig-saw puzzles. He stupidly mentioned something called the world's most difficult jig-saw puzzle. This only has eighteen thousand pieces but is mainly green and of jungle scenery – so can you guess what might happen should I dare attempt another six day race?

The result of this coverage reached many places, I had several other sources of media that made contact, went on the radio, did interviews in other areas and found it unbelievable that such a past-time could generate such interest, much more than my running ever did and it was far less strenuous! I always assumed that most people thought putting jig-saw puzzles together was a dumb exercise similar to Bill's view that was, "You spend hours (or days and weeks in this case) constructing a superb picture only to smash it into bits again". I could see his reasoning. But it kept me happy and he could watch his films and football in peace.

Half way through doing this puzzle I had been on the local radio and made a trip to BBC Tees for this sole purpose. While I was attending early in the morning, Bill had been off for an interview for another potential job. The first comment made was, "We heard your wife on the radio this morning doing that big jig-saw puzzle. How is she getting on?" Bill was promptly offered the job with Central Industrial Services in Redcar where he had worked many years ago. Just after the Commonwealth Championships 24 Hours race later that year I was to find work lecturing at Teesside University.

Selection soon came through for the World Challenge 24 Hours in Bergamo, Italy. Great Britain had a strong team with some recent good performances by the women. The team announced with me was Pauline Walker, Vicky Skelton and Lynne Kuz. For the men was sole representative Stephen Mason. We all performed below par again. The weather was hot and I took salt tablets after my last disaster in the heat. I lasted around 20 hours; too much salt this time compared to Canada, another hard way to learn this lesson. I ended up in the medical tent with a drip.

But three weeks after the race in Bergamo I thought I could make amends in the Surgeres 48 hour race in France, another equivalent world class event. This is not an event you can enter, you have to be invited and that is usually based on the world rankings. I had sustained my stress fracture here the previous year. Before going to Surgeres I had been to see a Rheumatologist for the results of a bone density scan and the results were not good. Two bone stress injuries in less than twelve months and the answer lay here. My bone density was nearly two standard deviations below normal. I had Osteopenia. I was fortunate enough to now change a medication I had taken for several years that could have been contributing to this and was put on new medication that could help improve this issue. Any future attempts on multi day races would depend on whether this condition could be improved. I started Surgeres with this "fear factor" and ran conservatively with running two long ultras a mere three weeks apart. I dared not sustain another injury. I never finished this race partly due to practicing a new nutritional strategy and possibly the fear of injury.

Finally, it was off to the Badwater Ultramarathon, "The Challenge of Champions, 135 miles, 125 degrees of heat, 60 hours time limit". The start was at 10am on Monday 13th July 2009. Training had been going well; a slightly reduced mileage to help the bones, but twice as much cross training to compensate. I tried to do at least one aqua-jogging session in the pool per week, do several hours on the elliptical trainer, as well as biking, rowing, two weights sessions a week and around the 70 miles a week mark in running. For the last four weeks I had been doing my elliptical trainer work in the conservatory with all the windows and doors shut and managed to get the heat nearly up to the fifty degrees Celsius mark (one hundred and twenty-two degrees Fahrenheit), but regularly it was over forty degrees Celsius. I did wilt with the higher temperatures, but also there was little air circulating which did make conditions very hard. The floor looked like I just tipped the drinks all over it, such was the sweat rate, but it got me used to drinking and I weighed myself to monitor how well I was hydrating. I have always been pretty good at this as long as water was available.

We had booked a couple of week's holiday for this event with having to travel so far. We arrived in Las Vegas; we walked out of the airport and WOW! This was hot! It was forty-two degrees Celsius and was sweltering. It would be even hotter in Death Valley and this was already really unbelievably hot and sticky. It was around 2:30pm in the afternoon (8 hours behind United Kingdom time). We immediately boarded the air conditioned bus to take us to the car hire centre and collect our Jeep Liberty (air conditioned of course) and then took a drive up "The Strip" to our hotel. The hotels here were enormous, something like fifteen of the world's twenty-five biggest hotels were here, and ours was not to let us down: tower block three, floor twenty-three and room seventeen.

We spent a few nights in Las Vegas and then went camping near the Grand Canyon for acclimatisation. At night time we could hear the coyotes howling and even watched one run purposefully through the campsite. I managed to drag Bill down to the bottom of the Grand Canyon to touch the forceful Colorado River and back up in a day, not without a few incidents! Highlights were seeing a condor, watching some elks, and some squirrel like animals fighting over some nuts.

Finally it was time to head to Death Valley. As we approached the National Park so the warning signs began, "DANGER, EXTREME HEAT" and we watched the temperature rise, the lower we sank into the valley. We stepped out of the Jeep at Badwater at 10am so that I could go for a 3 mile training run, and the heat was incredible. I didn't think it was humanly possible that any of the athletes could really survive this heat. It was scorching just standing around and Bill was plastering himself with sun oil while I got changed into my running kit. So off I went. It was exciting; I could not believe I was actually here and running! The scenery was of desolate sand and rocky mountain ranges, all without colour and the heat haze was rising, giving a kind of shimmering blurriness to the landscape. A mile on and there was Bill in the Jeep. It wasn't so bad running, in fact it almost felt like standing around was hotter than running, as the breeze gained by running cooled you down more. Onto the second and third mile and that was my first training run of the day, 28 minutes and 44 seconds. I had tried to mimic race pace, so I was definitely heading towards the 6 miles an hour that I usually averaged at 24 hour races, but I half guessed I would be walking some of the race to keep the core temperature down.

Back in the Jeep and we drove to the next timing station at Stovepipe Wells, around 42 miles. This first section is supposed to be the hardest and hottest of the entire race and I have heard that if you make it this far you have "cracked the race". We drove the rest of the route, checking out supplies and opening times of the small stores as we went over two mountain ranges and to Lone Pine. After this was the Mount Whitney Road. Here I jumped out again for another 3 mile run to experience the gradient. This was around 5,000 feet of climbing over 13 miles. The gradient was steep, it was challenging with this steady run on fresh legs but I guessed when I made it here after 122 miles of running I would be walking this. Bill did his usual job of drinks every mile and this time the 3 miles took nearly 34 minutes to run. The heat was still intense and the wind was swirling and nearly blew my hat off. It also blew sand in my eyes, despite wearing sunglasses; so I knew that the Marathon des Sables glasses would be needed with the sponge protection areas to keep sand out of my eyes. We continued the trip to the top as the gradient increased and hair-pinned upwards to arrive at Mount Whitney Portals. It was also curious watching the change in temperature the higher we climbed.

Race day had finally arrived. There had been no need for an alarm clock! Although the plan was to get up at 7am for the 10am start we were up and having cereal at 6am and had been awake for ages. The race was beginning to really scare me. Could I really run in these stunning temperatures? Surely it was impossible to avoid heat stroke? Would the stomach hold up with all the fluids it would have to take? Would dehydration set in? How would my feet do? I had seen the horror photographs of blistered feet. But this was the challenge, this was what I wanted. The distance was 135 miles, a challenge, but one that I knew I could achieve. The real challenge was the heat and the hills, the basic elements that would be thrown at me and deep down I was really excited. I had waited a long time to do this race, I had prepared well, doing the best I could with what I had. It had cost a fortune to get here, and now it was going to start. I wasn't going to race this one; that would be impossible for my first attempt in such extreme conditions, but just a very mediocre goal was to finish in the time limit of 60 hours (that meant a medal and finishers t-shirt). Then, I had to try to get sub 48 hours to get the belt buckle. Then, of course, came my overall placing in the women's race. I had this little goal of half the cut off time, which meant 30 hours and should place me in the top five women. Deep down I was also aware of the time William Sichel had run in 2006. He had been a member of the Great Britain 24 hour team a while ago and achieved a time of 31 hours and 36 minutes and claimed this as a British record. I am not sure this was really a record as such. Similar to the Libyan Challenge where I was the fastest ever British athlete and ladies winner, this was simply a course record, not a British or world record.

There were other forces against me here. Poor Bill hates the heat and this event required a mobile support crew, nothing like other events he had supported me on. It was like the 24 hour race but, instead of sitting stationary with all the supplies around him, he would have to work out of the back of a car, drive along with things clattering all over the place, stand at the road side and mix drinks and then have three Canadians with him helping out. How would it all work out? Would he get heat stroke? Would he suffer dehydration? Would the crew all get on with Bill? All this had been highlighted in the pre-race meeting. So many unknown elements; so many questions unanswered. How would it really pan out? How could I predict what could possibly happen? It was like being lowered into an arena, with people all around watching, wondering, what would the result be? Would I survive to tell the tale.......?

It was 8am and Barb, Isabelle and Mary breezed in. They were to be my support crew, along with Bill, all experienced ultra runners, cyclists and adventure racers. They were a really friendly, happy crew. The bags disappeared before me. The plan was to use the Jeep as the main car for all race supplies, while Barb's car was for everything else. There were three start times: 6am, 8am and 10am. The 10am start was reserved for the faster runners and I had wanted to be on the 10am start, as I can never quite extinguish the entire competitive nature inside of me; I wanted to see my opposition.

To gain entry to this race you must have had experience of both heat and ultra distance. Approximately ninety athletes are invited to run after a strict entry application is adhered to, proving your ability. Points are allocated based on your entry form and the ninety athletes with top points are accepted into the race. Previous finishes and crewing for other athletes also gained extra points. This was how I was fortunate enough to have my wonderful Canadian crew, they had applied to take part and as they had been rejected, despite some very high credentials, they had kindly offered to crew for me to gain extra points for the future.

The hotel room was bare, just waiting for me to leave now. There had been no point in leaving earlier than 9am, as the 17 mile drive would have little traffic on it other than the runners and there was no point standing around in the heat at the start, as there was no shade. Runners had to check in and be weighed 30 minutes before the start. One last visit to the toilet and then all the kit I was wearing was soaked in water to keep me cool. From top to bottom I was wearing a white cap with flap on the back, soaked in water and ice on my head under the cap and a bandana soaked in water and filled with ice around my neck. Below that I stripped off my white t-shirt to soak in water and I wore the Moben arm sleeves that were again soaked in water. On my bottom half were white Skins leggings sprayed with water, Thorlo Socks and the red Spira Stinger shoes, size six compared to my normal training size five. These were the only items not soaked in water. It was then off for the obligatory group photograph of all the runners and then onto the start line. Isabelle had asked me if I was nervous. I was probably more scared witless than nervous, but also really, really excited and couldn't wait to see the event unfold. She thought I looked very calm!

As I stood on the start line I don't know what was going through my mind. I took one last look around me at the dramatic landscape: a big, wide, desolate valley surrounded by high mountains. There was no colour, just pale, haze-like outlines and sand. The heat was intense, far hotter than anything I had ever experienced. I have raced in Taiwan and Japan when conditions have been hot, but this felt hotter. I had run across the Libyan Desert for 36 hours and run the Marathon des Sables in one of the hottest years ever, but this was far hotter.

The final countdown started and the journey into the unknown began. Some runners pelted off into the distance like a 10 kilometre race and I was staggered at this, as I had expected a very slow start like the 24 hour event and for runners to be bunched up and gradually find their own space. These were supposed to be experienced runners! It was interesting and I remembered seeing Pam Reed shoot off into the distance and Dean Karnazes; both were previous winners of this race. Jamie Donaldson was another face I recognised from the 24 hour international races. She had been fourth in the 24 hour race in Bergamo a couple of months previously and set the course record here the previous year in just under 27 hours. I set off and tried to remain calm and settled in as slowly as was practical. I felt great, it felt wonderful in fact to be finally started and really running this challenging race. I was kind of smiling to myself and it didn't somehow feel real. Here I was in this hostile environment with warning signs around about the extreme danger of heat and advising us to avoid the heat of the day between 10am and 4pm and not to exercise and yet here were around ninety runners all defying the odds. It was great. The instructions to my crew were to stop every 1.5 miles to cool me down and give me drinks. The routine was to be that the Jeep was there, Isabelle was there with the spray bottle, Bill was there with my drink, Barb was ready to take my hat and get it dunked in water and refilled with ice and Mary sprinted alongside when the hat was ready for putting back on. It worked like clockwork, amazing, all smiles and encouragement and so the race began. It felt a bit like Whacky Races with all the cars overtaking and stopping and, although I could not tell who many of the runners were, the names on their cars were the giveaway and no-one could hide. All cars had to be labelled with their runners name and number and in large size. The clock started to tick. The first hour ticked by: then the second. This was really happening. I almost had to pinch myself to believe I was running, and my crew were so cheerful, who could but smile at them?

A female runner called Lorie came alongside for a bit and chatted. She had run this race in around 32 hours the previous year; so she was a good guide mark for me. She went ahead as I stopped for my first "pee stop" shortly after the first hour. There was no privacy out here; to the side of the Jeep was the only object I could squat behind. Everything I did was recorded; what I ate, when I ate, what I drank, how often I drank, how much I drank, how often I went to the toilet. There was nothing I could do that went unnoticed!

The first 42 miles were virtually flat, passing Furnace Creek and the first timing point at 17.4 miles and 165 feet below sea level. My official time here was 2 hours 49 minutes. I wasn't feeling too hot in the slightest and the crew were working very hard to keep me that way. To add to the "cooling routine" a sponge had been found so that I could drench my arms and wash my face and head and another was used to douse my back, although the spray gun was doing a great job. It must have been hard running alongside on the rough ground at awkward angles spraying me. I had long given up with the sunglasses, the water was getting on them and they were just getting in the way, but the cap was keeping the sun out of my eyes quite well.

Although the field had thinned out, there were always runners around, always runners in sight and still cars constantly overtaking. It was after 3 hours of running that I started my solid food, just one item per hour and I started off with a sandwich (about a quarter of a normal sandwich). It was around 4 hours that I had my second "pee" stop, a very good sign that I was drinking enough at present and then shortly after my first "unofficial stop". I wasn't sure if it was a stone I had in my shoe or a blister developing, but it was right under the sole of my right heel, not a pleasant place for a blister. My hopes of it being a stone were dashed. It was a blister, nothing major. I just needed to get it popped and hopefully it wouldn't develop any further. I used the pin off my number to stab right through it, put the shoe back on and was away again. This was around the 25 mile mark.

I now got back into relaxing mode and remembered, "If you get to Stovepipe Wells you have cracked it". I was now approaching the 30 mile

248

mark and Salt Creek turnoff and 5 hours of running. At this rate I would be at Stovepipe Wells in 7 hours, just 2 hours away. This still just didn't feel real. Nothing major had happened and everything was running like clockwork. Bill was happy. He was being pampered by our three wonderful ladies and was having a ball. I was still trying to pinch myself to believe this could really be happening. Everything was far too comfortable. Something had to happen. Something was going to happen. It just couldn't work this well for an athlete from the United Kingdom to come here in this heat and not have problems.

The next thing I knew, I kept seeing the vans labelled Pam Reed. Surely not? Surely I wasn't catching the master of this event? But yes, there in the distance was the distinctive style I had seen in other international races, Pam Reed and her many pacers. After Furnace Creek you were allowed "pacers" which are athletes to run alongside you to support you, but they must remain to the left of the white line. My crew (not Bill) were all able and willing to pace me, but I rather like running on my own, I like to be at one with my thoughts and don't do a lot of talking. However, I liked knowing my crew were around me and it was a great comfort to know they were willing and able to run with me had I needed them.

I had been running along the white line. This was supposed to be better for cooling the feet rather than the black tarmac that has been reported to melt shoes. I could feel it was now even hotter than at Badwater, the small pool of salt water at the start of the race, but I had no idea of the exact temperature. I had heard whispers of one hundred and eighteen degrees Fahrenheit at Badwater, but nothing had been confirmed.

That same blister was beginning to bug me again; it had obviously started to grow again. My feet had been permanently wet from the soaking of the kit; good in some ways as it probably kept my feet cooler, but the downside was they were now shrivelled like when you've been in the bath too long. My shoes were really comfy and airy and I really didn't want to change these as I didn't feel they were the problem. It was either the result of the heat and water on the feet or the permanent camber on the road or a combination of all these things, but I decided to stop and pop this again. It was now three times the size and had turned into a blood blister, oops! Not a lot I could do about that; so another quick stab with the pin, back on with the shoes and off again. "Do you want ibuprofen?" I heard. "No, not yet" was the answer, "Not in enough pain yet". It was a great moment as I caught and passed Pam. I said, "Hi", but I wasn't sure if she responded or not. Her pacers were constantly talking to her and I had to run very wide to overtake her. I carried on by Devil's Cornfield and some small sand dunes (nothing like the dunes in the Marathon des Sables). It was also around this time that I overtook Mark Cockbain; he was going okay but was about to hit problems. Mark was also from Great Britain and had done this event several times and was one of only a handful of runners to have done "the double", now there's food for thought! Can you imagine having reached the finish line, climbing Mount Whitney, and then immediately returning to Badwater again, non-stop!

Stovepipe Wells came into sight. I had run 41.9 miles in 6 hours and 54 minutes. This was just incredible; 6 miles an hour and 90 minutes ahead of my schedule. I looked around in disbelief. I had cracked it! But the blister was beginning to worry me as the mountains began to appear ahead. There were now about 5,000 feet of climbing and 17 miles of winding roads. Stovepipe Wells was right at sea level and Townes Pass at 58.7 miles was 4,965 feet. I decided to relent and take some ibuprofen to settle into the climbing. Pam overtook me and forged ahead. I just relaxed and settled into a nice steady rhythm. The heat of the sun was beginning to fade and with each 1,000 feet climbed the temperature was dropping. Signs on the road gave a warning to turn off the air conditioning and I remember Martin Dietrich telling me the story of driving through the mountains and having to stop his car every 10 minutes as it kept over-heating. The Jeep had already done this journey once and as it had to keep stopping for me I didn't think it would be a problem. Onwards and upwards and then the strong winds began. It had been almost still at the start but the wind was becoming gradually stronger on the approach to Stovepipe Wells. It had been quite a pleasant wind initially (the kind of hair dryer blowing in your face feeling) but it was becoming quite forceful and getting harder to battle against with the gradient. The clock ticked until 7pm, which marked the official wearing of night kit: fluorescent, reflective kit with flashing red lights front and back.

I had taken my cap off now. I hate wearing hats, but as the sun was retreating there was not the need to keep quite so wet. I was still having a spray down and soaking my face and head with the sponge regularly as the temperature was still quite high and climbing was creating a lot of internal heat. I don't think the temperature fell below thirty degrees Celsius (eighty-six degrees Fahrenheit). The signs came and went indicating 1,000 feet, 2,000 feet, 3,000 feet, 4,000 feet and I was still climbing and running well despite the fierce head wind. The darkness set in shortly after 8pm and I had to put a head torch on, I didn't really need it for seeing as such, as the moonlight was quite strong, but it was difficult for the crew to see me; so it felt like having a hat on again and it was easier to see the odd rock or stone that had fallen on the road here. In the dark I missed the sign marking the Townes Pass Summit at 4,965 feet and 58.7 miles of running, but soon knew when I was running down hill as the tenderness on my right foot screamed at me. It now felt like the whole of the sole of the right heel was a complete blister (and indeed it was) and I really just could not bear to put this on the ground, as the pain was too much. Instead I was trying to run on my toes downhill, not a smooth running action, but at least I was still moving. It was quite worrying to have such pain at such an early stage. I knew things had gone just too smoothly, but I didn't ever think it would be blisters that would stop me, well not blisters, just one blister, but a very big one!

The clock ticked quickly now, the miles ticked by, the arm sleeves and bandana came off and the spray downs with water ceased. It was still very warm, but not baking hot. The elevation signs were going down, 4,000 feet, 3,000 feet, 2,000 feet and down to 1,640 feet before reaching Panamint Springs at 1,970 feet and 72.3 miles. I was in 28th position at Furnace Creek, 11th at Stovepipe Wells and now remained in 11th position at Panamint Springs with 13 hours 57 minutes (approaching mid-night). This was one very long hard race; one mountain range conquered, still two more to go and yet another day in the heat. I knew I was still well hydrated but it was much easier to go for a "pee" in the darkness and didn't need the protection of the Jeep now.

With Panamint Springs behind me, it was straight into the next climb. Darwin turnoff was 18 miles away and at an elevation of 5,050 feet. It was the cars that made the next section all the more amazing. As I walked and ran up the next mountain range, although it was dark, all I could see was a long streak of flashing red lights from the cars. The rules were that headlights had to be on all the time the car engine was running (day and night) and that four way flashers had to be on when parked. Most of the indicators here were red as opposed to the orange we have in the Great Britain. Barb's car was one of the few that had orange flashers, a feature that made it a little easier to pick them out (there was one other close by that deceived me every now and then). The higher I climbed and the more switchbacks made, the more magnificent the line of red lights became. Only on this night in Death Valley could I have witnessed this. I felt lucky to be here and experience this and I looked ahead at the next switchback and the red lights above me in the distance.

It was while on this section that I finally had enough of the hourly sandwiches I had been eating from the 3 hour mark. I was fed up with them and needed something moist; so I opted for the custard now. Sleepiness was also getting to me, not something I usually suffer with at night time, but my body clock had been thrown out completely with the 8 hours difference and I had woken really early most mornings and hadn't always slept. There were no markers on this bleak road; so I had to keep asking how far I had run as I knew Darwin turnoff was around 90 miles. Although I felt as though I was pestering, the crew gave me the reassuring message that was nice to hear "You are so low maintenance compared to other athletes". I requested little. There was a runner close by who was getting weighed very often and being given this, that and everything else. I was just water one stop, carbohydrate drink the next and food once an hour (and the soaking of course). My other requests were few and far between and not stressful.

The sun started coming up behind me as I made the final approach to Darwin turnoff and I could finally ditch the head torch. I was disappointed I could not see the sun rise behind me, but did take the odd glance behind to see. Darwin turnoff was nothing spectacular, a small gazebo tent by the road side, reached in 19 hours and 1 minute and 13th position, an hour ahead of my schedule. Then the downhill and flat began, all 32 miles of it as the heat began again. Within 3 miles I was in agony. My right heel was just so tender and the left one was now going the same way. I was trying to tiptoe down but the tenderness was increasing. There was no way I wasn't going to finish this, but it was going to be a painful affair and I could see the clock ticking against me. I stopped to take a look at my feet and change my socks. My feet were as expected; the whole of the right heel was loose, shrivelled skin and both feet were white as if I had trench foot. I was still very happy with my shoes and reluctant to change them, as I still didn't think they were the problem. The toe-box was spacious, there were hardly any blisters on my toes, only one toe had a blister and there was one to the side of the left forefoot, probably more to do with running the entire way on a camber.

Slowly, painfully, taking more ibuprofen, I continued, tiptoeing gingerly to start with, then a little splutter of very slow running. The rest of my legs felt great, quadriceps and hamstrings felt good, and stomach was comfortable, although I was going off most of my food now. I had tried a mouthful of couscous, but this had gone off in the heat and I did eat a couple of pieces of ginger cake and the date and walnut loaf I had purchased at Furnace Creek. As Lone Pine was not so far now Barb and Mary drove off in search of breakfast while Bill and Isabelle cheerfully attended my needs. It was shortly after the 100 miles that I really needed "the toilet". There were very few cars around now, the runners were really spaced out with barely anyone in sight and it was still very early in the morning so I thought I would chance my luck just a few metres off the road side. I didn't really want to put the crew through this next to the Jeep! How unfortunate was I? There had been no cars by for ages, but when I pulled my tights down for the business one car was suddenly approaching. Too late now, it was a Sheriff's car! How embarrassing was that? I guess he looked, but there was no point in telling me off. Where else could I go? That done, I never saw another car for a good 20 minutes! My luck was running out.

The next 30 miles were a long hot painful walk, hobble, stop, change socks, change shoes (into yellow Stinger Elite), dunk feet and change socks again, a very slow affair. I overtook another runner and was also overtaken by a runner. That was Lorie who had overtaken me long ago. I had not even realised I was back in front.

It was almost the last section now and, although I could not see Lone Pine, I knew I was closing in and if there was anything left in me I had to give it a shot now. This was the only time I could really have a race. I tried to focus. I tried to run. I tried to put the pain in my feet out of my mind. I was frustrated at stopping to cool my feet but it seemed to do the trick and kept me running a bit more; so it was worth the 10 minutes or so that it took so that I could run rather than walk. Barb and Mary returned with breakfast for Bill and Isabelle. Bill's omelette looked good; indeed it was, as I ate a few mouthfuls for him. The last suggestion made to me was, as my feet were now so wet from the continuous soakings again (the hat, bandana and arm sleeves were all back on and I was back into the previous day's routine of ice under the cap, ice in bandana and wet clothing), why did I bother taking my shoes off to dunk my feet? Why not dunk my feet with the shoes on to save time? Why didn't I think of that? It would save loads of time and do the trick perfectly, so there would be no need to stop before the finish now. All I had to do was fight it out, battle the pain. The quicker I got there, the quicker I could finish and the quicker I the pain would stop. Was I still enjoying it? Why yes! It was fantastic! I still looked around me and found it incredible that so much had gone well; the crew were just perfection. I had come here for a challenge. I had come here for an experience. This was all just part of it and I was still in my element. The crew were all incredibly happy and still having a ball; so why shouldn't I? I now knew I would finish. The battle against the elements was won and it looked as if I would achieve all my initial goals. I was going to finish in the top five women and, although I wasn't going to beat 30 hours, I wasn't going to be too far out and could still make the fastest time ever by a British athlete. There were lots of reason still to fight and with the rest of the route being uphill the feet shouldn't be so bad. That was even more good news.

I could finally see the last climb up Mount Whitney with the steep hairpins and a small area below that must be Lone Pine. On and on, I was running again and fighting with every step. The pain was being blocked and I was on a high. Lone Pine came and went (27 hours and 24 minutes and 14th place) and I had only lost one place since Darwin turnoff. My time was now around 90 minutes behind my planned schedule. I knew I had lost time, but the goal was now to beat that best British time. The final climb was hard! I had written 4,000 feet in 13 miles in my schedule. Lone Pine was at 3,610 feet and the finish was at 8,360 feet; so that was getting close to 5,000 feet of climbing. My schedule allowed 4 hours to do this section; so that made 31 hours 24 minutes which would just shave a few minutes off the 31 hours 36 minutes by William Sichel.

I battled on. It was just far too steep to run which I had known beforehand but I certainly wasn't slouching. My arms were pumping hard and I was striding out the best I could. I can be a pretty good walker when I want to be. The drinks were still going down and just the odd Ritz biscuit now. I was now doing my best, savouring the moment, taking in the glorious scenery that stretched out for miles and miles. Head down again, concentrating I noticed some curious signs. I had got used to seeing the Union Jack appear in the most weird places, but now, neatly written on paper, held down in the sand by stones, were around ten messages about ten feet apart alongside the road. I can't remember what they all said, but all were highly encouraging, along the lines of my performance was awesome and inspiring, I was an incredible person, it was a privilege to crew for me, they had all been proud to crew for me and my ability to fight the pain was amazing. Isabelle had written them and taken the time to put these in the sand. How wonderful! It really did the job in perking me up. The last message was one from Bill. I could tell he had written it, as the hand writing wasn't so neat, but just to tell me how proud he was. As ever, he had been just champion too!

The temperature was dropping slightly as the heights were reached and I guessed the air was just a bit thinner at around twice the height of Ben Nevis. But on and on I went, to find a surprise last checkpoint at 131 miles, before the last major hairpin. It was a long, winding road and I had forgotten just how far this last section was. All the cars coming down were beeping and waving. Many were the earlier finishers; Lorie came down as I approached the last mile and I got a hug out of the car window.

Around yet another corner and again, just where was that finish? Finally I saw Bill running towards me with two bottles of water in his hands. Yes, the drink had gone long ago, so long was this last section, "How far?"

I whined, "Ooh, still about a mile" he hardly dared tell me. However, he did give me more words of encouragement about how proud he was of my achievement and that the ladies were just around the corner. More shouting and cheering and the smile was back on my face. This crew had just been fantastic, the best ever. They had just understood me so well with such little communication beforehand, did everything just right, knew exactly what to say to me and what not to say, never once put a foot out of place, had kept me cheerful throughout and gave Bill the time of his life. The last half mile was absolutely exhilarating as we all walked along together. It had been an amazing adventure, a real journey and the event had lived up to all I had expected of it; a really tough challenge.

The finish was round the next hairpin. Oops! No, it wasn't. Maybe the next one? I decided to wait and see until I saw that finish line. Finally another hairpin and there was the finishing tent. I made one last effort to run with me and crew all finishing together and the Union Jack held high. Unfortunately we didn't have a Canadian flag for Mary, Barb and Isabelle. The finishing banner was held across the line for me to break. I had a big hug from all my crew while I had to fight back the tears of joy. It had been

Finish of Badwater Ultramarathon. Chris Kostman, Adventure CORPS ©.

just fantastically painful, unforgettable and incredible and I had crossed the line 4th lady, 14th overall and achieved the fastest time ever by a British athlete, 31 hours and 12 minutes, just heaven. It had been an incredibly phenomenal event, not one I will forget in a long time. That night I rested content in my thoughts that I had survived Death Valley and all it had thrown at me.

What were the thoughts and reflections on this one? The big flame of desire had been extinguished. I have been there, done that, got the t-shirt. But there is still a little glow that says, "Well you could go faster now you have done it and race it" and, "What about the double?" Who knows, there are many more races still on the agenda, many more places to go. I doubt that any of the others can be more extreme than this one; just different challenges. I was blessed with such a wonderful crew; it would be hard to find another crew quite as good as Mary, Isabelle and Barb. They kept Bill highly amused and looked after him as well as me. Their constant enthusiasm just bubbled over and they always seemed so cheerful and continuously spurred me on with their encouraging words and actions. My preparation had been as good as I could have expected. My feet were really the only point that let me down and I struggle to know what I could have done to have prevented this. Perhaps taping the whole of the sole of the foot was the answer.

It is worth noting there are no prizes for this event. The prize is the glory and prestige of finishing against all odds. Medals, t-shirts and belt buckles are the rewards, only for those that accomplish this feat beyond all imagination. It truly was an inspirational challenge, a really awesome event. There certainly isn't a hotter race and I doubt there are many more challenging courses of this distance; so it has to rate up there with the toughest ever.

So what event was next? What could be tougher? What could be more extreme? Who knows, but I will try to find something! The next one for now was a more sedate, 24 hour event, but it would be the first ever Commonwealth Championships for ultra distance running as the race takes a further step into recognition. The event was to be held in Keswick, England in September 2009. My selection had already come through for England as part of the team and being ranked as number one in the Commonwealth the previous year meant there was a lot to stand up for. England had high hopes for individual and team gold medals on this one, so no pressure!

Chapter 12

The Commonwealth
Championships and the Future

The inaugural Commonwealth Championships, Mountain and Ultra Distance were to be held in Keswick, England, September 2009. The preparation for this had been short, a week to let the skin on the feet heal after the Badwater Ultramarathon and it was back to racing. Two weeks later and I was back into high mileage. A good solid month of training in August, and bang! It was straight into September and the Commonwealth Championships 24 Hours, with just a day over nine weeks between events. Three marathons in the previous four weeks, no restrictions from England Athletics on racing and training and I came into the event full of confidence for a good performance.

Selection distances and time frames had been advertised long ago and men's and women's team both comprising four per team were announced in July. The men were Chris Finill, Chris Carver, Jim Rogers and Ken Fancett. The women were Sharon Gayter, Vicky Skelton, Sandra Brown and Marie Doke. For some absurd reason a further male and female were selected just three weeks prior to the event, Pat Robbins, winner of the Grand Union Canal Run (145 miles) but who had never run a specific 24 hour race and Ramona Thevenet-Smith, who had never returned to form since her selection performance in Apeldoorn back in 2004. There were mixed feelings about this. On the one hand it was incredibly hard for the athletes to prepare at just three weeks notice, a time when others would be tapering, and on the other hand, neither had reached the criteria specified. So why were they selected? Why was their selection so late? In some ways it was an insult to those who had to sacrifice other events to achieve selection distances. After all, you were supposed to earn a vest and not be given one. But both were welcomed to the team to do their best for England.

The weather was predicted to be dry but cool for this one, my first ever international 24 hours on home soil. There was none of the usual travelling, foreign food and meal times dictated by necessity by the local organising committee. I had Bill by my side, Bill had his own space in our tent and I had many supporters who were to visit.

Mid-day and it was time for the off, with a quick introduction to our lap recorder, as there was to be manual back-up just in case the champion-chip system failed. Organiser Dave Annandale felt it was much friendlier and personal with lap recorders and I have to agree immensely, they were an incredibly vocal, happy, bunch who supported us well. So off onto the scenic 1,005 metre loop around Fitz Park: gentle left bend, past the smelly line of port-a-loos, a little kind of s bend where you cut the corners, left by the children's play area, keep right to avoid the hump in the path, keep right on the bend, then head to the left side of the path, another left and downhill to the river, left by the river and back to the champion-chip mats and lap recorders, then the feed station, then it started all over again. The plan was around 10 kilometres to 10.5 kilometres an hour, no faster than 5 minutes 45 seconds per lap and no slower than 6 minutes per lap. It took 30 minutes for me to settle down and finally hit the 5 minutes 45 seconds per lap, by which time many of the female competitors had overtaken me. It was frustrating, but I came into this event ranked number one with an 8 kilometre advantage over Vicky Skelton from England, my 219 kilometres versus Vicky's 211 kilometres. There were twenty-two women and twenty-two men, bigger than the 100 kilometres field.

Round and round and I settled in nicely, just ticking the miles by. Bill was doing a fantastic job, running up and down after me, much more than I anticipated. His fitness was coming along nicely since his double hip replacement and I'd got used to less support from him; so he got a quick warning to look after himself, but he was as happy as me. I saw many familiar faces. There was now some intermittent bonfire smoke crossing the course. It was far too early for a bonfire and I certainly didn't want the smell of this to add to the pollution of the odd generator at the hospitality tent. I quickly moaned at Bill to get it put out and for a while it improved, but a second and third dose and I was now beginning to worry it would bring on my asthma. Spotting Dave updating the enormous leader board, I asked for some help. No sooner said than both he and referee Ian Champion were investigating and tracking down the source and reassured me that the burning of leaves would cease, and it duly did for the rest of the race.

The plan after 4 hours was to hit 42 kilometres, and spot on 42 kilometres was the result. So onto the next 4 hours and I hit my first low. It had been wonderful to see so many supporters and I did my best to acknowledge them, after all they had made a long journey just to see me; so they all got the odd wave and smile. I was feeling just a little fatigued and wanted a quick walk, unusual for me, as I usually go 12 hours solid with not so much as a walk, but to make use of any walking I asked for a pot of custard.

My left groin was feeling a bit "achy" and both gluteus (buttock) muscles seem to be grumbling a bit. It was nothing major, but I had felt better. It was dark by 8 hours and the distance 81 kilometres; this was just a kilometre less than anticipated, but nothing to worry about. What was more worrying was the next 10 hours or so of darkness. About five generators were now roaring away, lighting up most of the course and generating lots of exhaust fumes in the process. This, added to the smell of the port-a-loos every lap, was a good mixture to bring on the asthma, but I just had to progress as gently as possible. I was very slowly moving up the leader board. I had been in 6th place in the ladies race and was now hovering at around 3rd place. I had added arm sleeves to keep warm, having started out wearing a t-shirt, vest and long tights, but the temperature was beginning to drop. Bill also had to scrounge a fluorescent jacket, as, dressed in black, I found him hard to identify in the crowds of helpers.

The course now had some additional light sticks. Although the big motorway-style flood lights lit the corners well, there was a kind of alternating light and dark feel to this race. The light was not constant, the light sticks were reassuring, not that you could go off course, but the edges of this track in places fell away from the track or were gravel and uneven. I did hear reports of a couple of runners falling over. The course itself was a very good surface with no potholes; good for running and easy to see in daylight, but the edges were difficult to see in darkness. Mick Francis from Australia was wearing a head torch. Although I had one, I hate wearing things on my head and was happy to run without it. By the time I hit 12 hours the distance was now 119 kilometres, the target had been 120 kilometres, so again nothing to worry about, just a kilometre out after 12 hours of running was pretty much on course and I was now in 2nd place just trailing Vicky. We were on the same lap, but she was about half a kilometre in front. Half way is the point where I can make a good estimate of my distance based on how I feel. I had gone through a couple of bad spells, but in the peace and quiet of the night could get my head down and focus and, although I was confident of winning, I thought it would be touch and go as to whether I could get a personal best. By this stage in Bislett I was 2 kilometres ahead of my schedule. The temperature was continuing to drop and I now had a jacket on top of my clothing to keep warm.

The next 4 hours seem to fly by; the clock was ticking fast now but nothing to really report. I had gone off my usual sandwiches and replaced them with couscous, as I was in need of some warmer sustenance and this was going down well. Vicky had lapped me once and Bill reported at one time the lead was 2 kilometres. There had never been any point in the race when I had been more than 2 kilometres from leading, but I had yet to actually take the lead. There were now a few stalwarts who had come out to watch. Andy Eccles found a quiet lit corner to cheer us on our way and at one stage I even saw Stuart Buchan, a face from Hull and 24 hours a few years ago. The leader board was updated hourly. It was massive but while running it was still difficult to read; females were in red; and males in black. It was good for the public to see what was happening. I had a good 4 hours, I actually felt better in those 4 hours than usual. The distance at 16 hours, 155 kilometres, was still just a kilometre down on the schedule.

Onwards and upwards, into the last third of the race and I needed to start making my move soon. I was beginning to psych myself up for the daylight hours and the battle of the last 4 hours where this race should be won. By 18 hours I was now on the same lap as Vicky again. She was in the lead, but was beginning to slow down. It was 19 hours by the time I finally hit the lead in the ladies race. The first few signs of daylight started to peek through. The temperature had dropped to seven or eight degrees Celsius overnight, but with daylight would come the turning off of the generators. I was pleased to have got through the night with no breathing troubles, as this was one smelly course with the fumes and port-a-loos.

But day light came and Dave was quick off the mark to turn off the floodlights, fantastic! The spectators were starting to return. Finally 20 hours was reached, the distance 190 kilometres, amazing, as this was now 2 kilometres ahead of schedule. The schedule had been written for 216 kilometres which I guessed would be enough to win this race; so 2 kilometres up meant 218 kilometres, my final goal had been 220 kilometres to break my personal best.

I progressed steadily, I didn't race. I had the lead and just needed to maintain rhythm and focus and the gold medal was mine. I switched off from the spectators and informed Bill to tell anyone supporting me I wasn't being rude but I wanted to concentrate on this last 4 hours; I dearly wanted a personal best, not just the gold medal. I was trying to figure out the laps to get 220 kilometres when Eleanor Robinson (who was on the official team since retiring years ago) informed me I was on for 225 kilometres if I kept pace. 225 kilometres! This was further than anything I anticipated and I was excited by the prospect.

I was frequently lapping Vicky now, content there was no way back and extending the lead with every stride, but with every stride my breathing was becoming more laboured. I noticed runners could hear me coming, and not the pitter-patter of feet, but laboured, wheezing breathing. I was turning asthmatic. I could not believe I had lasted this long and now that most of the generators were off I was to have an asthma attack. Bill had noticed too. I was hardly able to walk and eat; my breathing was so bad. I needed my pump and needed it fast. But had I packed it? Confused, I could not remember packing it; usually it is in the first aid box. I began to panic and think where else one could be? I was thinking may be the medical tent would have one and surely there must be another runner here with asthma when suddenly I remembered John Pares telling me his story in Canada of getting an exemption form and having to be tested. He was running here for Wales (and running very well), and just at that moment he overtook me and I quickly asked if he had an asthma pump and if I could use it, "Yes," he said and he promptly asked his crew as I arrived at the feed station.

In the meantime Bill had found mine. I had packed it in the first aid box after all and on top of that a couple of wonderful Guisborians supporting had overheard and given Bill their pump, so three came at me at once! I sat and tried to breathe and take the pump, my head was spinning, going dizzy. I needed to lie down, the chair was removed from beneath me and I was gently lowered to the ground. Eyes closed trying to breathe, trying to use my pump, slowly but surely my breath was coming back, getting under control. I think others were worrying more. I was in the lead. Would I get up again? Did I need the medical tent? No such worries here, just give me a few minutes and I will be back. Back up to sitting, feeling better, still laboured but maybe I would be able to walk now? Off again, 21 hours 30 minutes and I just had to create a bit of drama. Back to a slow jog, breathing improving all the time, lap by lap, kilometre by kilometre, I was going again.

I was counting laps now. This was in the bag. Just what was the final distance going to be? With 23 hours on the clock the distance was now 216 kilometres, just three laps to equal my personal best. One more lap and 220 kilometres, I could relax now, I was so far in front I could stop now and still win the gold medal. I could once again acknowledge the gathering crowds and smile. This race was mine. This was my best ever performance on home soil in front of my home crowd. It was a fantastic feeling. For once in my life I could enjoy the last hour of running. I was free from all pain, running on a high; I came in as favourite, came in to take the gold medal, came here to improve my personal best and came here to retain my Great Britain ranking for the thirteenth year. All goals achieved, all boxes ticked, I was one happy runner from England! I proudly flew the flag for the last few laps, hands high in the air waving the St George's Cross until the final hooter sounded. I could officially sit down at last and Bill had brought the chair to me.

I found all of two of the smallest blisters ever. I didn't even know they were there. The Spira Striker has served me well. I had never needed to change shoes at all and my feet felt the best ever. I was now hooked on these shoes. It had taken time to get used to them and run a few ultra races, but I now had confidence in them and would not want to change them.

The next day I watched the finish of a dramatic men's 100 kilometres race with Jez Bragg taking the lead only 5 kilometres from the finish and a gold, silver and bronze medal for England. On the final day there were more races and the up and down mountain race. The weather had stayed superb for us all. The mountain races were phenomenal; it would scare me to death running down hill as fast as these runners.

Finally it was time for the presentation of the medals and closing ceremony. So it was on with my England jacket and the 24 hours was first up for presentation in the marquee on Fitz Park. I got my reward and stood on the top of the podium while the National Anthem was played. It was a proud moment. Then the medals for the men: Martin Fryer had set a new Commonwealth record for Australia. Then it was my turn to go back for the team gold medal. Vicky got a personal best with 212 kilometres, as did Marie with 201 kilometres for 2nd and 4th place respectively; so good performances

On the podium for the Commonwealth Championships gold medal (picture courtesy of Dave Woodhead© www.woodentops.org.uk).

all round. Medals for all the other races were then given out followed by a short closing ceremony. I was itching to see where 226 kilometres placed me in the rankings and just had to look at the International Association of Ultrarunners website. At the time I was 3rd in the world (eventually to be knocked down to 4th by the end of the year). I slept well.

So where to now? I have had a good life since leaving home. If I were to stop tomorrow would I have had a good time? Would I have lived my life to the full? I can say with full confidence I have achieved the many things in life I wanted. I have been a success. From barely being able to run a mile, to completing my first marathon and now I have represented my country for sixteen years and over twenty-five appearances. I have taken a world record, a British record, an English team record, a world veteran record and British titles. I have global team medals and now an individual and team Commonwealth gold medal.

I have a husband who cannot be beaten, the most supportive person I have ever met in my life. I cannot imagine for one second that getting to know me was easy, to break down my defences into my little world and become my partner of many years. To understand me so well, to go through many painful experiences himself, just to look after me. He really is one in a million and I seriously think that without Bill by my side I would not have become the athlete I have. From being a bus driver back when we met, to finally being awarded a degree, going back to work as a sandwich delivery person, then becoming a lecturer, then run my own business and now turn full circle to lecture at Teesside University. It has been a wonderful life.

So where to go on from here? What more is there for me to achieve? What are my next goals? When will I retire? So many questions yet to answer. There are many more races I would like to run, many more desert adventure runs appearing all the time, several long road races such as the Spartathlon and Comrades, races such as the Great Wall of China. Then there are races such as the Himalayan stage race and Everest Marathon. There are many British races yet to try: the Grand Union Canal Run, the Cleveland Way, the Ridgeway and many more. The world is full of wonderful places to run; the next one may possibly be "The High", the highest ultra race in the world, an event of 135 miles and altitudes of up to 18,000 feet, for an invited field of experienced ultra distance runners only. Then of course there are still the international races and representing my country. How much longer will this continue? I do not want to continue until I no longer can make the selection distance. I want to retire at a point where I know it will be hard to keep up the high standards. I am not finished with running yet. The Commonwealth Championships win is a great place to finish for now, the next step up in recognition of our sport, but I still have a desire to go back and finish the 48 hours with a good performance. I still have the six day race that is pending. Ultimately I do quite like the idea of what Eleanor Robinson did, to run a world record of 1000 miles and say, thanks very much, that is it. So will 1000 miles be my final distance? The answer to these questions remains in the future. There is plenty more life in me yet and I have more plans for extreme distance world records - so watch this space......... .

Appendix 1

Running Progression

1984   First half marathon, Sinclair Cambridge Half Marathon, 2 hours 4 minutes (3 races for year).

1985   Longest run, Rutland Water Mini Marathon, 16.8 miles, 2 hours 50 minutes (7 races for year).

1986   First marathon, Mars London Marathon, 4 hours 27 minutes (7 races for year).

1987   Ten half marathons, no marathons (13 races for year).

1988   Six half marathons and Harlow Marathon in 3 hours 43 minutes (7 races for year).

1989   First ultra, Fat-Ass Fifty Miler in 11 hours 56 minutes, ADT London Marathon and three half marathons (5 races for year).

1990   Two off-roads ultras, Crosses at 53 miles and Cleveland Classic at 56 miles, one marathon and a few shorter races (16 races for year).

1991   First ever win in ladies race, one ultra, one marathon and shorter races (11 races for year).

1992   Six race wins, 15 races between 20 miles and 56 miles (25 races for year).

1993   First outright win in a race (no men in front), first 100 mile race Cleveland 100 (1st lady and 5th of 499 starters), set 7 course records, first lady in 19 races and ran over 10 ultras (43 races for year).

1994   National champion 100km (8 hours 42 minutes) and 24 hours (204km) on my debut, first international vest (47 races for year).

1995   First international medal, best 100km time 8 hours 12 minutes, 3rd lady Malta Marathon, 3 hours 7 minutes (50 races for year).

1996   First injury and 6 months out, 3 international races (43 races for year).

1997   National champion 24 hours, 2 internationals (45 races for year).

1998   First 12 hour race (128km), outright win and third on British all time list, 3 more internationals (48 races for year).

1999   Win for England in Anglo Celtic Plate 100km, new team England record, national champion 24 hours, 3 international races (43 races for year).

2000   Injured from motorbike accident (30 races for year).

2001   First half ironman triathlon and started race walking (42 races for year).

2002   National champion 100km (57 races for year).

2003   Longest event, Flora 1000 Mile Challenge (32 races for year).

2004   Moravian Ultra Marathon, 7 marathons in 7 days, became Centurion 1006 (44 races for year).

2005   Gortex-Transalpine Run from Germany to Austria, Switzerland and Italy (56 races for year).

2006   World record, Land's End to John O'Groats, 837 miles (36 races for year).

2007   Libyan Challenge 190km, going more extreme (66 races for year).

2008   Marathon des Sables, British indoor 24 hour track record, world veteran 45 indoor track record (61 races for year).

2009   Badwater Ultramarathon, fastest time by British athlete, Commonwealth champion 24 hours (77 races for year).

Appendix 2

Ultra Distance Races,
50 Kilometres and Beyond

Road and track ultras, 50 kilometres and more (* denotes selection for country for race).

06/03/94	Barry 40, 40 miles track. 5 hours 14 minutes, 2nd lady.
08/05/94	British 100km Championship, Sutcliffe Park, London, 100km road. 8 hours 42 minutes, 1st lady.
03/07/94	X Subida, Granada-Pico Veleta, Sierra Nevada, Spain, 50km road. 6 hours 10 minutes, 2nd lady.
03/09/94 *	IAU European Championships, Winschoten, Holland, 100km road. 8 hours 28 minutes, 6th lady, 4th team.
22/10/94	AAA Championships of England, Sri Chinmoy, Tooting Bec, London, 24 hours track. 204 kilometres, 1st lady.
27/05/95*	IAU European Championships, Chavagnes-en-Paillers, France, 100km road. 8 hours 21 minutes, 10th lady, 2nd team.
16/09/95*	IAU World Challenge, Winschoten, Holland, 100km road. 8 hours 12 minutes, 18th lady, 5th team.
04/05/96*	IAU World Challenge, Moscow, Russia, 100km road. 9 hours 36 minutes, 25th lady, 5th team.
25/08/96*	IAU European Championships, Cleder, France, 100km road. Stopped injured at 50 kilometres.
21/09/96*	IAU European Challenge, Courcon, France, 24 hours road. 190 kilometres, 10th lady, 2nd team.
31/05/97*	IAU European Championships, Firenze to Faenza, Italy, 100km road. 9 hours 22 minutes, 13th lady, 3rd team.
13/09/97*	IAU World Challenge, Winschoten, Holland, 100km road. 9 hours 47 minutes, 45th lady.
11/10/97	BAF and AAA Championships, Sri Chinmoy, Tooting Bec, London, 24 hours track. 193 kilometres, 1st lady.

15/03/98	Catterick Garrison, North Yorks, 12 hours track.
	128 kilometres, 1st person.
25/04/98	Sheffield Don Valley Stadium, 6 hours track.
	71 kilometres, 1st lady.
19/06/98*	IAU European Championships, Torhout, Belgium,
	100km road.
	9 hours 2 minutes, 18th lady.
29/08/98*	IAU European Championships, Lille, France, 24 hours road.
	212 kilometres, 5th lady, 2nd team.
18/10/98*	IAU World 100km Challenge, River Shimanto, Japan,
	100km road.
	11 hours 3 minutes, 31st lady, 4th team.
20/03/99	L'Aunis, France, 100km road.
	8 hours 54 minutes, 3rd lady.
15/05/99*	IAU World Challenge, Chavagnes-en-Paillers, France,
	100km road.
	8 hours 42 minutes, 35th lady.
19/06/99*	Anglo Celtic Plate, Phoenix Park, Dublin, 100km road.
	8 hours 27 minutes, 1st lady, 1st team, England team record.
11/09/99*	IAU European Championships, Winschoten, Holland,
	100km road.
	8 hours 51 minutes, 10th lady.
09/10/99	UK and AAA Championships, Sri Chinmoy, Tooting Bec,
	London, 24 hours track.
	201 kilometres, 1st lady.
14/05/00	Scottish Championhips, Fife, 50km road.
	3 hours 58 minutes, 1st lady.
02/06/00	Apeldoorn, Holland, 24 hours road.
	191 kilometres, 1st lady.
09/07/00*	Anglo Celtic Plate, Edinburgh, 100km road.
	33 kilometres in 3 hours 23 minutes (fell over).
09/09/00*	IAU World Challenge, Winschoten, Holland, 100km road.
	9 hours 44 minutes, 30th lady.
21/10/00*	IAU European Challenge, Uden, Holland, 24 hours road.
	90 kilometres in 10 hours, 26th lady, 6th team.
08/04/01	Intemelia, Italy, 100km track.
	9 hours 22 minutes, 3rd lady.
13/05/01	Scottish Championships, Fife, 50km road.
	4 hours 29 minutes, 2nd lady.
25/05/01	IAU European Challenge Apeldoorn, Holland,
	24 hours road.
	123 kilometres in 14 hours, 21st lady.
26/08/01	IAU World Championships, Cleder, France, 100km road.
	9 hours 11 minutes, 37th lady.
24/11/01	Du Cher, France, 24 hours road.
	191 kilometres, 1st lady.

07/04/02	UK National Championships, Moreton-in-Marsh, Gloucester, 100km road.
	8 hours 53 minutes, 1st lady.
10/05/02	Apeldoorn, Holland, 24 hours road.
	217 kilometres, 1st lady.
03/06/02	100th Bradford Race Walk, 50km road.
	6 hours 5 minutes, 3rd lady.
07/09/02*	IAU European Challenge, Gravigny, France, 24 hours road.
	158 kilometres in 16 hours, 20th lady.
20/10/02	RRC Track Race Crystal Palace, London, 100 miles track.
	50 miles in 7 hours 47 minutes
02/03/03	Flora 1000 Mile Challenge, 1000 miles road, London Marathon route 38 times.
	1 mile every hour, 2nd person.
18/05/03	AAA of England Championships, Sutton Coldfield, 50km road.
	4 hours 10 minutes, 4th lady.
06/07/03*	UK National Championships, Anglo Celtic Plate, Edinburgh, 100km road.
	9 hours 47 minutes, 3rd lady.
11/10/03*	IAU World/European Challenge, Uden, Holland, 24 hours road.
	205 kilometres, 15th lady in world, 11th lady Europe.
16/11/03	IAU World Challenge, Taiwan, 100km road.
	11 hours 49 minutes, 38th lady.
21/08/04	UK National Championships, Centurions Race Walk, Colchester, 100 miles.
	22 hours 41 minutes, 3nd lady, 2nd lady in championships.
23/10/04*	IAU World/European Challenge, Brno, Czech Republic, 24 hours road.
	202 kilometres, 16th lady and 6th team in World, 11th lady and 4th team in Europe.
05/12/04	Amageny, France, 12 hours road.
	119 kilometres, 1st lady.
02/04/05	Anglo Celtic Plate, UK Champs, Phoenix Park, Dublin, 100km road.
	8 hours 45 minutes, 3rd lady.
16/07/05*	IAU World/European Challenge, Worschach, Austria, 24 hours road.
	200 kilometres, 14th lady and 7th team in world, 8th lady and 5th team in Europe.
29/10/05	East Hull Harriers Track Race, 24 hours track.
	198 kilometres, 1st lady.
12/02/06	Draycote Water, Warwickshire, 35 miles road.
	4 hours 46 minutes, 2nd lady.
25/02/06	IAU World Challenge, Taiwan, 24 hours road.
	214 kilometres, 6th lady.

03/09/06	Land's End to John O'Groats, 837 miles road.			
	12 days 16 hours 22 minutes 3 seconds, Guinness World Record.			
31/03/07	AIM Crawley Track Race, 6 hours track.			
	61 kilometres, 2nd lady.			
28/07/07*	IAU World Challenge, Drummondville, Canada, 24 hours road.			
	92 kilometres in 10 hours, 50th lady, 9th team.			
25/08/07	Finnforest Through the Night, Boston, Lincolnshire, 12 hours track.			
	120 kilometres, 1st person.			
06/10/07	Self-Transcendence, Tooting Bec, London, 24 hours track.			
	212 kilometres (course record), 1st lady.			
06/12/08	Bislett Indoor Challenge, Oslo, Norway, 24 hours track.			
	219 kilometres, 1st lady, British indoor track record, world vet 45 record.			
02/05/09*	IAU World/European Challenge, Bergamo, Italy, 24 hours road.			
	172 kilometres in 20 hours, 42nd lady, 33rd lady in Europe, 7th team.			
13/07/09	Badwater Ultramarathon, Death Valley, America, 135 miles road.			
	31 hours 12 minutes, 4th lady, fastest time by British athlete.			
17/09/09*	Commonwealth Championships, Keswick, England, 24 hours road.			
	226 kilometres, 1st lady, 1st team.			

Off road ultra distance races, 50 kilometres or more.

07/01/89	Fat-Ass Fifty Miler	50 miles	11 hours 56 minutes	2nd lady
14/07/90	Crosses	53 miles	14 hours 24 minutes	2nd lady
22/09/90	Cleveland Classic	56 miles	11 hours 53 minutes	4th lady
28/09/91	Cleveland Classic	56 miles	16 hours 7 minutes	
11/07/91	Lyke Wake Race	42 miles	7 hours 33 minutes	6th lady
29/09/92	Cleveland Classic	56 miles	13 hours 3 minutes	3rd lady
29/05/93	Cleveland 100	100 miles	25 hours 15 minutes	1st lady
10/07/93	Lyke Wake Race	42 miles	6 hours 33 minutes	1st lady
25/09/93	Cleveland Classic (record)	56 miles	9 hours 11 minutes	1st lady

29/05/94	Dartmoor 100	100 miles	26 hours 55 minutes	1st lady
20/11/94	Darlington Dash	39 miles	6 hours 27 minutes	1st lady
17/12/94	Round Rotherham	50 miles	8 hours 20 minutes	1st lady
16/04/95	Speyside Way	50 kilometres	4 hours 03 minutes	1st lady
12/11/95	Darlington Dash	37 miles	5 hours 36 minutes	2nd lady
16/12/95	Round Rotherham (record)	50 miles	7 hours 44 minutes	1st lady
25/02/96	Doncaster Doddle	40 miles	6 hours 22 minutes	1st lady
14/04/96	Speyside Way (record)	50 kilometres	3 hours 56 minutes	1st lady
13/07/96	Crosses	54 miles	9 hours 56 minutes	1st lady
10/11/96	Darlington Dash	36 miles	6 hours 5 minutes	2nd lady
21/06/97	West Highland Way	95 miles	21 hours 3 minutes	1st lady
12/07/97	Crosses (record)	54 miles	9 hours 23 minutes	1st lady
27/09/97	Cleveland Classic	56 miles	10 hours 28 minutes	1st lady
09/11/97	Darlington Dash	35 miles	6 hours 10 minutes	3rd lady
13/12/97	Round Rotherham	50 miles	7 hours 57 minutes	1st lady
22/02/98	Doncaster Doddle	40 miles	7 hours 9 minutes	2nd lady
11/07/98	Crosses	54 miles	9 hours 38 minutes	1st lady
28/02/99	Doncaster Doddle	40 miles	7 hours 36 minutes	2nd lady
11/12/99	Round Rotherham	50 miles	8 hours 9 minutes	1st lady
27/02/00	Doncaster Doddle	40 miles	7 hours 14 minutes	2nd lady
17/03/00	Darlington Dash	34 miles		1st lady
29/07/00	Swiss Alpine Marathon			
25/02/01	Doncaster Doddle	42 miles	7 hours 34 minutes	1st lady
23/06/01	West Highland Way	95 miles	21 hours 10 minutes	1st lady

08/12/01	Round Rotherham	50 miles	8 hours 52 minutes	1st lady
24/02/02	Doncaster Doddle (record)	42 miles	6 hours 36 minutes	1st lady
13/07/02	Lyke Wake Race	42 miles	6 hours 51 minutes	1st lady
14/12/02	Round Rotherham	50 miles	9 hours 14 minutes	1st lady
17/04/04	Woldsman (record)	50 miles	8 hours 36 minutes	1st lady
04/07/04	Moravian Ultra Marathon	301km	31 hours 13 minutes	1st lady
	Brno, Czech Republic (7 marathons in 7 days)			
04/09/05	Gortex Transalpine Race	202km	33 hours 48 minutes	4th ladies
	Germany, Austria, Switzerland, Italy		7 stage race in pairs	
10/12/05	Round Rotherham	50 miles	7 hours 59 minutes	1st lady
21/06/06	Verdon Canyon Trail Adventure Aiguines, France	115km	21 hours 5 minutes 4 stage race	2nd lady
06/03/07	Libyan Challenge (record)	190km	36 hours 46 minutes	1st lady
18/09/07	Welsh International 4 Days 4 days stage race	100 miles	16 hours 13 minutes	1st lady
16/02/08	Thames Meander, London	54 miles	8 hours 33 minutes	2nd lady
04/03/08	Libyan Challenge (record)	190km	36 hours 10 minutes	1st lady
30/03/08	Marathon des Sables Morocco, 6 stage race	245km	38 hours 13 minutes	17th lady
11/04/09	Compton	40 miles	6 hours 17 minutes	2nd lady